# THE MOUNTAINS AND WATERS SŪTRA

# THE MOUNTAINS AND WATERS SŪTRA

## A PRACTITIONER'S GUIDE TO DŌGEN'S "SANSUIKYŌ"

Commentary by Shohaku Okumura

FOREWORD BY ISSHO FUJITA
EDITED BY SHODO SPRING
TRANSLATION OF "SANSUIKYŌ" BY CARL BIELEFELDT
APPENDIXES BY CARL BIELEFELDT AND GARY SNYDER

Wisdom Publications
199 Elm Street
Somerville, MA 02144 USA
wisdomexperience.org

Library of Congress Cataloging-in-Publication Data
Names: Okumura, Shohaku, 1948– author. | Bielefeldt, Carl, translator, writer of supplementary
    textual content. | Snyder, Gary, 1930– writer of supplementary textual content. | Fujita, Isshō,
    1954– writer of foreword. | Spring, Shodo Janet Cedar, 1948– editor.
Title: The Mountains and waters sūtra: a practitioner's guide to Dōgen's Sansuikyō / commentary
    by Shohaku Okumura; translation of Sansuikyō by Carl Bielefeldt; appendixes by Carl Bielefeldt
    and Gary Snyder; foreword by Issho Fujita; edited by Shodo Spring.
Description: Somerville, MA: Wisdom Publications, 2018. | Includes bibliographical references and
    index. |
Identifiers: LCCN 2017034910 (print) | LCCN 2017036120 (ebook) | ISBN 9781614293125 () |
    ISBN 1614293120 () | ISBN 9781614292937 (pbk.: alk. paper) | ISBN 1614292930 (pbk.: alk.
    paper)
Subjects: LCSH: Dōgen, 1200–1253. Sansuikyō. | Zen Buddhism—Doctrines. | Spiritual life—Zen
    Buddhism.
Classification: LCC BQ9449.D654 (ebook) | LCC BQ9449.D654 M68 2018 (print) | DDC
    294.3/85—dc23
LC record available at https://lccn.loc.gov/2017034910

ISBN 978-1-61429-293-7     ebook ISBN 978-1-61429-312-5

24 23 22   5  4  3

Cover art, "To the sky" by Eiji Imao. More of his work is available at https://etimao25.wixsite.com/mizunokioku. Cover design by Tim Holtz. Interior design by Gopa & Ted2, Inc. Set in Diacritical Garamond Premier Pro 11.9/15.54.

Permission to reprint Carl Bielefeldt's translation of "Sansuikyō" was given by the Sōtō Zen Text Project of Sōtōshū Shūmuchō. Permission to reprint essays by Gary Snyder and Carl Bielefeldt was given by Sōtō Zen Buddhism International Center. The format and style of those essays has been adjusted to conform to this book.

# CONTENTS

# FOREWORD

I HAVE KNOWN Rev. Shohaku Okumura for more than thirty years. I met him for the first time when I visited Antaiji temple in Hyōgo Prefecture, Japan, at the age of twenty-seven, to check out whether it would be good for me to stay as a resident practitioner.

I had practiced Rinzai-style Zen in Tōkyō for a year as a lay practitioner, and I'd decided to drop out of graduate school to become a full-time training monk. A Rinzai Zen master (*rōshi*) with whom I had been studying strongly recommended Antaiji. He said, "Mr. Fujita, you're not interested in becoming a priest to manage a temple, right? If you want to live a life purely based on zazen, nothing to do with qualifying as a priest, maybe Antaiji is more suitable for you than a traditional monastery."

Thus, in the winter of 1982 I came up to Antaiji. The temple was completely isolated from the outer world and covered with heavy snow, almost nine feet high. I had to walk up from the foot of the mountain with snowshoes. About twenty people, monks and lay people, were living up the mountain, together with some dogs. During this visit I stayed at Antaiji for twenty days. My original plan had been to stay one week. I extended it because I wanted to experience more Antaiji-style *sesshin* (a period of intensive meditation practice) and to see more of their everyday life there. I liked the atmosphere of Antaiji.

While I was staying, I attended special lectures on Zen that were given for six Italian people, three monks and three laywomen. A tall and handsome Japanese monk taught the history and teachings of Zen in English. I had never heard Zen being explained in English. I became very intrigued by this monk. That was Rev. Shohaku Okumura. Since then I have always called him Shohaku-san, with great respect and affection.

Three months after this visit I started living at Antaiji as a resident and got ordained the following year. At that time I could not have imagined that a few years later, in 1987, I would go to the United States and live at the place Shohaku-san cofounded in the early 1970s: Pioneer Valley Zendō in Massachusetts. I lived there as a resident priest for more than seventeen years.

In 2010, five years after I came back from the United States to Japan, I was assigned to be the director of the Sōtō Zen Buddhism International Center in San Francisco. Shohaku-san had been the first director for twelve years. Somehow it seems that I have always been following in his footsteps—first Antaiji, then Pioneer Valley Zendō, and finally the International Center. And now I was asked by him to write a preface to his wonderful commentary to Dōgen Zenji's *Shōbōgenzō* "Sansuikyō." I do it with heartfelt gratitude. I also feel humbly honored.

Shohaku-san is a kind of very rare and precious spiritual resource for English-speaking people who are interested in Dōgen's Zen. It is not so easy to find a Japanese Zen teacher who can lead a Genzō-e (an intensive retreat to study *Shōbōgenzō*) without relying on a translator. He has rich and deep experience of practicing and studying Zen in both Japan and America. This background enables him to be a strong and effective bridge between two different cultures.

Even for Japanese people, Dōgen Zenji's *Shōbōgenzō* is one of the most challenging books to read, because he uses the language acrobatically to point to what cannot be described by language. It is like learning a completely new language with its own distinct grammar and vocabulary—even though it looks like Japanese. I call it Dōgenese. Sometimes I even wonder if it is possible to translate it into a non-Japanese language at all. That is why I very much admire the sincere effort of many people who work hard to translate Dōgen Zenji's writing into English.

I think the best way to get access to *Shōbōgenzō* is to keep reading aloud the original Japanese many times, whether you understand it or not, until some understanding of Dōgenese spontaneously emerges from it. But that approach is limited to only those who understand Japanese. The second-best way, I think, is to read a detailed and in-depth commentary with the good translation of *Shōbōgenzō*. Shohaku-san has been providing such commentaries on "Genjōkōan" and other fascicles of *Shōbōgenzō* for years. Now you have such a great gift from him in your hands. Congratulations!

"Sansuikyō" is a completely unique fascicle in the sense that Dōgen Zenji picks up concrete things like "mountains" and "waters" as a theme, rather than abstract concepts such as "being," "time," "mind," "good and evil," "buddha nature," and so forth, as he does in other fascicles. Mountains and waters are physical, not metaphysical at all, but he eloquently expounds them as Buddhadharma.

Delving into "Sansuikyō," we can encounter the mountains and waters with a freshness of the heart that is beyond the human-centered mind. That is the world of "mountains are mountains, waters are waters," as the old buddha in the text says, unfolded through practicing zazen. Through zazen, we can eventually realize with our own bodies what is written in "Sansuikyō."

I am confident that with this book you will get some insight into the depth of Dōgen Zenji's articulations of the Dharma and be inspired toward practicing zazen.

Issho Fujita
Director, Sōtō Zen Buddhism
International Center, San Francisco, CA

O N FIRST HEARING the title "Mountains and Waters Sūtra,"
I found my heart opening. The truth is written in the mountains, the rivers, and the whole earth: this is what I have
known all my life. Yet on attempting to read it, I became quite confused. Blue mountains walk? Dōgen's poetic writing did not yield to
me. Only by working with this commentary did I begin to enter the
profound and intimate teaching Dōgen offers; through mountains and
waters he discusses everything in the teaching and in our whole life of
practice.

With no interest in summarizing, I offer a few of my favorite quota-
tions from "Sansuikyō":

> We must bring to realization the road on which the self
> encounters the self.

> These words should be engraved on skin, flesh, bones, and
> marrow, engraved on the interior and exterior of body and
> mind, engraved on emptiness and on form; they are engraved
> on trees and rocks, engraved on fields and villages.

> Although we say that mountains belong to the country,
> actually they belong to those who love them.

It was his kindness that attracted me to study with Shohaku Okumura. Yet over the years, the results of his scholarship have seeped into my bones. His translations and commentaries are completely trustworthy. He is careful with words and their meaning, he knows the context in which Dōgen and other ancients spoke, and he is not fooled by the glamour that surrounds so many ancestors. Knowing his way of translating and studying, I feel safe with his work.

Shodo Spring

# Introduction

THIS BOOK IS based on my lectures on *Shōbōgenzō* "Sansuikyō," or "Mountains and Waters Sūtra," during a one-week Genzō-e retreat at the San Francisco Zen Center held from March 8 to March 15, 2002. That was the first Genzō-e in the United States. *Genzō-e* literally means "a gathering for studying *Shōbōgenzō*"; *Genzō* is an abbreviation of *Shōbōgenzō* (*True Dharma Eye Treasury*), the most famous work by Dōgen Zenji, the founder of the Japanese Sōtō Zen tradition.

Genzō-e has become one of my main teaching activities. In 2003 I moved from San Francisco to Bloomington, Indiana, to establish my practice center, Sanshinji. From 2003 to 2013 I led Genzō-e four times a year, twice at Sanshinji and twice at other Zen centers. In 2014 I reduced the number of Genzō-e to three times a year, twice at Sanshinji and once at another center, to maintain the quality of my lectures.

## GENZŌ-E IN JAPAN AND AMERICA

This tradition started in Japan more than a hundred years ago. Until the Meiji Restoration in 1867, Japanese Buddhism was protected and controlled by the Tokugawa Shogunate government. But after the Meiji Restoration, a new imperial government was established that wanted to make Shintōism, the indigenous Japanese religion, the state religion, with the emperor as a god. They considered Buddhism a religion from outside that would not help promote nationalism. In 1868 the government declared that it no longer controlled Buddhist orders, and it stopped supporting Buddhism. Since Buddhist orders were forced to become independent, they had to start teaching and sharing their practice with common people.

The main teachings of the Sōtō School were based on Dōgen Zenji's writings, among which *Shōbōgenzō* is the most important. However, *Shōbōgenzō* was quite difficult even for Sōtō School priests.

In 1905, as a commemoration of the six hundred and fiftieth anniversary of Dōgen Zenji's death, Eiheiji monastery started the practice of Genzō-e to convey *Shōbōgenzō* to Sōtō priests. The temple invited an eminent Sōtō Zen master and expert on *Shōbōgenzō* to lecture twice a day for seventy days. The first lecturer was Sōtan Oka Rōshi. He was the president of Sōtōshū Daigakurin (present-day Komazawa University) and was also the abbot of Shuzenji monastery. He lectured on the entire ninety-five fascicles of *Shōbōgenzō*. About one hundred and fifty people participated. Today Genzō-e lasts only two or three weeks at Eiheiji, and a week or less at some other temples.

Since that time many lay people have also become interested in Dōgen; not only Zen Buddhist scholars but philosophers as well study Dōgen. Today many books on *Shōbōgenzō* or Dōgen Zenji have been published. In large bookstores in Japan you can find at least a few shelves of books on Dōgen.

Beginning at the end of the nineteenth century, many Japanese people emigrated and formed communities in Hawaii and California. In the early twentieth century, Sōtō Zen priests followed them and established temples for the Japanese-American communities. However, not many Americans were interested in the actual practice of Sōtō Zen Buddhism until the second half of the century. In the 1960s Japanese Sōtō priests, including Shunryū Suzuki, Hakuyū Taizan Maezumi, and Dainin Katagiri, began to teach Zen practice to Americans. In the 1960s and 1970s some of the leading Zen centers in the West were established, and many young Americans went to Japan to practice Zen.

Now Sōtō Zen in the United States has a history of more than fifty years.

When I started to practice at Antaiji in 1972 with my teacher Kōshō Uchiyama Rōshi, he encouraged me to study English. At that time, many Westerners came to Antaiji in Kyōto. They lived in the neighborhood and came to sit with us every day. During the sesshins, almost one-third of the participants were Westerners. Uchiyama Rōshi didn't speak any European language, so he asked his disciples to study English. I was one of three people he sent to an English school in Osaka, run by a student of Suzuki Rōshi. I actually had no desire to speak English, but somehow when he asked I couldn't say no. I was never able to say no to my teacher. So I hesitatingly agreed. That was the original mistake; it shaped the whole direction of my life. Everything I am doing now is a result of that ambivalent "yes" when I was just twenty-four years old.

Somehow I managed to learn English. Then I wanted to study Dōgen's teaching in English, but I found only three English books on Sōtō Zen. These days there are many books, but there are still very few English commentaries on *Shōbōgenzō*. The problem is that Dōgen's writings are extremely difficult. Even in Japan, when we study Dōgen's writings, we start with commentaries and translations into modern Japanese. Dōgen lived eight hundred years ago. For a modern Japanese person, reading Dōgen is like a Westerner reading thirteenth-century English literature mixed with Latin and Greek. Adding to this natural language barrier, Dōgen often intentionally ignored or twisted Chinese and Japanese grammar to express his unique perspective on well-known terms or expressions. To understand his writings we need a large range of knowledge on Buddhist teachings and Zen literature, but that is not enough. We also need to understand his teaching through the practice of zazen and other aspects of Sōtō Zen tradition.

I have been studying and practicing Dōgen's way for about forty-five years. At Komazawa University I studied Buddhism and Dōgen's teaching; since then I have been studying and practicing zazen in Dōgen's way. I myself have been working on translations of Dōgen's writings, but sometimes I feel sad because much is lost, added, or twisted in the process of translation. I try to fill the gaps by offering my understanding based on my study of *Shōbōgenzō* in Japanese and the zazen practice I learned from my teacher Kōshō Uchiyama Rōshi, which was based on Dōgen's teachings. My English is not really good, but somehow I have managed to talk about Dōgen. If I can fill that gap in American Zen even a little bit, then I will feel I have contributed. This is the reason I teach Genzō-e retreats. I hope my effort is helpful.

When I give lectures, my audience is mostly practitioners at Sōtō Zen centers, but this study is not only for people with a particular interest in Dōgen or even in Sōtō Zen. Dōgen is a unique and profound teacher. His teaching is helpful for anyone who wants to understand what Zen Buddhism is. Many philosophers, poets, and social and environmental activists have been inspired by Dōgen's insight.

In 2002, when I gave the lectures that became this book, I had been living at the San Francisco Zen Center for two and a half years. But I usually didn't participate in the practice activities there because I had a job somewhere else; since 1997 I had been the director of the Sōtō Zen Education Center, now called the Sōtō Zen Buddhism International Center. This office was established by the Japanese Sōtō School as a bridge between American Sōtō Zen sanghas and the Japanese tradition.

Every day I walked to Sokoji, the temple that housed the Center, in Japantown. Sokoji was the original home of the Zen Center, which had moved to Page Street in 1969. Since then unfortunately there hadn't been much interaction between Sokoji and the Zen Center. So when I walked, I thought that I was going back and forth, not only between the Zen Center and Sokoji but also between American and Japanese Zen, connecting them.

I'm part of American Zen; I've been living in the United States altogether for about twenty-five years, practicing and teaching at various American Zen centers and now at my temple, Sanshinji. But I was born in Japan. I studied Buddhism and was ordained and trained as a priest in Japan. Within me are both American and Japanese Zen, and I still have to walk back and forth between them. It's a difficult practice.

Sometimes I think American Zen is too different from the practice I learned in Japan, but when I go back to Japan, I find Japanese Zen too traditional, and I think it's losing relevance in the modern world. I wonder if both Japanese and American practitioners will think I am strange. Still I find this experience precious, both as a person and as a practitioner. Not many people can have such a practice. It is very hard, but I consider myself fortunate to practice in this way.

## "Sansuikyō" in Dōgen's Life

Dōgen was born in 1200 CE. He was ordained as a Tendai monk at age thirteen. After that he had big changes every ten years: at twenty-three he went to China, ten years later he founded his first monastery, and ten years later he left that monastery and moved to Echizen, where he practiced and taught for ten more years before dying. In my book *Realizing Genjōkōan*, Dōgen's life, as written by Hee-Jin Kim, is included as appendix 3. So I will just mention a few things here.

It is said that when Dōgen was about fourteen or fifteen years old he had a question about Mahāyāna teaching. If we already have buddha nature, why do we have to study and practice? He was not satisfied with the answers he received, and finally he left to study Zen. He went to Kenninji monastery and practiced Rinzai Zen for six or seven years with Myōzen. Then Myōzen and Dōgen went to China together to study with a Chinese Zen master. Myōzen died there; Dōgen stayed for about five years. Right at the beginning he had a famous encounter with a Chinese *tenzo* (monastery cook) in which he came to realize that working with the everyday materials of rice and vegetables was a practice equal to the chanting, studying, and sitting practice he had known before. Here he had found the true spirit of Zen, and it influenced everything that followed.

While in China, Dōgen met the master he considered his true teacher, Tiantong Rujing (in Japanese, Tendo Nyojo). Dōgen practiced with Rujing for about two years, received transmission, and returned to Kenninji. For three years he stayed at Kenninji, which combined

Rinzai Zen with the Tendai tradition. But Dōgen was a radical; he wanted to establish a place of genuine Zen practice. He left Kenninji and for a while lived in a small hermitage. During this time he wrote *Bendōwa* or *The Wholehearted Way*, describing real practice and countering common misunderstandings.

In 1233, while still very young for a Zen master, Dōgen established his own monastery, Kōshōji, beginning his career as a teacher. He also began writing the essays that later became *Shōbōgenzō*. "Sansuikyō" was written at Kōshōji in 1240, at the beginning of his most creative years, which continued till 1245. In 1243 he moved for unknown reasons and started a new monastery. He first named it Daibutsuji, Great Buddha Temple, then changed the name to Eiheiji, Temple of Eternal Peace. In 1246 he changed the focus of his teaching method from writing essays to giving frequent Dharma discourses, later compiled in *Eihei Kōroku* (*Extensive Record*). He practiced at Eiheiji for another ten years and died of illness in 1253.

Dōgen's life as a Zen master was rather short, only twenty years. He spent his entire life searching out the way and studying the Dharma. After he found the Dharma through his teacher, he focused on transmitting that Dharma to Japan. He tried to establish a community where people could practice with the genuine spirit of Dharma. That was all he did in his life, nothing dramatic. Just sit, study, and teach—that's all.

Dōgen titled his collection *Shōbōgenzō* with an expression that is very famous in Zen literature, but its meaning and origin are not clear. I translate it as *True Dharma Eye Treasury*. For a discussion of the history of this term, and more details about *Shōbōgenzō*, please see appendix 3.

## SANSUIKYŌ MEANS "MOUNTAINS AND WATERS ARE SŪTRA"

This chapter of *Shōbōgenzō* is not a sūtra about mountains and waters. Rather, Dōgen says mountains and waters are themselves sūtra—they unceasingly expound the Buddha's teaching.

One source of Dōgen's inspiration for writing "Sansuikyō" is a poem by the well-known Chinese poet Su Shi or Su Dongpo (in Japanese, he's known as So Shoku or So Tōba) called "The Verse of Keisei Sanshoku." *Keisei sanshoku* literally means "sounds of valley streams, color of mountains" or "sounds of valley streams, form of mountains." Dōgen also wrote *Shōbōgenzō* "Keisei Sanshoku" ("Valley Sounds, Mountain Colors"), inspired by this poem. The original poem in Chinese and the Japanese way of reading it is as follows.

谿声便是広長舌
山色無非清浄身
夜来八万四千偈
他日如何挙似人

*kei sei wa sunawachi kore ko cho zetsu*
*san shoku wa sho jo shin ni arazaru kotonashi*
*yarai hachimanshisen no ge*
*tajitsu ikan ga hitoni koji sen.*

I found five English translations:

The murmuring brook is the Buddha's long, broad tongue.
And is not the shapely mountain the body of purity?
Through the night I listen to eighty thousand gathas,
When dawn breaks, how will I explain it to the others?[1]

The sound of the stream is his long, broad tongue;
The mountain his immaculate body.
These evening's eighty-four thousand verses—
How will I tell them tomorrow?[2]

The sounds of the valley streams are His long, broad
   tongue;
The forms of the mountains are His pure body.

At night I heard the myriad sūtra-verses uttered;
How can I relate to others what they say?[3]

Valley sounds are the long, broad tongue.
Mountains colors are no other than the unconditioned body.
Eighty-four thousand verses are heard throughout the night.
What can I say about this at a future time?[4]

The voices of the river-valley are the [Buddha's] Wide and
    Long Tongue,
The form of the mountains is nothing other than his
    Pure Body.
Through the night, eighty-four thousand verses.
On another day, how can I tell them to others?[5]

Studying the differences among these five translations of one poem
can tell us something about what Dōgen is saying in "Sansuikyō"—
that our views are limited, biased by our karmic consciousness. For
example, if we read only one of the translations, we understand Su Shi's
expression only through that translator's interpretation. And even if
two people read the same translation, their understanding might vary,
based upon their karma and on their different experiences with valley
streams or mountains. Understanding this, what is the "true color" of
the mountains? And what is the valley stream really saying? Which
understanding is correct? Is there any absolutely true understanding,
when each of us hears differently? This is a very important point in
"Sansuikyō."

When I used the Japanese–English dictionary to look up the English
translation of the Chinese *tani,* the original word for "valley stream,"
I found almost ten different English words. And when I looked it up
in a Chinese–Japanese dictionary I also found almost ten different
Chinese characters for this one word. Twenty different words! Poets
choose their words carefully. Why did this Chinese poet, Su Shi, want
to use this particular Chinese word? I really don't know, because I'm

not him, I'm not Chinese, and I have never been to the temple on Mount Lu where he wrote the poem. I can only try to interpret this poem through my limited knowledge, imagination, and experiences of the sounds of valley streams and colors of mountains in my life. So I am not sure if I actually understand what Su Shi wanted to express. And I have no confidence that I share the same understanding of this poem with any of the five translators. I also don't know how my English words right now seem to you.

We are very uncertain about almost everything; this uncertainty is a key element of the reality of our life. Actually, this uncertainty is a very important experience of the Buddhist teaching of emptiness. So please be patient. Don't simply believe and memorize what I am saying. Try to really see the colors of mountains yourself; try to hear the actual sounds of valley streams yourself, as your own experience; and try to share this experience with others.

This book you are reading now is my understanding of the sounds of valley streams and the color of mountains. Both Su Shi and Dōgen say the sounds of valley streams are Buddha's voice and teaching, and the colors of mountains are Buddha's body. How can we hear Buddha's message? And how can we see Buddha? This is the central point of Buddhist study.

In India, after Śākyamuni Buddha died, many people thought, "There's no Buddha anymore." They couldn't imagine a way to see Buddha or meet him personally, so they tried to study the Buddha's teachings as they were recorded in the sūtras and to practice following those teachings. But Mahāyāna Buddhists believed they *could* see the Buddha, that they could hear the voice of the Buddha in a different way, that they didn't have to rely on written records. That's why they produced so many new sūtras, which, as you know, are not a historical record of what the Buddha said.

In our common way of thinking, their belief that those teachings were spoken by Śākyamuni himself is not true; it is a lie. So Mahāyāna Buddhism is based on a collection of fake sūtras. However, this is a very important point of Mahāyāna Buddhism: How can we see the

Buddha's body? How can we hear the Buddha's voice? Is it possible or not? Mahāyāna Buddhists, including Dōgen, thought that it is. At least in Dōgen's tradition, the sounds of valley streams—the sounds of everything in nature, like wind, birdsong, temple bells—expound what the Buddha taught. They expound the reality that the Buddha awakened to. If our eyes are open to see, whatever we see is the Buddha's body.

For example, in *Shōbōgenzō* "Kenbutsu" ("Seeing Buddha"), Dōgen quoted another expression from the *Lotus Sūtra*: "Deeply entering the samādhi, we see all buddhas in the ten directions." And he comments, "Deeply entering the samādhi is itself seeing all buddhas in the ten directions."⁶ In the same fascicle, Dogen quotes a sentence from the *Diamond Sūtra* (*Vajracchedikā Prajñāpāramitā Sūtra*): "To see all forms as no form is to see Tathāgata." And he suggests that this sentence should be read as, "To see both all forms and no-form is to see Tathāgata."

Dōgen wrote these poems on the *Lotus Sūtra*:

> *tani ni hibiki*
> *mine ni naku saru*
> *taedae ni*
> *tada kono kyō wo*
> *toku to koso kike*

> In the valley, vibrating sounds,
> On the peak, monkeys' intermittent chattering,
> I hear them as they are exquisitely expounding
>     this sūtra.

> *Kono kyo no*
> *kokoro wo ureba*
> *yononaka ni*
> *uri kau koe mo*
> *nori wo toku kana.*

Grasping the heart
of this sūtra
even the voices of selling and buying
in the world are expounding the Dharma.

*Mine no iro*
*tani no hibiki mo*
*mina nagara*
*waga Shakamuni no*
*koe to sugata to*

Colors of the mountain peak
and echoes of the valley stream
all of them as they are
are nothing other than
my Śākyamuni's
voice and appearance.

*Shōbōgen*, from the title *Shōbōgenzō*, means "true Dharma eye." We need the eyes that can see true Dharma; then we can see the Buddha's body in everything. If we have the ears to hear Buddha's teaching, then we can really hear the sūtra. When we have these eyes and ears, we can see the reality of each and every thing—not only pleasant things but terrible and painful things, too. If we have the eyes and ears, we can see and hear the Buddha's teaching even through negative things.

The important question is *how* we can have such eyes and ears. That is the point of our study and practice, at least in Mahāyāna Buddhism. That is what Dōgen is discussing in "Sansuikyō."

Dōgen answers that the valley streams, or the wind and water, are always expounding Dharma. Even though Su Shi and Dōgen use poetic expressions such as "the sounds of valley streams" and "the color of mountains," these expressions are nothing special. Su Shi and Dōgen did not see and hear some deep, secret, mysterious vision only special people can experience. All of us can see the Buddha himself in everything. This way of seeing is, of course, the point of our zazen practice. Although it is nothing special, this is the profound transformation of opening the true Dharma eye.

In the final paragraph of "Keisei Sanshoku" Dōgen writes, "When we are truly practicing, the sounds and the colors of the valley streams, the colors and the sounds of the mountains, all un-begrudgingly expound their eighty-four thousand verses." This means that the sounds of valley streams and the color of mountains do not hide the Dharma, the teaching, the truth, the reality of all beings. The reality is always revealed. Nothing is hidden. What's important is the condition of the person. Are we ready to listen to what the valley stream is really saying to us? Are we ready to see the Buddha's body through the form of mountains—through the form of everything?

Dōgen continued, "When the self does not cling to fame, profit, body, and mind, valleys and mountains as well do not withhold [their verses] in a similar way." We often make a kind of fence between ourselves and all other things. We cling to whatever we own as our personal possession. When we can get something good, we want to take it into *my* territory and keep it. This is our basic problem, caused by the three poisons: greed, anger or hatred, and ignorance. If we are free from these, we can see that the fence is only in our mind. In reality we are not separated from other things. And if we are free from this separation, then not only mountains and rivers but each and every thing in the world is always expounding Buddha's teaching. This is the reality of impermanence, egolessness, and interdependent origination.

In summary, Dōgen says that to hear the teaching of Buddha through everything we encounter every day, we have to free our eyes and ears of defilement by the three poisons. And not only eyes and ears but all the senses. For example, in *Fushukuhanpō*, or *Dharma for Taking Food*, Dōgen said that food is Dharma and Dharma is food. How can we eat as Dharma? Dōgen describes the formal practice of *ōryōki*, in which we encounter food as Dharma, recognizing that the three wheels—the giver, the receiver, and the gift—are all empty and undefiled by the three poisons. This is like seeing valley streams and mountains as Buddha's body. There is no fence interfering with that direct encounter.

Even though we see things, we don't normally see them as the Dharma. How can we get this true Dharma eye? How can we really see the Dharma? That is the point of our practice. In the Sōtō Zen tradition we do monastic practice to transform our eyes, ears, nose, tongue, body, and mind. The foundation of monastic practice is zazen, and all the activities in daily monastic life are the manifestation of zazen practice: chanting sūtras, listening to Dharma talks, eating with ōryōki, cooking, cleaning, even resting and sleeping. Doing all these activities with awakening mind, being mindful and attentive—this is the way we transform our six sense organs into the true Dharma eye, ear, nose, tongue, body, and mind.

Dōgen's specific prescriptions for transforming eye, ear, nose, tongue, body, and mind might not work so well in America, where the time and culture are very different. Zen practitioners in modern America cannot do exactly the same things Japanese monks did eight hundred years ago at a monastery in the deep mountains; even if we did, our cultural background would make them different. But I think that in this country we can still practice with the same spirit as Dōgen did, even though the forms may be different. If we can find a way to live with such a spirit in modern society, then American Zen might help Japanese Zen too. In Japanese society there's a long-established tradition of Zen practice, but it doesn't work anymore. We need something new, but we don't know what. Because we live within such a strong tradition, it is very difficult to create something new in Japan. I think that if American Zen creates new styles of practice with the same spirit, it will inspire Japanese Zen practitioners and be very helpful to them. This is my wish.

*Shōbōgenzō* "Sansuikyō," or "Mountains and Waters Sūtra," was written in 1240, when Dōgen was forty years old and still in Kyōto at Kōshōji. To me this is an important point.

For me these mountains and waters have always been associated with Dōgen's life at Eiheiji in Echizen, which is very deep in the mountains. Dōgen loved the mountains, and he often talked about the mountains and cold winters in Echizen. But Dōgen lived there from 1243 to 1253, until a few months before his death, and I eventually learned that when he wrote "Sansuikyō" he was still in Kyōto. I know the geography of Kyōto and its vicinity because I grew up in Osaka, not far from Kyōto. There are no high mountains there. The highest mountains are Mount Hiei and Mount Atago, both to the north. In the southern part of Kyōto, where Kōshōji is located, there are no real mountains, only hills.

So even though Dōgen is discussing "mountains and waters of the present," as the first line of "Sansuikyō" says, he is not talking about a particular mountain where he actually lived. This seemed strange to me, and I tried to understand what it means. It seems that the mountains and waters in "Sansuikyō" were not real mountains and waters but a metaphor or symbol. This is important for understanding "Sansuikyō": "mountains and waters" is a Buddhist expression rather than a reference to real mountains where Dōgen lived.

In old Chinese and Japanese religions like Daoism, Shintōism, and Shugendō, mountains are very important. For example, Shugendō is the combination of Buddhism and a very old Japanese folk religion that worships mountains; it was formed shortly after Buddhism arrived in Japan. *Shu* (修) means "practice," *gen* (験) means "supernatural powers attained by various practices in the mountains," and *dō* (道) means "way." Shugendō essentially combines Shintō teachings and practice with tantric or esoteric Buddhism. Its practitioners purify their minds and bodies by staying in the mountains and doing ascetic practices in which they eat only nuts or walk a long distance every day or climb the steep mountains. They believe by practicing in this way, their bodies and minds are purified, and they can gain magic powers. The famous expression chanted in this kind of mountain practice is *rokkon shōjō*, "the six sense-organs are purified."

The Shugendō practice of *kaihōgyō* or mountain pilgrimage, in which the practitioner walks within Mount Hiei and the city of Kyōto for one thousand days, is still practiced today. It was established in 831 by a monk named Sō-ō. It is said that in a dream Sō-ō heard, "All the peaks on this mountain are sacred. Make pilgrimages to its holy places following the instructions of the mountain gods. Train hard like this each and every day. This is the practice of Never-Despise Bodhisattva. Your sole practice is to be the veneration of all things; through it you will realize the True Dharma."[7] This is how the ascetic mountain practice combined with Buddhist teaching, in this case using the *Lotus Sūtra*, in which Never-Despise Bodhisattva appears and which is fundamental to the Tendai school.

However, Dōgen's "Sansuikyō" is very different from such traditional religious practices in the mountains, with their elements of animism, shamanism, and occultism. What he says in "Sansuikyō" has nothing at all to do with such mountain worship, with ascetic practice for the purpose of attaining supernatural powers. Instead, he writes things like "mountains are walking." What does this mean? He does not encourage people to walk in the mountains as a spiritual practice. He discusses the virtue and movement of mountains and waters themselves.

"Sansuikyō" is a simple word with a clear meaning: *sansui* means "mountains and waters" and *kyō* means "sūtra" or "sūtras." You know what mountains and waters are. One understanding of this title could be the "Sūtra about the Mountains and Waters." But Dōgen is saying that the mountains and the waters are *themselves* sūtras. We need to understand this difference.

*Sūtra* means a collection of the Buddha's teaching, in which the Buddha showed us the reality of all beings, to which he had awakened. For about three to four hundred years, the Buddha's teachings were memorized by his students and transmitted orally. At the beginning of the first century CE, Indian people started to write them down in both Pāli and Sanskrit. The Pāli canon was transmitted to the Southeast Asian countries; Sanskrit sūtras were transmitted to the north and translated into Chinese. The word *sūtra* is Sanskrit; *Jing* is the Chinese translation and *kyō* is the Japanese pronunciation. Both *sūtra* and *jing* literally mean a "thread" or "string" used, for example, to make a garland of flowers. With this thread, Buddha's teachings are collected or compiled, so a sūtra is a collection of Dharma flowers.

When the Buddha was dying, his students were very sad because they were losing their teacher. People thought that Śākyamuni was a unique person, that no one could take his place. Śākyamuni was the only person called Buddha, and within the saṅgha no one else took the title. But the Buddha told them, "If you see Dharma, you see me." If we study and practice Dharma, if we study and practice the Buddha's teaching and live following the teaching, then we see the Buddha. The Buddha's teaching, or Dharma, is not simply the words that Buddha said. The reality of this entire world is itself Dharma. This reality of all beings is also the Buddha. Early Buddhists named it *dharmakāya*—the way each and every thing is. That is Dharma, and this Dharma is actually the Buddha. When we awaken to this reality we meet the Buddha, even though Śākyamuni as *rūpakāya* (material body) died twenty-five hundred years ago in India.

When Dōgen called this writing "Sansuikyō," or "Mountains and Waters Sūtra," he was saying that when we see mountains and waters with our true awakened eye, we see the Buddha and hear his teachings, and that is our sūtra. Mountains and waters as the sūtra are not objects that we need to study objectively; we are parts of the mountains and waters sūtra.

## DŌGEN AND LANGUAGE

Dōgen reads Buddhist and Zen texts in a unique way. He confuses us, inviting us to see the same expression from multiple perspectives. For example, in the beginning of *Shōbōgenzō* "Busshō" ("Buddha Nature"), he quotes a sentence from the *Mahāparinirvāṇa Sūtra*: "All living beings have buddha nature." This is an accurate translation of the Chinese, but Dōgen turns it into "All living beings and entire being *are* buddha nature," which is very different.

This kind of interpretation was possible because he was not Chinese.

When we study a foreign language we can read it in ways that differ from those of native speakers. For example, once when I was just starting to study English, I visited an American person in his apartment. He said he was going to eat, and I thought, "Where is he *going*?" I thought he was going somewhere to eat, but he started to eat right there. I thought English was a strange language. In English you say "It is raining" or "It is snowing." What is this *it*? This is very mysterious to me. In Japan we say that rain is falling or rain falls. When I studied English grammar I learned that "it" is just a formal subject that means nothing. If it means nothing, why is it there?

When we read a foreign language we think in ways native speakers cannot. First we consider the meaning of each word, then we try to see the meaning of the whole sentence. In a dictionary one word may have several meanings, so we have to guess what a word means in the context of the sentence. In this process, we read the sentence in various ways. Reading in a foreign language is like assembling a jigsaw puzzle. I think this is what Dōgen is doing; he deconstructs the sentence into a collection of words with more than one meaning, and then he chooses one meaning.

This transition from one culture to another is very interesting. Something very stupid could happen, and yet something very creative could happen too. We are in the process of that transition here as well; I am thinking in Japanese and writing in English, so I'm not sure whether what I am writing is the same as what I am thinking. Many of you don't know Japanese so you cannot imagine what I am thinking in Japanese; you only read my "unique" English. There might be misunderstanding, and this very misunderstanding might create profound understanding.

Here is one example from Dōgen. Some scholars think that Dōgen's expression *shinjin datsuraku* (身心脱落), "dropping off body and mind," might be a misunderstanding of the Chinese. In the written record of Dōgen's teacher Rujing, which was compiled by his Chinese disciples, he never used the expression "dropping off body and mind." He did use a seed of that expression: "dropping off mind dust." "Mind dust," or *shinjin* (心塵), means delusive thought, as in Shenxiu's verse: "We should always polish the mind mirror not to collect any dust."[8] So this could have been a misunderstanding. Rujing's saying might simply mean dropping off delusive thoughts, which is an ordinary instruction in Zen.

But "dropping off body and mind" is unique and profound. I don't agree with the scholars who think this expression is a misunderstanding. In *Hōkyōki,* Dōgen's record of his practice with Rujing, Dōgen recorded several conversations with his teacher regarding dropping off body and mind. Both expressions are pronounced *shinjin* in Japanese, but the tones in Chinese are different. If Dōgen made such a mistake, Rujing could have corrected him. I cannot imagine that their communication was so poor that such a mistake could persist.

## A NOTE ON TRANSLATIONS

Shūmuchō, the administrative headquarters of Sōtōshū, sponsors a translation project for Sōtō Zen texts; Carl Bielefeldt and a few other American scholars have been working on a translation of *Shōbōgenzō*. In his essay "Circumambulation of Mountains and Waters," Professor Bielefeldt wrote that he first translated "Sansuikyō" in 1971 at Tassajara with the help of Shunryū Suzuki Rōshi. He has been working on "Sansuikyō" for a long time; I'm honored to use his translation for this book. Though of course there is no perfect translation, I think his translation is excellent. I used his translation as the text for the Genzō-e that prompted this book because I did not think I was ready to make my own translation of "Sansuikyō." I would like to express my gratitude to Professor Bielefeldt and Sōtōshū Shūmuchō for their generous permission to use this translation in this book.

## ACKNOWLEDGMENTS

Many people contributed this book. First of all, I would like to express my gratitude to the San Francisco Zen Center and the late Rev. Zenkei

Blanche Hartman, who was the abbess of the SFZC at the time I held the Genzō-e. She had been a sewing student of Rev. Jōshin Kasai, my Dharma aunt, who visited SFZC several times to teach sewing okesa and rakusu, and has been helping and supporting my teaching activities ever since I moved to the United States. Particularly after I moved to San Francisco, she allowed me to live at the City Center without participating in their formal practice for three and half years. Without her support, I could not have worked for Sōtō Zen Buddhism International Center in the way I did.

I also want to say "thank you" to all the practitioners who participated the Genzō-e in 2002. Their enthusiasm for studying Dōgen was great encouragement for me while I was suffering in the hell of talking about Dharma in English. I also thank the practitioners at Sanshinji, from 2003 through today, for their support and appreciation of the Dharma.

Rev. Myōkō Sara Hunsaker transcribed all fourteen ninety-minute lectures of mine on Dōgen's not-so-easy writings with my not-so-normal English. I deeply appreciate her love of the Dharma. My disciple Rev. Shodo Spring worked on editing this material for several years and made my Japanese English into real, readable English. I think it must be much harder work than writing her own book.

Rev. Eijun Linda Cutts, during the practice period at Tassajara Zen Mountain monastery, looked at the manuscript on "Sansuikyō" while it was being edited and gave us wise advice. Another disciple of mine, Rev. Jokei Molly Whitehead, also went through the entire manuscript and made many helpful suggestions.

I would like to express my special gratitude to Rev. Issho Fujita, the director of Sōtō Zen Buddhism International Center, who very kindly wrote the foreword to this book, and to Mr. Gary Snyder, who kindly gave us permission to use his essay "Mountains Hidden in Mountains: Dōgen Zenji and the Mind of Ecology." The essay was written as a draft of his presentation at the Dōgen Zenji Symposium held at Stanford University on October 23 and 24, 1999. The international symposium was one of the commemorative events on the eight hundredth anniversary of the birth of Dōgen Zenji cosponsored by Sōtōshū, Daihonzan Eiheiji, Daihonzan Sōjiji, and the Stanford Center for Buddhist Studies. This symposium was one of the largest events the Sōtō Zen Education Center organized. As the director of the center, I was honored by the participation of Mr. Snyder, and now I am honored again to have this essay as an appendix to this book. His appreciation of Dōgen Zenji's "Sansuikyō" as an ecologist shows the relevance of Dōgen's teaching not only for Zen practitioners but also for all people who sincerely wish to live in harmony with nature on this planet Earth in the twenty-first century.

Finally, I want to express gratitude to my family, particularly my wife, Yuko Okumura, for support, encouragement, and patience while I studied, practiced, and taught the Dharma.

# THE TEXT

*The chapter titles and the chapter and paragraph numbers are added for the convenience of the readers. They exist neither in Dōgen's original nor in Bielefeldt's translation.*

## 1. Mountains and Waters Are the Expression of Old Buddhas

(1) These mountains and waters of the present are the expression of the old buddhas. Each, abiding in its own Dharma state, fulfills exhaustive virtues. Because they are the circumstances "prior to the kalpa of emptiness," they are this life of the present; because they are the self "before the germination of any subtle sign," they are liberated in their actual occurrence. Since the virtues of the mountain are high and broad, the spiritual power to ride the clouds is always mastered from the mountains, and the marvelous ability to follow the wind is inevitably liberated from the mountains.

## 2. Mountains

### 2-1. Blue Mountains Are Constantly Walking
(2) Preceptor Kai of Mount Dayang⁹ addressed the assembly, saying, "The blue mountains are constantly walking. The stone woman gives birth to a child in the night."

(3) The mountains lack none of their proper virtues; hence, they are constantly at rest and constantly walking. We must devote ourselves to a detailed study of this virtue of walking. Since the walking of the mountains should be like that of people, one ought not doubt that the mountains walk simply because they may not appear to stride like humans.

(4) This saying of the buddha and ancestor [Daokai] has pointed out walking; it has got what is fundamental, and we should thoroughly investigate this address on "constant walking." It is constant because it is walking. Although the walking of the blue mountains is faster than "swift as the wind," those in the mountains do not sense this, do not know it. To be "in the mountains" is "a flower opening within the world."[10] Those outside the mountains do not sense this, do not know it. Those without eyes to see the mountains, do not sense, do not know, do not see, do not hear the reason for this. To doubt the walking of the mountains means that one does not yet know one's own walking. It is not that one does not walk but that one does not yet know, has not made clear, this walking. Those who would know their own walking must also know the walking of the blue mountains.

(5) The blue mountains are not sentient; they are not insentient. We ourselves are not sentient; we are not insentient. We can have no doubts about these blue mountains walking. We do not know what measure of Dharma realms would be necessary to clarify the blue mountains. We should do a clear accounting of the blue mountains' walking and our own walking, including an accounting of both "stepping back and back stepping."[11] We should do an accounting of the fact that, since the very time "before any subtle sign," since "the other side of the King of Emptiness," walking by stepping forward and back has never stopped for a moment.

(6) If walking had ever rested, the buddhas and ancestors would never have appeared; if walking were limited, the Buddhadharma would

never have reached us today. Stepping forward has never ceased; stepping back has never ceased. Stepping forward does not oppose stepping back, nor does stepping back oppose stepping forward. This virtue is called "the mountain flowing, the flowing mountain."

(7) The blue mountains devote themselves to the investigation of walking; the East Mountain studies "moving over the water." Hence, this study is the mountains' own study. The mountains, without altering their own body and mind, with their own mountain countenance, have always been circling back to study [themselves].

(8) Do not slander mountains by saying that the blue mountains cannot walk, nor the East Mountain move over the water. It is because of the baseness of the common person's point of view that we doubt the phrase "the blue mountains walk"; because of the crudeness of our limited experience, we are surprised by the words "flowing mountain." Without having fully penetrated even the term "flowing water," we just remain sunk in our limited perception.

(9) Thus, the accumulated virtues [of the mountain] brought up here represent its very "name and form," its "vital artery." There is a mountain walk and a mountain flow. There is a time when the mountains give birth to a mountain child. The mountains become the buddhas and ancestors, and it is for this reason that the buddhas and ancestors have thus appeared.

(10) Even when we have the eyes [to see mountains as] the appearance of grass and trees, earth and stone, fences and walls, this is nothing to doubt, nothing to be moved by: it is not the complete appearance [of the mountains]. Even when there appears an occasion in which [the mountains] are seen as the splendor of the seven treasures, this is still not the real refuge. Even when they appear to us as the realm of the practice of the way of the buddhas, this is not necessarily something to be desired. Even when we attain the crowning appearance of the vision

of [the mountains as] the inconceivable virtues of the buddhas, their reality is more than this. Each of these appearances is the particular objective and subjective result [of past karma]; they are not the karma of the way of the buddhas and ancestors but narrow, one-sided views.[12] "Turning the object and turning the mind" is criticized by the Great Sage; "explaining the mind and explaining the nature" is not affirmed by the buddhas and ancestors; "seeing the mind and seeing the nature" is the business of non-Buddhists. "Sticking to words and sticking to phrases" are not the words of liberation. There are [words] that are free from such realms: they are "the blue mountains constantly walking" and "the East Mountain moving over the water." We should give them detailed investigation.

(11) "The stone woman gives birth to a child in the night." This means that the time when "a stone woman gives birth to a child" is "the night." There are male stones, female stones, and stones neither male nor female. They repair heaven, and they repair earth. There are stones of heaven, and there are stones of earth. Though this is said in the secular world, it is rarely understood. We should understand the reason behind this "giving birth to a child." At the time of birth, are parent and child transformed together? We should not only study that birth is realized in the child becoming the parent; we should also study and fully understand that the practice and verification of birth is realized when the parent becomes the child.[13]

### 2-2. *East Mountains Walking in the Water*
(12) The Great Master Yunmen Kuangzhen[14] has said, "The East Mountain moves over the water."

(13) The import of this expression is that all mountains are the East Mountain, and all these East Mountains are "moving over the water." Therefore, Mount Sumeru and the other nine mountains are all appearing, are all practicing and verifying [the Buddhadharma]. This is called "the East Mountain." But how could Yunmen himself be liberated

from the "skin, flesh, bones, and marrow" of the East Mountain and its life of practice and verification?

(14) At the present time in the land of the great Song there is a certain bunch of illiterates who have formed such a crowd that they cannot be overcome by the few real [students]. They maintain that sayings such as this "East Mountain moving over the water" or Nanquan's "sickle" are incomprehensible talk. Their idea is that any saying that is involved with thought is not a Zen saying of the buddhas and ancestors; it is incomprehensible sayings that are the sayings of the buddhas and ancestors. Consequently, [they hold that] Huangbo's "stick" and Linji's "roar," because they are difficult to comprehend and cannot be grasped by thought, represent the great awakening preceding the time "before the germination of any subtle sign." The "tangle-cutting phrases" often used as devices by earlier worthies are [they say] incomprehensible.[15]

(15) Those who talk in this way have never met a true teacher and lack the eye of study; they are worthless little fools. There have been many such "sons of Māra" and "gang of six" shavepates in the land of Song for the last two or three hundred years.[16] This is truly regrettable, for it represents the decline of the great way of the buddhas and ancestors. Their understanding is inferior to that of the hīnayāna śrāvakas, more foolish than that even of non-Buddhists. They are not laymen; they are not monks. They are not humans; they are not gods. They are dumber than beasts that study the way of the buddha. What you shavelings call "incomprehensible sayings" is incomprehensible only to you, not to the buddhas and ancestors. Simply because you yourself do not comprehend [the sayings] is no reason for you not to study the path comprehended by the buddhas and ancestors. Even granted that [Zen teachings] were in the end incomprehensible, this comprehension of yours would also be wrong. Such types are common throughout all quarters of the state of Song; I have seen them with my own eyes. They are to be pitied. They do not know that thought is words; they do not know that words are liberated from thought. When I was in the Song,

I made fun of them, but they never had an explanation, never a word to say for themselves—just this false notion of theirs about "incomprehensibility." Who could have taught you this? Though you have no natural teacher, you are natural little non-Buddhists.[17]

(16) We should realize that this [teaching of] "the East Mountain moving over the water" is the very "bones and marrow" of the buddhas and ancestors. All the waters are appearing at the foot of the East Mountain, and therefore the mountains mount the clouds and stride through the heavens. The mountains are the peaks of the waters, and in both ascending and descending their walk is "over the water." The tips of the mountains' feet walk across the waters, setting them dancing. Therefore, their walking is "seven high and eight across" and their "practice and verification are not nonexistent."[18]

## 3. WATERS

(17) Water is neither strong nor weak, neither wet nor dry, neither moving nor still, neither cold nor hot, neither being nor nonbeing, neither delusion nor enlightenment. Frozen, it is harder than diamond; who could break it? Melted, it is softer than milk; who could break it?

(18) This being the case, we cannot doubt the many virtues realized [by water]. We should study the occasion when the water of the ten directions is seen in the ten directions. This is not a study only of the time when humans or gods see water: there is a study of water seeing water. Water practices and verifies water; hence, there is a study of water telling of water. We must bring to realization the road on which the self encounters the self; we must move back and forth along, and spring off from, the vital path on which the other studies and fully comprehends the other.

(19) In general, then, the way of seeing mountains and waters differs according to the type of being [that sees them]. In seeing water, there

are beings who see it as a jeweled necklace. This does not mean, however, that they see a jeweled necklace as water. How, then, do we see what they consider water? Their jeweled necklace is what we see as water. Some see water as miraculous flowers, though it does not follow that they use flowers as water. Hungry ghosts see water as raging flames or as pus and blood. Dragons and fish see it as a palace or a tower, or as the seven treasures or the *mani* gem. [Others] see it as woods and walls, or as the Dharma nature of immaculate liberation, or as the true human body, or as the physical form and mental nature. Humans see these as water. And these [different ways of seeing] are the conditions under which [water] is killed or given life.[19]

(20) Given that what different types of beings see is different, we should have some doubts about this. Is it that there are various ways of seeing one object? Or is it that we have mistaken various images for one object? At the peak of our concentrated effort on this, we should concentrate still more. Therefore, our practice and verification, our pursuit of the way, must also be not merely of one or two kinds, and the ultimate realm must also have a thousand types and ten thousand kinds.

(21) If we reflect further on the real import of this [question], although we say there is water of the various types, it would seem there is no original water, no water of various types. Nevertheless, the various waters in accordance with the types [of beings] do not depend on the mind, do not depend on the body [of these beings]; they do not arise from [different types of] karma; they are not dependent on self; they are not dependent on other. They are liberated dependent on water. Therefore, water is not [the water of] earth, water, fire, wind, space or consciousness; it is not blue, yellow, red, white, or black; it is not form, sound, smell, taste, touch, or idea. Nevertheless, the waters of earth, water, fire, wind, space, and the rest have been spontaneously appearing [as such].

(22) This being the case, it becomes difficult to explain by what and of what the present land and palace are made. To say that they rest on

the wheel of space and the wheel of wind is true neither for oneself nor for others; it is just speculating on the basis of the suppositions of an inferior view and is said only out of fear that, without such a resting place, they could not abide.[20]

(23) The Buddha has said, "All things are ultimately liberated; they have no abode."[21]

(24) We should realize that, although they are liberated, without any bonds, all things are abiding in [their own particular] state. However, when humans look at water, they have the one way that sees it only as flowing without rest. This "flow" takes many forms, of which the human view is but one. [Water] flows over the earth; it flows across the sky; it flows up; it flows down. [Water] flows around bends and into deep abysses. It mounts up to form clouds; it descends to form pools.

(25) The *Wen Tzu* says, "The tao of water, ascending to heaven, becomes rain and dew, descending to earth, becomes rivers and streams."[22]

(26) Such is said even in the secular world; it would be shameful indeed if those who call themselves descendants of the buddhas and ancestors were more stupid than the secular. [This passage] says that, although the way of water is unknown to water, water actually functions [as water]; although the way of water is not unknown to water, water actually functions [as water].

(27) "Ascending to heaven, it becomes rain and dew." We should realize that water climbs to the very highest heavens in the highest quarters and becomes rain and dew. Rain and dew is of various kinds, in accordance with the various worlds. To say that there are places to which water does not reach is the teaching of the hīnayāna śrāvaka, or the false teaching of the non-Buddhist. Water extends into flames; it extends into thought, reasoning, and discrimination; it extends into awareness and the buddha nature.

(28) "Descending to earth, it becomes rivers and streams." We should realize that, when water descends to earth, it becomes rivers and streams, and that the essence of rivers and streams becomes sages. The foolish common folk think that water is always in rivers, streams, and seas, but this is not so: [water] makes rivers and seas within water. Therefore, water is in places that are not rivers and seas; it is just that, when water descends to earth, it works as rivers and seas.

(29) Moreover, we should not study that, when water has become rivers and seas, there is then no world and no buddha land [within water]: incalculable buddha lands are realized even within a single drop of water. Consequently, it is not that water exists within the buddha land, nor that the buddha land exists within water: the existence of water has nothing whatever to do with the three times or the Dharma realm. Nevertheless, though it is like this, it is the kōan of the actualization of water.

(30) Wherever the buddhas and ancestors are, water is always there; wherever water is, there the buddhas and ancestors always appear. Therefore, the buddhas and ancestors have always taken up water as their own body and mind, their own thinking.

(31) In this way, then, [the idea] that water does not climb up is to be found neither in Buddhist nor non-Buddhist writings. The way of water penetrates everywhere, above and below, vertically and horizontally. Still, in the sūtras it is said that fire and wind go up, while earth and water go down. But this "up and down" bears some study—the study of the up and down of the way of the buddha. [In the way of the buddha,] where earth and water go is considered "down"; but "down" here does not mean some place to which earth and water go. Where fire and wind go is "up." While the Dharma realm has no necessary connection with up and down or the four directions, simply on the basis of the function of the four, five, or six elements, we provisionally set up a Dharma realm with directions. It is not that the "heaven of nonconception" is above

and the "Avīci hell"[23] is below: Avīci is the entire Dharma realm; the heaven of nonconception is the entire Dharma realm.

(32) Nevertheless, when dragons and fish see water as a palace, just as when humans see palaces, they do not view it as flowing. And, if some onlooker were to explain to them that their palace was flowing water, they would surely be just as amazed as we are now to hear it said that mountains flow. Still, there would undoubtedly be some [dragons and fish] who would accept such an explanation of the railings, stairs, and columns of palaces and pavilions. We should calmly consider, over and over, the reason for this. If our study is not liberated from these confines, we have not freed ourselves from the body and mind of the commoner, we have not fully comprehended the land of the buddhas and ancestors, we have not fully comprehended the land of the commoner, we have not fully comprehended the palace of the commoner.

(33) Although humans have deeply understood what is in seas and rivers as water, just what kind of thing dragons, fish, and other beings understand and use as water we do not yet know. Do not foolishly assume that all kinds of beings must use as water what we understand as water.

(34) When those who study Buddhism seek to learn about water, they should not stick to [the water of] humans; they should go on to study the water of the way of the buddhas. We should study how we see the water used by the buddhas and ancestors; we should study whether within the rooms of the buddhas and ancestors there is or is not water.

## 4. Mountains and Waters Are Dwelling Places for Sages

(35) From the distant past to the distant present, mountains have been the dwelling place of the great sages. Wise men and sages have all made

the mountains their own chambers, their own body and mind. And through these wise men and sages the mountains have appeared. However many great sages and wise men we suppose have assembled in the mountains, ever since they entered the mountains no one has met a single one of them. There is only the expression of the mountain way of life; not a single trace of their having entered remains. The "crown and eyes" [of the mountains] are completely different when we are in the world gazing off at the mountains and when we are in the mountains meeting the mountains. Our concept of not-flowing and our understanding of not-flowing should not be the same as the dragon's understanding. Humans and gods reside in their own worlds, and other beings may have their doubts [about this], or then again, they may not.

(36) Therefore, without giving way to our surprise and doubt, we should study the words "mountains flow" with the buddhas and ancestors. Taking up one [view], there is flowing; taking up another, there is not-flowing. At one turn, there is flowing; at another, not-flowing. If our study is not like this, it is not "the true Dharma wheel of the Thus Come One."

(37) An old buddha has said, "If you wish to avoid the karma of Avīci hell, do not slander the true Dharma wheel of the Thus Come One."[24]

(38) These words should be engraved on skin, flesh, bones, and marrow, engraved on interior and exterior of body and mind, engraved on emptiness and on form; they are engraved on trees and rocks, engraved on fields and villages.

(39) Although we say that mountains belong to the country, actually they belong to those who love them. When the mountains love their owners, the wise and virtuous inevitably enter the mountains. And when sages and wise men live in the mountains, because the mountains belong to them, trees and rocks flourish and abound, and the birds and

beasts take on a supernatural excellence. This is because the sages and wise men have covered them with their virtue. We should realize that the mountains actually take delight in wise men, actually take delight in sages.

(40) Throughout the ages, we have excellent examples of emperors who have gone to the mountains to pay homage to wise men and seek instruction from great sages. At such times [the emperors] respected [the sages] as teachers and honored them without standing on worldly forms. For the imperial authority has no authority over the mountain sage, and [the emperors] knew that the mountains are beyond the mundane world. In ancient times we have [the cases of] Kongtong and the Hua Guard: when the Yellow Emperor made his visit, he went on his knees, prostrated himself, and begged instruction.[25] Again, the Buddha Śākyamuni left his royal father's palace and went into the mountains; yet his royal father felt no resentment toward the mountains nor distrust of those in the mountains who instructed the prince. [The prince's] twelve years of cultivating the way were largely spent in the mountains, and it was in the mountains that the Dharma King's auspicious event occurred. Truly, even a "wheel-turning king" does not wield authority over the mountains.

(41) We should understand that the mountains are not within the limits of the human realm or the limits of the heavens above. They are not to be viewed with the calculations of human thought. If only we did not compare them with flowing in the human realm, who would have any doubts about such things as the mountains' flowing or not flowing?

(42) Again, since ancient times, wise men and sages have also lived by the water. When they live by the water they hook fish. Or they hook people, or they hook the way. These are all "water styles" of old. And going further, there must be hooking the self, hooking the hook, being hooked by the hook, and being hooked by the way.

(43) Long ago, when the Preceptor Decheng suddenly left Yueshan and went to live on the river, he got the sage of Huating River.[26] Is this not hooking a fish? Is it not hooking a person? Is it not hooking water? Is it not hooking himself? That the person got to see Decheng is [because he was] Decheng; Decheng's accepting the person is his meeting the person.

(44) It is not the case simply that there is water in the world; within the world of water there is a world. And this is true not only within water: within clouds as well there is a world of sentient beings; within wind there is a world of sentient beings; within fire there is a world of sentient beings; within earth there is a world of sentient beings. Within the Dharma realm there is a world of sentient beings; within a single blade of grass there is a world of sentient beings; within a single staff there is a world of sentient beings. And wherever there is a world of sentient beings, there, inevitably, is the world of buddhas and ancestors. The reason this is so, we should study very carefully.

(45) In this way, water is the palace of the "true dragon"; it is not flowing away. If we regard it only as flowing, the word "flowing" is an insult to water: it is like imposing "not flowing." Water is nothing but water's "real form just as it is." Water is the virtue of water; it is not flowing. In the thorough study of the flowing or the not-flowing of a single [drop of] water, the entirety of the ten thousand things is instantly realized. Among mountains as well, there are mountains hidden in jewels; there are mountains hidden in marshes, mountains hidden in the sky; there are mountains hidden in mountains. There is a study of mountains hidden in hiddenness.

## 5. CONCLUSION: MOUNTAINS ARE MOUNTAINS, WATERS ARE WATERS

(46) An old buddha has said, "Mountains are mountains and waters are waters."[27]

(47) These words do not say that mountains are mountains; they say that mountains are mountains. Therefore, we should thoroughly study these mountains. When we thoroughly study the mountains, this is the mountain training. Such mountains and waters themselves become wise men and sages.

*Treasury of the Eye of the True Dharma*
Book 29
"Mountains and Waters Sūtra"

Presented to the assembly
eighteenth day, tenth month, first year of Ninji (1240),
at Kannon Dori Kōshō Horinji.

Translated by Carl Bielefeldt

# THE COMMENTARY

# MOUNTAINS AND WATERS ARE
# THE EXPRESSION OF OLD BUDDHAS

I N HIS TRANSLATION, Professor Bielefeldt divided "Sansuikyō" into four parts: introduction, mountains, waters, and mountains and waters as the dwelling of wise people. Professor Bielefeldt didn't make another division, but I think the last two paragraphs are Dōgen's conclusion, so we have five sections.

Here is the first paragraph of "Sansuikyō":

(1) These mountains and waters of the present are the expression of the old buddhas. Each, abiding in its own Dharma state, fulfills exhaustive virtues. Because they are the circumstances "prior to the kalpa of emptiness," they are this life of the present; because they are the self "before the germination of any subtle sign," they are liberated in their actual occurrence. Since the virtues of the mountain are high and broad, the spiritual power to ride the clouds is always mastered from the mountains, and the marvelous ability to follow the wind is inevitably liberated from the mountains.

Do you understand this? Somehow, even though we don't understand it, it sounds beautiful, very poetic. We want to understand. This thirst to understand is a desire; it stands in the way of our encountering the text.

Dōgen emphasizes not-understanding (*fu-e*, 不会). When we read writings like this, it is important to realize that not-understanding is not negative. Dōgen uses the term *fue suru*; *suru* means "do," *fu* means "not," and *e* means "understand." In common usage this expression means "I don't understand" and is negative. But Dōgen uses *fu-e* as a compound, making it one word, and puts "do" with it, so he tells us to "do not-understanding." He uses this expression in various meanings in various fascicles of *Shōbōgenzō*. One meaning is "to go beyond understanding": that is, to embody and actually practice it without stagnating within "understanding." This is very important when we study Dōgen.[28]

I use this expression in a different way here; I use it to mean keeping something in my mind without grasping it with my personal "understanding." I have been "doing not-understanding" for forty years. Sometimes I think I understand, but the next moment or the next day I find that I don't. This kind of not-understanding is also important. In zazen we let go of our thought. This letting go is "not-understanding." Thought is "understanding." By letting go we "do not-understanding." This sitting and letting go of thought, this opening the hand of thought, is the true Dharma eye. That means that we are not grasping things with our karmic consciousness or with the thoughts that arise from it.

"Karmic consciousness" refers to the storage of our past experiences. According to Yogācāra teaching, our consciousness can be categorized into eight layers. The first five are created by our sense organs: eye, ear, nose, tongue, and body. The sixth consciousness, the *manovijñāna*, is our discriminating mind, our usual psychology, the functioning of our brain. The seventh is called *manas*, sometimes translated into English as "ego consciousness." The last is *ālayavijñāna*, translated into Japanese as *zō*, like the *zō* in *Shōbōgenzō*. It means "storehouse"; the deepest layer of our consciousness is called our "storehouse consciousness." All the experiences from birth or even before are stored in this deepest layer. When we encounter a new object or situation, we interpret it according to what kinds of seeds are stored in our storehouse. The way we view and react to things depends on the seeds we have. This is karmic consciousness, and it is how we are unique: each of us has different seeds stored in our storehouse. That is the teaching of Buddhist psychology.

The founders of Yogācāra created the concept of the storehouse consciousness to explain how our life has continuity without having permanent self (*ātman*). According to them, consciousness is there, but nothing is fixed as "self." Our life is like a river or a waterfall. There is something continuous, just as water is always flowing in the river, but each moment the water is new and different. Our life is always changing, always moving, never fixed. Still there's some kind of continuation in our consciousness.

## PRACTICE IN ZAZEN AND DAILY LIFE

Our zazen is a unique thing. We face the wall without an object. Still, many things rise in our consciousness. For example, I might think about an incident that made me angry, maybe yesterday. That event may be so powerful that no matter how many times I have tried to let go it still comes up. Actually, when I am sitting and facing the wall the incident is already over. It's not reality anymore. But it continues in my consciousness as if it were real. During zazen I can see clearly that there's no object, no person in front of me now. It's an illusion, just energy that still remains from those seeds in my storehouse consciousness. So I can let go. When we let go without grasping, without taking action based on our thoughts, we are released from our karmic consciousness. This is the completely unique activity of zazen.

In my teacher's style of practice, we have five-day sesshin. On each of these five days we sit one period of fifty minutes, then we have ten minutes of *kinhin*, walking meditation, then another fifty minutes of sitting, and we practice this way for fourteen periods a day. We have no chanting, no lecture, no interviews with the teacher, and no work period. We have three meals, fortunately, and a short break after each meal. We sit from four A.M. until nine P.M. It is really quiet.

At Antaiji we had this kind of sesshin ten times a year. After one sesshin, there would be just three weeks before the next. It was very difficult for me. I was in my twenties then and had much energy and desire to do things, but I had to somehow stay on the cushion, facing the wall. I had many thoughts, emotions, and desires come up. It was difficult to sit still, but it was a very powerful practice.

In 1975 Uchiyama Rōshi sent three of his students to build a very small zendō in Massachusetts: Pioneer Valley Zendō. There we had twelve sesshins a year. Later in Japan I had a place in Kyōto where I could practice with non-Japanese people and work on translation. Because of my responsibilities as caretaker, our sesshins included temple cleaning and morning service; still, it was basically just sitting. For me, that was what sesshin meant. I practiced that way for more than twenty years, from 1970 to 1992.

In 1993 I went to Minneapolis to teach at Dainin Katagiri Rōshi's Minnesota Zen Meditation Center. While there I decided to practice following Rōshi's style. So, for ten years, I practiced and taught in this style of sesshin, with zazen, chanting, ōryōki meals, *dokusan* (private interviews), work periods, and so on. I had twenty years of just sitting experience and then ten years of sesshin with other activities. The two styles are very different for the priest leading the sesshin.

In "Genjōkōan," Dōgen writes about riding in a boat and watching the shore. When you keep your eyes closely on the boat, you can see that it is the boat moving and not the shore; this is the practice of a sesshin that includes chanting, dokusan, and work. In my teacher's style, it is like being in the middle of the ocean where you can't see the shore. In this style, no one has to think, "I am a teacher" or "I am a student." You just sit, and you can go very deep. Since I founded Sanshinji in Bloomington, Indiana, in 2003, I sit five sesshins a year in the style I learned from my teacher, and five retreats of different kinds.

Sesshin has a different reality from ordinary life. Of course day-to-day things influence what's going on in our minds. If someone recently triggered my anger, thoughts come up about that person while I'm sitting. I might try to figure out why the person said or did such a thing. Anger also may arise. Anger is a kind of energy; it comes back no matter how many times I try to let go. When I am sitting facing the wall, the person and the incident are already gone, yet the person is also still sitting within me. The instant that brought up my anger is gone yet still seems to be there. While sitting, I may try to figure out what kind of person this is and why he or she did this or that.

When I continue this way in zazen, moment by moment for fourteen hours a day, I get tired. Somehow my mind calms down. Eventually I realize that the reason this person did the thing that angered me is gone. The anger, though, is still there as energy. When I sit with this energy it goes deeper and deeper. This is no longer the anger caused by the particular action or particular person. Instead, I find that this anger is my self. And still I sit and try to let go of whatever comes up, to just keep sitting. Sometimes, not always, I experience that the anger disappears.

I have found that anger is not really caused by a particular person's action. The anger is inside me. That person's action or speech simply opens the lid of my consciousness. Feelings and thoughts always come from our own consciousness. They come up in zazen; when we let go, we can let go, and that's okay. Zazen is a unique and precious practice. In the zendō we can let go of everything. This is really liberation—not only from our daily lives but also from the karmic consciousness created by our twisted karma. In zazen we are determined not to take action based on the thoughts coming and going; therefore we don't create new karma. This is what it means that in zazen we are liberated from our karma.

My teacher, Uchiyama Rōshi, and his teacher, Kōdō Sawaki Rōshi, taught that zazen itself is the true Dharma eye. In other words, the true Dharma eye means not seeing things with our karmic consciousness. This is the meaning of Uchiyama Rōshi's phrase "opening the hand of thought." In ordinary life, thought leads to actions. When we open the hand of thought, we let go and no actions arise.

Sawaki Rōshi said, "In our zazen we see things from our coffin." This means we are as if already dead. We have no opinion, no desires, and no right to request anything of anyone. In Japan when someone dies their casket is placed in a room, usually in the person's house, or sometimes in a temple. During the wake, relatives and friends stay overnight with the casket and usually talk about their experiences with the dead person. The dead person cannot disagree, argue, or complain to the people around the casket. According to Sawaki Rōshi, in zazen we are like the dead person in the casket. Whatever people say about me, good or bad, I cannot argue with them. I just keep silently sitting in zazen.

Only in zazen can we stop making karma. When we leave the zendō we have to do something; to do something we have to make choices, and the choices I make depend on my values, which are influenced by my karmic consciousness. I can't be free of karma even when I try to do things simply for the sake of Dharma. That is still my choice, and whenever I make a choice I am making new karma, whether good or bad karma, as a continuation of my past karma.

When we stand up from the cushion and go outside we cannot let go of everything; it would be dangerous. When we leave the zendō we have to think again. We have to make choices about what we should and shouldn't do. In daily life I need to think and take actions using my knowledge, understanding, values, and picture of the world. The expression "created by karma" means created or influenced by my experiences. It's not necessarily a bad thing; it's just how we create our life. In taking action based on these things, we create our life. For example, because I am a Buddhist priest, as one of my responsibilities, I often talk about my knowledge, understanding, and experiences of Dharma. I always try to figure out the best way to make my talk most interesting and helpful to the audience. Not only when I give a talk but also when I play a certain role during ceremonies and other activities, I try to do my best. To do so, I make choices based on discrimination about who I am and what my responsibility is in each occasion. When I'm with my family, I behave differently as a husband and a father.

Our practice in daily life is about creating wholesome karma. In this context, wholesome karma means to manifest in daily life what we experience in zazen: no separation between myself and other people and myriad things. That is how the Buddha is expressed in everyday activities. With all the choices we have to make, we try to make these choices in the direction of the bodhisattva path. That is our life based on zazen and the bodhisattva vows.

## True Dharma Eye

Viewing things with the true Dharma eye and viewing things with our karmic consciousness are very different. As bodhisattvas we need to see things with a true Dharma eye. Still, we are not completely free from our karmic consciousness; we have to live out our karma. Precisely speaking, our karmic condition is the only device we can use to practice. For example, part of my karma is that I'm Japanese. Because English is not my mother tongue, it is very difficult for me to exactly express what I feel or think. If possible, I'd avoid thinking, speaking, or writing in it. But I think it is a part of my mission as a Buddhist priest working with American people to share my understanding of Dharma in English. I often think in Japanese and speak or write in English. My brain works really hard. This is one of the ways I use my karma for the sake of Dharma. I cannot cancel my karmic conditions even for the sake of the Dharma.

If this is our attitude toward our daily lives and in our zazen, we can let go of our karma and be liberated from our attachment to it. We need both manifestation and liberation (*genjō* and *tōdatsu*) as our life. This is what Dōgen is discussing in this writing: not only mountains and waters but this whole world, including human society.

Sawaki Rōshi said that in our zazen we realize that we are no good. "We are no good" is the reality of our life. We are conditioned and self-centered. Whatever I try to do, even for the Dharma, is influenced by "my" desire and preference. In the Yogācāra teaching, ego consciousness clings to the seeds stored in the storehouse consciousness as "me." And the ego consciousness, the seventh consciousness, controls the first six. That's how our way of thinking becomes self-centered and distorted. In Yogācāra understanding, when we attain buddhahood we are free from this structure, and all the layers of our consciousness function as wisdom. Until then, we make a story of our lives, and the hero or heroine of the story is always "me." We even distort the story; we're really creative. We are still pretty immature bodhisattvas.

In zazen, or with our true Dharma eye, we see that distortion: we see how self-centered we are. I think this is wisdom in a very practical way.

That is why zazen is the practice of repentance and also the practice of the bodhisattva vow. Vow and repentance are always together. Without taking a vow, there is no way we can repent. Repentance is a kind of awakening to the incompleteness of our practice of vow. Unless we practice following our vow, we cannot see our incompleteness. Rather, we think we're okay and others are wrong. But practicing and awakening to our incompleteness encourages our practice of vow. Repentance does not mean saying, "I'm sorry. I made a mistake." Repentance is really deeply awakening to how much we are influenced by the seventh consciousness. To see this is the true Dharma eye.

According to Uchiyama Rōshi, the way zazen functions in our daily lives is described as the three minds. The three minds are magnanimous mind, joyful mind, and parental or nurturing mind. These minds are explained by Dōgen in the *Tenzo Kyōkun* (*Instructions for the Cook*).

Dōgen said magnanimous mind is like a great mountain that doesn't move. It's very stable. The mountain allows different living beings to live and grow; plants and animals, large and small, and other kinds of beings live on that mountain. Yet the mountain doesn't move. Even though in "Sansuikyō" he says mountains are moving, their moving is steady, much steadier than our emotional minds. Magnanimous mind is also the mind of the great ocean. It doesn't reject water from any rivers; instead it makes all waters from different rivers its own. There's no separation, no discrimination.

Nurturing mind or parental mind is a mind of caring for others; it's the bodhisattva spirit. A parent takes care of children and can find joy in that. But children can find joy only in being taken care of. That's the difference between parents and children. We are too often childish; we are like babies. We cry or complain when we are not well taken care of. Childish mind is the opposite of nurturing or parental mind.

The third, joyful mind, is also necessary. We need it especially when our situation is not joyful. When we are in a fortunate condition, we don't need joyful mind because our condition is joyful. But without joyful mind it is difficult to find joy in pain, difficulty, and sorrow. We experience difficult conditions more often than favorable ones, so we need a mind that can find joy even in misfortune. Joyful mind can also help us in difficulties, as we vow to take care of others. Then we find joy by sharing our spirit. These three minds are the way our zazen works in our daily lives.

When I began my sangha in 1996, I named it Sanshin Zen Community. *Sanshin* is the Japanese word for "three minds." I kept the Japanese expression for three minds because the English expression "three minds" doesn't sound right to me. These are not three different minds but actually three ways that one Buddha mind manifests itself.

The true Dharma eye is the way we view things from zazen, from a casket, without egocentric mind. Every fascicle of *Shōbōgenzō* is about zazen. Dōgen writes about how to live following the spirit and practice of zazen in our daily lives, and he writes about how the world looks from our zazen. In "Sansuikyō" he talks about mountains and waters as examples of what we encounter and where we live together with other beings. What we encounter is our life. A person in the mountain and all beings in the mountain are not separate. We are the mountain and the mountain is us.

## ENLIGHTENMENT AND DELUSION

In "Genjōkōan," the very first fascicle of *Shōbōgenzō*, Dōgen defined delusion and enlightenment. He said, "conveying oneself toward all things to carry out practice-enlightenment is delusion" and "all things coming and carrying out practice-enlightenment through the self is realization."[29] In Dōgen's definition, delusion and enlightenment are opposites. In delusion we see all beings in terms of "our" karmic consciousness; we evaluate them and try to arrange things so we feel safe. We usually practice in this way; we try to make our lives orderly. We organize things we encounter into drawers of concepts: good, terrible, ugly, valuable. When everything is in its drawer, we think our life is well-organized and successful. The things exist for us.

This is not just an idea. When I give a lecture, as a preparation, I take notes in a notebook. A notebook is not expensive, so it's not valuable economically, especially after I write something in it. However, because I write something about *Shōbōgenzō* and what I need to talk about, my notebooks are very important to me. I try to keep them safe. If someone tries to take my notebook or throws it in the trash, I will get angry and protect it. I might even fight with the person. This is how we act: we arrange our lives to protect the valuable and get rid of the worthless. We carry out practice-enlightenment in this way too, using our desires to make life peaceful, calm, and safe, and to make ourselves powerful and important.

Dōgen said this way of practice is based on delusion. Dōgen's definition of enlightenment is that all beings come toward the self and carry out practice-enlightenment through the self. The subject of this practice is not this person. Even though Shohaku is sitting using Shohaku's body and mind, still this is not Shohaku's activity. Myriad dharmas come toward Shohaku and make Shohaku sit.

My sitting is not really Shohaku's personal action based on Shohaku's personal choice, according to Shohaku's values. Often I do not want to sit. Sometimes I am looking for an excuse not to sit. Still, something makes me wake up, put on my robes, and walk to the zendō. Somehow I can't resist. I know this is my choice, but it is not really "my" choice. For example, as I said, Uchiyama Rōshi asked me to study English; I didn't really want to, but somehow I couldn't refuse. And when Uchiyama Rōshi asked me to come to the United States, I didn't really want to, but again I couldn't say no. I wonder what made me halfheartedly agree. This was me but not me. What was it? What is it that makes me get up when I want to stay in bed, that makes me do what my teacher asks when I would rather do something else? What is it that wants to practice more than it wants to rest? What wants to do the hard work rather than take the easy way? For a long time this was my kōan.

It is difficult to be a serious Zen practitioner in this country, but even in Japan it is hard. When I asked to become Uchiyama Rōshi's disciple, he said, "I never encourage people to become monks because it's very difficult to be a true monk, and there are already so many meaningless monks in Japan." He said he didn't want me to be a monk if I were a meaningless one. If I wanted to be a real, true practitioner of zazen, he would accept me. He didn't encourage me to be a monk. I had to make the choice. Therefore, I made the decision by myself and took responsibility for it. Even when I had many difficulties as a monk, I had no excuse to quit. Although I had to make the decision by myself, although no one could make such a decision for me, I still feel that it wasn't mine. The decision wasn't my personal determination simply using my own willpower; it was all beings coming toward me and enabling me to make it. I think all those actions, even getting up in the morning to sit zazen, came from all beings coming toward me and enabling me to practice. My willpower is a tiny part of it. Otherwise, I could not have continued for more than forty years.

According to Yogācāra teaching, when we are released from delusion or karmic consciousness, the functioning of these consciousnesses changes. When we are enlightened, storehouse consciousness starts to function as *daienkyochi*, wisdom of the great perfect mirror. The seventh consciousness, ego consciousness, which discriminates things and makes us egocentric, now functions as *byōdōshōchi*, wisdom seeing equality. Released from grasping, it sees the equality of all things. The sixth consciousness, our usual thinking mind, when released from ego attachment becomes *myōkansatsuchi*, the wisdom to see things as they are. And the first five consciousnesses, the sense consciousnesses of seeing, hearing, and so forth, begin to function as *jōshosachi*: the sense consciousnesses transformed, so that we function from wisdom instead of karmic preferences.

Actually karmic consciousness is exactly the same as these four wisdoms of Buddha. This may seem confusing. The difference is whether or not I cling to this body and mind as my personal possession. This is what Dōgen means when he says in "Genjōkōan," "Conveying oneself

toward all things to carry out practice-enlightenment is delusion."
When we use these eight consciousnesses with self-clinging, whatever
we do is egocentric, even if we practice zazen or study Buddha's teaching. It is egocentric because it is based on our ego attachment, with
ourselves as the center of everything.

"All things coming and carrying out practice-enlightenment
through the self" means that the practice is no longer motivated by my
personal desire to improve myself. When we have full understanding
that each of us is living together with all beings, interconnected, we
cannot live in the egocentric way. That is the difference. That is also
the meaning of Dōgen Zenji's expression *shinjin datsuraku,* "dropping
off body and mind." That is what our zazen really is. Rujing, Dōgen's
teacher, said, "Studying Zen is dropping off body and mind" and
"Dropping off body and mind is zazen."[30] This dropping off body and
mind, for me, is actually a release from clinging to this being called
Shohaku. So we open our hand.

## A PERSON IN THE MOUNTAIN

> These mountains and waters of the present are the expression of
> the old buddhas.

This first sentence is an introduction to "Sansuikyō." If we understand
this we understand the entire *Shōbōgenzō.* This doesn't mean if we
memorize this sentence and think a lot about it we don't need to read
the rest of *Shōbōgenzō.* It means that in order to understand this one
sentence we must study the entire *Shōbōgenzō.*

It is the same with each and every thing. Every word that Dōgen
writes is connected with other words and expressions in his writings
and also with all his experiences in life. If we want to study *Shōbōgenzō*
thoroughly, we have to study each fascicle very carefully and also think
of the connections among fascicles. Then we apply the teaching in our
lives, searching for the meaning of the words in our own experience.
Eventually we don't need dictionaries or commentaries anymore.

The first sentence of "Sansuikyō" begins with "these mountains." In my introduction, I referred to Su Shi's poem on the sound of the valley streams and the color of the mountain. There is another well-known poem by Su Shi on the same mountain that has been appreciated by many people within the Zen community in China and in Japan. The mountain is Mount Lu, the sacred mountain famous for its beauty. Su Shi practiced with a Rinzai Zen master, Donglin Changzong (in Japanese, Tōrin Jōshō, 1025–91), at Donglin temple on the mountain. I would like to introduce this poem because, I think, it was another source of inspiration for Dōgen to write "Sansuikyō":

> Regarded from one side, an entire range;
> From another, a single peak.
> Far, near; high, low, all its parts
> different from the others.
> If the true face of Mount Lu
> cannot be known,
> It is because the one looking at it
> is standing in its midst.[31]

In this poem, "Mount Lu" refers to the entire network of interdependent origination. This translation says if one cannot see its true face, it is because one is in the middle of it. Actually, we are always in the mountain—so there's no way we can see the true face of Mount Lu.

Zen Master Hongzhi Zhengjue (in Japanese, Wanshi Shōgaku, 1091–1157) composed his own poem following Su Shi's expression:

> With coming and going, a person in the mountains
> Understands that blue mountains are his body.
> The blue mountains are the body, and the body is the self,
> So, where can one place the senses and their objects?[32]

Hongzhi said that we are persons coming and going in the mountain. We are the people in the mountain, and the mountain is us. Hongzhi said that the mountain is his body and his body is his self. That is why I don't see the mountain: an eye does not see the eye. So for Hongzhi, not seeing is positive.

In *Eihei Kōroku* volume 9, Dōgen quoted this poem and then composed his own, following both Su Shi and Hongzhi:

> A person in the mountains should love the mountains.
> With going and coming, the mountains are his body.
> The mountains are the body, but the body is not the self
> So where can one find any senses or their objects?[33]

Dōgen said the person in the mountains must be a person who loves the mountains. In "Sansuikyō" he also wrote that the mountains belong to the people who love mountains. This love is important. We are in the mountains and we love them. When we love mountains, mountains belong to us and we belong to the mountains. We are living within the network of interdependent origination and we love this network. To love means to be intimate and to be one. The person who is coming and going in the mountains must be a person who loves the mountains.

"The mountains are the body, but the body is not the self." Dōgen's poem is almost the same as Hongzhi's, but Dōgen says that his body is *not* his self. This tiny difference is very important. This is Dōgen not grasping body and mind as the self. This is how we open our hands.

We are living in the mountains together with all other beings, and the mountains are our body, but this body is not the self. The body is there but it is not our self. This is dropping off body and mind. Dropping off body and mind does not mean this person's body and mind disappear; they're still there, functioning as part of interdependent origination, living together with all beings. Only the misidentification of body and mind as self has dropped away.

The last line of Dōgen's poem is "So where can one find any senses or their objects?" He is talking about how there is no separation between eye, ear, nose, tongue, body, and mind and their objects: color, sound, smell, taste, touch, objects of mind. There's no separation between the selfless self and all beings. We are the mountains and the mountains are us.

Dōgen is using mountains and waters to talk about the reality of our lives before any separation between self and others—this one seamless life and one seamless time. This nonseparation is happening all the time, but we don't usually see it. In zazen it becomes clearer that we are living the same life with all beings—this is called Mount Lu.

Thus, when Dōgen discusses mountains, we are already in the mountains. We are in the mountains and we love the mountains. Our practice is based on love. This reality is the expression of the ancient buddhas and the Buddha's way. This is the reality to which all buddhas awaken.

## MOUNTAINS AND WATERS OF THE PRESENT

In "these mountains and waters of the present," *nikon*, or "present," is a very important expression, one of the key words in Dōgen's philosophy. We have to investigate deeply what it means in this sentence.

"Sansuikyō" was written in 1240, on the eighteenth day of the tenth month. At the beginning of the same month Dōgen wrote three fascicles, including "Uji," or "Being Time." Since he wrote "Uji" and "Sansuikyō" within a few weeks of each other, it seems very clear that the two are closely connected. While "Sansuikyō" contrasts mountains and waters seen by the true Dharma eye (by Buddha's eye) and by our karmic eyes, "Uji" compares time as perceived by these different eyes.

"Uji" in Japanese or Chinese is *u* and *ji*. The common way of reading this is "one time" or "once upon a time." *U* also means "to be" or "being," and *ji* is "time." Dōgen reads this *uji* as "being time," with *being* meaning "existence." He said that *u* (being) and *ji* (time) are one thing. Being is time and time, being. We cannot separate time and existence. This is an essential point in Dōgen's teaching.

In the excerpt from "Uji" below, "being-time" is one word:

As the time right now is all there ever is, each being-time is without exception entire time. A grass-being and a form-being are both times. Entire being, the entire world, exists in the time of each and every now. Just reflect: right now, is there an entire being or an entire world missing from your present time, or not?[34]

Being-time, *uji*, is any being including you or me, and also the whole world and all time. If you sit in zazen you manifest this reality—called the buddha mudra—with your body and mind. As Dogen said in *Bendōwa*:

Even if only one person sits for a short time, because this zazen is one with all existence and completely permeates all time, it performs everlasting Buddha guidance within the inexhaustible Dharma work in the past, present, and future.

So each and every being-time is entire time. That means each and every one of us, not only human beings but each and every thing, is entire time. Time cannot be separated into three parts: past, present, and future. Our common idea is that time flows from the past to the future through the present. But Dōgen said that if we see time and being with the true Dharma eye through zazen, then each and every one of us is all of time and space. That means everything is connected with everything else in time and space—which is the Buddha's teaching of interdependent origination. Everything is connected with everything else within this network of interdependent origination, so when we see one thing we see everything. Of course, the word "seeing" does not mean seeing with our physical eyes.

For example, take this body and mind named Shohaku. It includes everything in this entire universe and entire time, not just from my birth but from the Big Bang. There's no time and space, but everything that has happened since then is really my self. If we say it this way it sounds like a kind of delusion. Yet if we let go of our common frame of thinking, ultimately we really are one with everything. When we sit in zazen and let go of thought, we let go of that frame of thinking. So actually Dōgen is writing here about our zazen—how all the beings in space and time look from the viewpoint of zazen.

Without the experience of zazen it's very difficult to understand Dōgen's writing, but if we have that experience, I think we can understand. "A grass-being" and "a form-being" refer to each and every being without exception. Everything is time. And within the present moment of each one of us, all beings throughout space and time are there. All beings, myriad dharmas—is there any one of those that doesn't exist within your present time?

At this time and being, what is lacking? According to Dōgen, nothing. Everything is right here at this moment with each and every one of us. This is very strange. And yet, according to Dōgen, this is reality—reality beyond our thinking. Dōgen tried to explain why it sounds strange; in the next paragraph of "Uji," he says, "In spite of this, a person holds various views at the time he is unenlightened and has yet to learn the Buddha's Dharma."[35] This means we don't understand because we cling to our karmic views, which were created by our experiences, education, and thinking.

Our karmic views include ideas of change and progress:

> Hearing the words "the time being," he thinks that at one time the old Buddha became a creature with three heads and eight arms, and that at another time he became a sixteen-foot Buddha.[36]

"At one time" is *uji*, being-time. The creature with three heads and eight arms refers to some Buddhist statues that show either *asura* (fighting spirits) or guardian gods of Dharma. Sometimes Buddha appears in frightening and angry forms to convince deluded beings like us to arouse the mind of awakening. He also sometimes appears standing or sitting on lotus petals in a buddha hall; "sixteen-foot Buddha" refers to a standing buddha statue, which is said to be about sixteen feet tall.

He imagines it is like crossing a river or a mountain.[37]

In this passage from "Uji," the image of crossing a river or climbing a mountain suggests that we are traveling through many difficulties. It presents practice as being like a journey from one point to another, with a start and a goal. That is a common understanding about our practice. Our starting point is saṃsāra, and our goal is nirvāṇa. Each moment and each day we try to walk forward, even if it's just one step further. We think of our life as a journey, going through changing scenery toward our destination, which we think will be better than here. With each step we try to get closer to buddhahood.

> The river and mountain may still exist, but "I" have left them behind and at the present time "I" reside in a splendid vermilion palace.[38]

This refers to the time when a person has reached the goal, become a buddha, and been enshrined in a buddha hall. The mountains and rivers the person crossed while practicing are still there, but the person views them as separate and apart:

> To him the mountain or river and I are as distant from one another as heaven from earth.[39]

Here Dōgen uses an expression from the Third Patriarch's *Xinxin Ming*, or *Faith in Mind*, that is common in Chinese culture, not only in Buddhism: "When we have the slightest deviation we are far distant like heaven from earth."

According to Mahāyāna teachings, a bodhisattva needs to go through fifty-two stages in order to become a buddha. It takes almost forever. But Dōgen disagrees with the common understanding that life is a journey toward a destination. He says that when we think in this way there is separation between the wayfarer, the distance of their journey, and the time it takes.

But the true state of things is not found in this one direction alone. At the time the mountain was being climbed and the river being crossed, I was there [in time]. The *time* has to be in *me*. Inasmuch as I am there, it cannot be that time passes away. As long as time is not a modality of going and coming, that time on the mountain is the immediate present—right now—of "the time being" (being-time). Yet as long as time takes upon itself a modality of going and coming, the *being* in me in the immediate *now* of "the time being" is being-time.[40]

Usually we think time comes and goes. The present moment moves to the past, and the future comes into the present, so we think time has a function of coming and going. "Immediate present" is *nikon*: this immediate present of time-being or being-time, which is not simply part of the linear flow of time. Here Dōgen explains that time doesn't necessarily flow, that it is beyond coming and going. *Nikon*, immediate present, means simply this moment that completely permeates all time.

"This moment" is a strange thing. Actually there's no such thing as "the present moment." Even the slightest length of time can be cut in two, with one part already in the past and another still in the future. Even as I say "now," when I pronounce "n," "w" is still in the future. When I say "o," "n" is already in the past. The only times that exist are past and future; the present doesn't really exist; it's only the border between past and future. But this is strange because the present is also the only reality; the past is already gone and the future is not yet come. This present moment is really nothing. But this nothing is the only reality and includes all time!

The real reality of our life is nothing. It's completely empty. It's a strange thing to think, but that's reality. When we see that time has no modality of going and coming, we are seeing one side of reality, according to Dōgen. But he also said, "Yet as long as time takes upon itself a modality of going and coming . . ." So, time is also going and coming; that is Dōgen's other side of reality.

> So does not the time climbing the mountain or crossing the
> river swallow up the time of the splendid vermilion palace?
> Does not that time spit out this time?[41]

"Swallow up" here means to become one. The time of practice and
the time within buddhahood are the same; that is what Dōgen pro-
poses here.

Actually, Dōgen is asking; we have to answer him, and the way we
answer is through our practice. Through each and every activity we
have to manifest buddhahood; that is our answer. And from the other
side, our question: how can the Buddha enshrined in the buddha hall
manifest itself through our each and every practice activity? That is
our question.

The time of being Buddha and the time of practicing are the same
time. That is what Dōgen is saying, and it's a unique way of thinking.
But this understanding of time, of the process of our life, is necessary
to explain why practice and enlightenment are actually one thing. And
that is the very foundation of Dōgen's teaching about our practice.

In the next paragraph of "Uji," Dōgen says,

> The creature with three heads and eight arms is yesterday's
> time. The sixteen-foot Buddha is today's time. Nonetheless,
> the nature of the truth of this yesterday and today lies in
> the time when you go directly into the mountains and look
> at the myriad peaks around you—hence there is no passing
> away.[42]

Even though yesterday is past, he uses the present tense: "is." That
means yesterday's time is still here.

Maybe I could use my life to explain what "yesterday's time" means.
I was born in 1948. That was three years after the end of World War II.
My family had lived in Osaka for about three hundred years. For six
generations my family had been merchants. On a single day in March
1945, my family lost everything in the bombing by the American Air

Force. My family had lived in the same place for six generations; they had accumulated certain wealth, but it was gone in one night. The only thing left was a broken buddha statue, which was later enshrined in our family altar during my childhood.

After the war my father wanted to become a farmer. He had been working at a bank and, being from a family of merchants, he had never done any farming. Still, he wanted to become a farmer. He moved to the countryside, to a place called Nose, in Osaka; that's where I was born. We had nothing except a small piece of land for farming. I lived there until I was four years old. In my earliest memory, from when I was about three years old, I was playing in a stream with other kids. The sound of the valley streams and the mountains is in that memory. For at least the first four years of my life I heard the sound of valley streams every day.

Thirty years later I again lived near the mountain that was in my memory. Once, since it was so close, I tried to go back to Nose, but I found that the area had become part of the development of Osaka and had houses everywhere. So I stopped trying to find that place, because that memory is a really important part of my life. Even though I don't remember it precisely, for me it is "the sound of valley streams." It seemed to me that if I went to that place and saw how things have changed, part of my life would be destroyed.

Memory is a strange thing. When I remember that scene it seems as if I am watching a movie; I see myself running to my house, crying. Within the scenery the small boy is running. This cannot be a real memory, because when I was a baby I couldn't see the baby—I would only have seen the baby's surroundings. But in my memory there's a river and a road and a mountain and a boy running. So I think this memory was created later in my childhood. It didn't come only from my direct experience; it was created using a function of my brain.

I think that is how we create our past. Our experiences are actually part of our present life through memory. I have that experience right now, in this immediate moment. It's not gone, and it's not separate from what I'm doing right now. It's part of my present, even though it's only one memory and I have forgotten almost everything else from that time. Even all the experiences I forget are part of my life at this moment. Dōgen's point that yesterday's time is still within us is the reality of our lives. And when we sit in the zendō we can experience this reality, that our past experiences are there even if we don't remember them.

I really like Carl Bielefeldt's translation of "Sansuikyō," but I have a few questions about it. One of my questions is about this first sentence: "These mountains and waters of the present are the expression of the old buddhas." I will explain the question, because often the question contains the answer.

Here is the original sentence that Dōgen wrote. It is very short and precise, so it is not difficult to translate.

*Nikon no sansui wa kobutsu no dō genjō nari.*

*Nikon* in this sentence is "present." *San* is "mountain." *Sui* is "waters." My translation of *kobutsu* is "ancient buddhas"; Professor Bielefeldt's is "old buddhas." *Dō* (道) is "way." *Genjō* is the same word as in "Genjō-kōan": manifestation or actualization. *Gen* (現) means "to appear" and *jō* (成) means "to become." *No* is "of" and *wa* shows the subject of the sentence, which is *nikon no san sui*, "the mountains and waters of the present." *Kobutsu no dō* can be "the way of old (or ancient) buddhas." Carl Bielefeldt translated *dō genjō* as "expression." So he translated the sentence as "These mountains and waters of the present are the expression of the old buddhas."

Here is my question:

"Way" (*dō* or 道 in Japanese or *dao* in Chinese) is a very important word in Japanese and Chinese philosophies and religions. The Sanskrit word *bodhi*, for instance, was translated into Chinese as "way." *Anuttarasamyaksaṃbodhi*, or "unsurpassable complete awakening," was translated into Chinese as *mujōdō* (無上道), "supreme way." In this case, *dō* means "enlightenment" or "awakening of all the buddhas."

Another possible meaning of *dō* is words or speech, "to say something." For example, one fascicle of *Shōbōgenzō* is "Dō-Toku." *Toku* (得) means "to get" or "to attain" and *dō* means here "to speak, talk, or express." Dōgen says that *dō-toku*, to express what we see and experience using words, is really important. If you experience something and fully understand that experience, the experience naturally becomes words. But if we change the order of these words from *dō-toku* to *toku-dō*, then it means "attaining the way," awakening to the Buddha Way.

So in this first sentence from "Sansuikyō" there are these two possible meanings for *dō*. In the commentary by Tenkei Denson (1648–1735), *dō* is interpreted as the expressions of the Chinese Zen masters that Dōgen quotes in this writing, such as Furong Daokai and Yunmen Wenyan. In that case this sentence means: "The mountains and waters at this present moment are the manifestation of the sayings of those old buddhas," with "those old buddhas" referring to the Chinese masters. This is the interpretation Professor Bielefeldt chose.

The other interpretation is given by Menzan Zuihō (1683–1769), another great Sōtō Zen master in the eighteenth century. Tenkei and Menzan were almost contemporary, and they argued with each other about many points of Sōtō Zen practice and Dōgen Zenji's teachings. Menzan said the meaning of *dō* here is "the great way of Buddha." So *kobutsu*, "old buddhas," is not those two Chinese Zen masters but the great way of all old buddhas.[43] I agree with Menzan here. I think the sentence should read as follows:

> These mountains and waters at this moment are the manifestation of the great way of ancient buddhas.

"Manifestation," or *genjō,* is a key word for Dōgen, a very important expression not only in "Genjōkōan" but in many of his writings. Moment-by-moment things are genjō, which literally means "manifestation of timeless reality." Timeless reality shows itself within momentary phenomena. That is our life; that is our activity. Within mountains and waters at this very moment is the manifestation of the great way of ancient buddhas. This is my understanding of this sentence.

"Old buddhas" is also an important phrase in Dōgen's teaching and writing. To understand more fully we have to read another fascicle of *Shōbōgenzō*: "Kobusshin," or "The Mind of Old Buddhas."

> Though [the term "old" in] "old buddhas" is the same "old" as in "new and old," they go beyond past and present, they are straightforward in past and present.[44]

Professor Bielefeldt translated *kobutsu* as "old buddhas"; I translate it as "ancient buddhas," and others translate it as "past buddhas" or "eternal buddhas." The first three translations are literal, but "eternal buddhas" is nonliteral. The term *kobutsu* suggests something beyond time and space, making "eternal buddhas" a possible translation. The term "past buddhas" may cause confusion with the *saptatathāgata*, the seven past buddhas, which is not the meaning here.

Dōgen referred to several respected Chinese masters as Kobutsu or Old Buddha: his teacher Tiantong Rujing, Hongzhi Zhengjue, Zhaozhou Congshen (in Japanese, Jōshū Jūshin, 778–897), and so on. In these cases "Old Buddha" means a person who has awakened to timeless reality and expressed that reality through their practice and teaching. In short, *kobutsu* means a person who has the true Dharma eye.

In the same fascicle, Dōgen quotes a dialogue between a monk and Nanyang Huizhong (in Japanese, Nayo Echu, 675–775).

> A monk once asked the National Teacher, "What is the old buddha mind?" The master answered, "Fences, walls, tiles, and pebbles."[45]

This means that the mind of old buddhas—which is eternal, beyond the three times—is nothing other than fences, walls, tiles, and pebbles, or all the ordinary phenomenal things.

The present is time: this moment, the next moment, and yet another moment are time. And mountains walk through time. In other words, mountains and waters of the present are actual phenomenal things, which move and change. The way of old buddhas means the eternal truth, beyond time and space. These are two poles: things right here and now, and timeless eternal truth. Dōgen says that these two are really one and the same.

This is like when the *Heart Sūtra* says, "Form is emptiness and emptiness is form." Logically, form is not empty and emptiness has no form, so emptiness and form negate each other. Yet the *Heart Sūtra* says they are one and the same. Usually our rational mind doesn't accept this kind of twist. We say it's contradictory and doesn't make any sense. Allowing such a question is the beginning of Buddhist study.

"Maka Hannya Haramitsu," or "The Perfection of Great Wisdom," Dōgen's commentary on the *Heart Sūtra*, is the earliest writing in *Shōbōgenzō*, written during the first summer practice period at Kōshōji monastery in 1233. In it Dōgen says that the *Heart Sūtra*'s statement, "Form is emptiness and emptiness is form," is not complete. So he adds, "Form is form and emptiness is emptiness." That's Dōgen's way to express this reality.

There is a concept "form" and another concept "emptiness." The *Heart Sūtra* says these two contradictory concepts are one. Dōgen's point is that if form is really emptiness we don't need to say "emptiness." When we say "form," emptiness is already included. When we say "emptiness," form is already there. If form and emptiness are really one thing, we don't need to say "form is emptiness." That is Dōgen's logic. He often expresses the teaching this way.

This means that moment-by-moment phenomena such as mountains and rivers are the expression of timeless reality, the way of old buddhas. Unless we thoroughly understand the significance of this first sentence, we can't understand Dōgen's discussion in the rest of this fascicle. This is the essence of "Sansuikyō."

## ABIDING IN DHARMA POSITION

> Each, abiding in its own Dharma state, fulfills exhaustive virtues.

Now we're reading the second sentence; we're going very slowly. Soon the mountains will start to walk, though, and their walking will become faster and faster.

This expression "Dharma state" is a translation of *hō-i* from the *Lotus Sūtra*; each and every being dwells within its own hō-i. My translation of *hō-i* is "Dharma position." Dōgen uses this expression "Dharma position" in "Genjōkōan," when he discusses firewood and ash:

> Firewood becomes ash. Ash cannot become firewood again. However, we should not view ash as after and firewood as before. We should know that firewood dwells in the Dharma position of firewood and has its own before and after. Although before and after exist, past and future are cut off. Ash stays in the position of ash, with its own before and after. As firewood never becomes firewood again after it has burned to ash, there is no return to living after a person dies. However in Buddhadharma it is an unchanged tradition not to say that life becomes death.[46]

He is saying that life doesn't become death. We die, but life doesn't become death. Life is life, one hundred percent, and death is death, one hundred percent, and there's no return. Life-and-death is no arising and no perishing even though we are born and we die.

> Life is a position in time; death is also a position in time. This is like winter and spring. We don't think that winter becomes spring, and we don't say that spring becomes summer.[47]

Unfortunately in English this sentence is not true. In Japanese we don't say that spring becomes summer, but in English we do.

Dōgen is saying that change is not what we commonly think. In our usual view firewood becomes ash when burned. Before it was cut and dried, firewood was a living tree, and before it became a big tree it was a seed. That seed was produced from the life activity of the previous generation.

There is a kind of a stream of being within change. We think that within impermanence there is a something continuous that changes form depending upon causes and conditions.

In contrast Dōgen says that a tree dwells within the Dharma position of a tree; when it becomes firewood, this firewood dwells in the Dharma position of firewood; and when it is ash, ash is within the Dharma position of ash. Each stage is absolutely independent. The tree is not an earlier stage of firewood, and firewood is not a previous stage of ash. Ash is completely ash, firewood is completely firewood, and a tree is completely a tree.

In human life this corresponds to babies, teenagers, adults, and the elderly. When we are a baby we are one-hundred-percent baby; we are not a future child. Babies and children are completely different in this sense, independent of each other. In each moment we dwell in a certain Dharma position.

Dōgen also says that within firewood there's a past and a future. The stage of being firewood includes a past in which it was a tree, and includes a future in which it is ash. This past and future are part of the present Dharma position or stage. There is a before and after, but the before and after are cut off. This moment is a complete, perfect time, with nothing lacking.

This reminds us of what Dōgen said in "Uji." Being and time are one thing; so each moment and each being is complete. It is one complete time-being. And yet it is flowing: tree becomes firewood, firewood becomes ash. In the case of mountains we don't see this change because the mountains change so slowly, much more slowly than humans. When we are born, the mountains are already mountains, and when we die the mountains are still mountains. So we don't think mountains change. But they do.

My past experience is part of my life at this moment. The time of yesterday or fifty years ago is still part of my present life at this moment. Each moment is completely independent; it doesn't flow. Still, this time that doesn't flow is flowing. It's a strange thing. Dōgen uses the expression *go-uji* to describe it; *uji* means being-time and *go* (吾) means "self." So go-uji together is the name of "this reality-self and all other beings and entire time." This is one thing, and this one thing is my self. That is what Dōgen is talking about when he uses the word "self."

Likewise, within this Dharma position of firewood there's this moment. It has no length, like zero, but this zero state includes the entire past as our karma. Additionally, the entire future is within this present moment; it is present as our vow, aspiration, hope, or desire. Within this present zero-moment, the entire past and future are reflected. In this self, which is as tiny as a drop of dew, the entire universe is reflected. That is the self in Dōgen's teaching. As he said in "Genjōkōan," the vast, universal moonlight is reflected even in a tiny drop of dew. All of time from beginningless beginning to endless end is included in this very moment. All beings in this entire universe are reflected in one tiny thing.

This moment is also a fiction, but without this fiction there's no reality. This fiction is the only reality. In *Shōbōgenzō* "Gabyō" ("Painting of a Rice Cake"), Dōgen compares our lives to a painting:

> If we say that paintings are unreal, then all the myriad things are unreal. If all the myriad things are unreal, then even the Buddhadharma is unreal. If the Buddhadharma is real, paintings of rice cake must be real.

Dōgen also uses the expression *muchūsetsumu*, "relating a dream within a dream." This life is like a dream, but while we are within the dream we try to understand what the dream looks like. Without this dream there's no reality; this dream is the only reality. Waking up within the dream, we realize it is a dream. Actually waking up means we recognize it as a dream. We don't usually see this; we assume our dream is simply reality, and we cling to it as permanent and substantial.

Each person has a different dream, and within our personal dream each of us is the center of our own story. Each one of us has different views even when we look at the same things. These different views are our dreams and our separate realities. How shall we deal with them?

Why do we practice zazen in the zendō and listen to a Dharma talk? We do something else—walk on the beach or in a forest, shop, or see a movie—and it might be a better dream. Sitting in the zendō and listening to a talk on Dōgen's writings could be a nightmare. I don't know which is better. Still, somehow, as my role in this dream, I go to zendō to sit, talk about Dōgen, and write about my understanding, my dream about Dōgen's teaching. You are reading my dream. If you don't enjoy this book, you can put it down. But you cannot leave the dream of your own life.

## EACH MOMENT HAS EXHAUSTIVE VIRTUE

In our common understanding, the food I ate yesterday was real then, but now it does not exist anymore. That food is digested; some has become part of my body and energy, and some is already out of my body. Dōgen says that the food I ate yesterday is still here; as "the food" it is gone, but it is still here within my body, changed into my energy. This is an example of how this moment right now includes everything and lacks nothing. The food I ate yesterday is still here as part of my karma. That karma helps me to work right now. If I hadn't eaten yesterday, I would be hungry now and I wouldn't have energy to write. So the food is actually working right now as my energy. The food is still part of this moment. I think Dōgen's point is that even though this moment is only a fiction, it is also the only reality.

This moment is not a step to the next moment. We usually think that practice is a step to the next stage; that is common sense in society, just as elementary school is a step to higher education. In the same way, if we have a goal, reaching that goal is most important, and if we cannot reach it, then what we are doing right now is meaningless. When we study driving, our purpose is to get a license. If I fail to get the license, my study and practice of driving is meaningless.

If we think that what we are doing right now has the purpose of becoming Buddha, that is ordinary, goal-oriented thinking. But if we think in Dōgen's way—if we see this moment as including the entire stream—then each step of our practice is the entirety of the Buddha Way. If we practice sincerely, mindfully, and wholeheartedly, buddhahood is already here, in what we are doing right now, even though we have not yet crossed over to the other shore.

Each of us dwells in a certain Dharma position. Yet each and every one of us has a virtue, called "exhaustive virtue" in Professor Bielefeldt's translation. This applies not only to human beings but to all things. Each one of us is in whatever Dharma position we are in. This life at this moment has exhaustive virtue.

The original word for "exhaustive" is *gūjin*. *Gū* (窮) means "to penetrate thoroughly or completely," and *jin* is "to exhaust completely with nothing lacking."

For "virtue," the original word is *kudoku*. *Ku* (功) means "function" or "result of function," and *toku* (德) is "virtue," meaning "good quality" or "power to command respect."

In the next sentence Dōgen uses the word *dōtoku*. *Dō* and *toku* are in the Japanese name of Lao Tsu's *Tao Te Ching*, "The Virtue of the Way": *Dō Toku Kyō*. Dōtoku is an important concept in Chinese culture. It means goodness, good quality, true nature of persons or things, excellent personality. This kudoku is completely fulfilled. Buddha's kudoku is complete, but because we are beginners our kudoku is not complete. Still, within our incomplete practice as beginners, Dōgen says the perfect virtue of Buddha is manifested. This is an incredible statement. We make so many mistakes. Our work is not impressive. But Dōgen said we have this virtue, that we completely manifest Buddha's virtue, if we practice for the sake of fulfilling our vow to live together with all beings.

The first half of each of the four bodhisattva vows is contradicted by the second:

> Beings are numberless; I vow to free them.
> Delusions are inexhaustible; I vow to end them.
> Dharma gates are boundless; I vow to enter them.
> The Buddha Way is unsurpassable; I vow to realize it.

If beings are numberless, there's no way we can save them all. If delusions are inexhaustible, there's no way to end them. If teachings (Dharma gates) are boundless, we can't master them. If awakening (the Buddha Way) is unsurpassable, we can never attain it.

It is very clear: when we take these vows, we vow to do something we cannot complete. A clever person cannot take such a vow; only a stupid one can. This contradiction is important; it shows us the incompleteness of our practice. No matter how hard we practice, no matter how much good we do, still our practice is incomplete.

Because we've taken this unreasonable vow, we always feel incomplete. To awaken to that incompleteness is our repentance. Vow and repentance will always be together; they are two sides of one coin. Repentance—awakening to the incompleteness of our practice—strengthens our vow. Or we could say it strengthens our practice toward our vow. This two-sidedness, this contradiction, is really important.

This contradiction is the same as "These mountains and waters of the present are the expression of the old buddhas." It is not logical; our logical mind can't follow. Within practice is the only possible way to awaken to the reality of the stupidity of this person, and to make this stupid person walk in the bodhisattva path in a practical, concrete way. Otherwise our vow becomes a dream.

As the person who is living in this body and mind, I experience a great difference between following my personal desire and following my vow as a bodhisattva. From the outside, my life and everyone else's are the same: we are born, eat some food, spend a certain period of time, and die. We are sometimes happy, sometimes unhappy. That's all. But as a person who is living with this particular body and mind, within this particular society, there are differences. Each one of us has to choose which way to go. The four bodhisattva vows are our compass for our journey on the path of practice. We take a vow and practice toward infinity; vow gives us this direction. We have to directly go into the mountains and see the mountain peaks from inside.

Practicing in the mountains, if we see only the beauty of the mountains, we are not bodhisattvas. Everybody likes beautiful expressions or poems, but it's careless to think our practice is just to appreciate the beautiful scenery in the mountains. Mountains are not only beautiful and virtuous; they can be sometimes violent and merciless, and we need to see the ugly part of the mountains too. And somehow we need to take care of that ugly and painful part.

Each one of us has different tendencies, capabilities, vows, desires, and hopes; we are all limited and shaped by our karma. The way each of us works for the sake of this mountain can be different. How can this particular person make this mountain better for all beings? This question is the meaning of the bodhisattva vow—for every Dharma practitioner. We have to discover how to practice with the ugliness within ourselves and this mountain, and work to make the world even a little better. In this way we can find the beauty of the mountain even within its ugliness.

In my case I think the best contribution I can make to human society is to practice as a Sōtō Zen Buddhist and try to transmit what I studied and practiced in Japan to this country. This is my activity as a person of limited capability.

> Because they are the circumstances "prior to the kalpa of emptiness," they are this life of the present; because they are the self "before the germination of any subtle sign," they are liberated in their actual occurrence.

We are still talking about the mountains.

Here there are also two sides. One is "prior to the kalpa of emptiness" and "before the germination of any subtle sign"; both mean before the Big Bang, before anything happened. The other side is this concrete life of here and now with this particular conditioned body and mind within this particular situation of the world.

*Kalpa* means an immeasurably long time. In Buddhist teachings, it is said that there are four kalpas: arising, abiding, destruction, and emptiness. In the first kalpa things are forming. In the second these forms are maintained. The third kalpa sees falling apart or destruction, and the fourth, emptiness. But "prior to the empty kalpa" doesn't mean during the kalpa of destruction, because Dōgen also says "before the germination of any subtle sign." So this means before all the four kalpas, or before anything at all happened. This is complete emptiness beyond discrimination. This comes from the image of a seed germinating: before a sprout comes up out of the earth, nothing is visible even though it is there. Like the meaning of ancient or old in "old buddha," this emptiness refers to eternity.

In "they are this life of the present," this present is again *nikon*.

"Life" means our daily activities. The original word is *kakkei*. *Kei* literally means "calculation," or managing things. So "life" here means our livelihood and our moment-by-moment or day-to-day responsibilities. This is a practice, and this is also eternity; eternity manifests itself as our everyday activity and livelihood.

Dōgen also says, "They are liberated in their actual occurrence." "Actual occurrence" is another translation of *genjō*, actualization moment by moment. "To be liberated" is a translation of *tōdatsu* (透脱). *Tō* (透) is "to permeate" or "to be seen through"; *datsu* is the same word as in *shinjin datsuraku*, "dropping off body and mind": to take or drop off. *Tōdatsu* as a compound means "to penetrate and liberate."

In the beginning of *Shōbōgenzō* "Zenki" ("Total Function"), "liberation" is *tōdatsu*, and "manifestation" is *genjō*:

> The great Way of all buddhas, when it is completely penetrated, is liberation and is manifestation. *Liberation* means that life liberates itself from life and also death liberates itself

from death. Therefore, there is leaving life-and-death, there is entering life-and-death; both are the great Way, which is completely penetrated. There is abandoning life-and-death; there is crossing over life-and-death; both are the great Way, which is completely penetrated. Manifestation is life; life is manifestation. At the time of the manifestation, there is nothing but the total manifestation of life; there is nothing but the total manifestation of death.

A baby completely manifests babyhood, and yet at the same time, the baby is completely liberated from babyhood. A baby is one hundred percent a baby, and yet in its perfect babyhood, it has the energy to negate this babyhood and to become a girl or boy. This life force enables a baby to manifest perfect babyhood and at the same time to be liberated from babyhood.

In short, Dōgen is saying that each activity of our lives is liberated from itself, because it manifests ultimate reality—if we practice living by bodhisattva vows. Living to fulfill this wondrous vow is a manifestation of the eternal buddhas. If we merely live to fulfill egocentric desires for fame and profit, then we cannot say our lives manifest timeless reality.

## RIDING THE CLOUDS AND FOLLOWING THE WIND

> Since the virtues of the mountain are high and broad, the spiritual power to ride the clouds is always mastered from the mountains, and the marvelous ability to follow the wind is inevitably liberated from the mountains.

"Spiritual power" is a translation of *dōtoku*, "virtue of the way," which appeared above, and "marvelous ability" is a translation of *myōku*. Dōgen splits the word *kudoku*, or virtue, into two parts and combines them with the terms *myō* ("wondrous") and *dō* ("way"). Both *dōtoku* and *myōku* are "the virtues of the mountain." This mountain has the virtue to ride the clouds and follow the wind. To ride the clouds means to go up, and to follow the wind means to go everywhere. "Go up" could mean go up toward buddhahood to fulfill bodhisattva vows, or it could mean go through time. To go up and down and follow the wind means to go everywhere in space at this moment.

That is the way mountains walk, moment by moment. That is what Dōgen meant when he said the mountain is always walking. Moment by moment it is a perfect mountain. It actualizes a perfect virtue that allows us to practice, to go higher and broader in order to help others.

This is Dōgen's introduction to "Sansuikyō." Remember that mountains are go-uji, this reality-self and all other beings and all time. "Mountains and waters" actually means our life, which is connected with all beings in the Dharma world. Mountains and waters are not outside our lives; we ourselves are mountains and waters. There is this strange thing, called "mountains," which includes our selves. We can call this entire thing "the self." We are the self including the entire mountains; the mountains include the self.

In *Shōbōgenzō* "Zenki," *zenki* means total, entire, complete function or work:

> Life is manifestation of the total function, death is manifestation of the total function. We should know that, among the numberless dharmas in the self, there is life; there is death. We should quietly think whether this present life and all beings that are coarising with this life are together with life or not together with life. Any single moment and any single mind is not apart from life.

Both life and death are within this life. "Numberless dharmas in the self" refers to all things that are living together with us. Each and every moment is part of this life; each and every thing is part of this life.

> Life is, for example, like a time when a person is riding in a boat. In this boat, the person operates the sail; the person

manages the rudder. Although the person rows with the oar, the boat gives the person a ride and, other than the boat, there is no such person as a self. The person rides in the boat and the person makes this boat into a boat. We should make efforts to study this very moment. This very moment is nothing but the world of the boat. The sky, the water, and the shore; all of those become the time of the boat: it is not the same with the time of something else other than the boat. Therefore, we give birth to life; life makes us into ourselves.

The image of the boat clearly depicts how interdependent origination works from both sides, the self and the network. In my case, I express my life by practicing, studying, and explaining these strange things written by Dōgen to Westerners. This work creates my life; it also causes people to consider me a Sōtō Zen priest. It is like this for each of us; our work creates our life, and creates how people see us. Society creates each person, and we create or re-create society through our actions.

> When riding in a boat, our body and mind, ourselves and the environment—all become the functioning of the boat. The entire earth and the entire space become the functioning of the boat.

Dōgen said when we are sailing on the boat the entire world becomes part of the boat. It's a strange thing; the boat is part of the world, and the entire world is also part of the boat. In our activity, in our practice, in our life, this entire world is part of me, part of my life, part of my practice.

> Thus, life is the self, and the self is life.

This is the same as the statement in "Sansuikyō" that we are part of the entire world and the entire world is part of our life. I think that is the basic premise of Dōgen's teaching. The world creates me and I create the world. The mutual work is our life and our practice.

## 2-1: Blue Mountains Are Constantly Walking

(2) Preceptor Kai of Mount Dayang addressed the assembly, saying, "The blue mountains are constantly walking. The stone woman gives birth to a child in the night."

WHEN I FIRST read this very short and simple statement by Furong Daokai, or as Dōgen refers to him, Preceptor Kai, I thought it might be a part of a longer discourse. However, it seems he said just these two sentences and descended from the teaching seat. No explanation or discussion is recorded. I wonder whether his students understood it. Regardless, the only thing we have now is the statement itself. What it means is a question to us, a kōan.

Dōgen Zenji used this statement to express his understanding of the reality of nikon, this present moment, which is the intersection of impermanence and eternity, discontinuation and continuation, phenomenal beings and ultimate truth. Interpenetration of these opposite pairs is the expression of the way of ancient Buddha. It is also the reality of our life.

## IMPERMANENCE AND ETERNITY

> (3) The mountains lack none of their proper virtues; hence they are
> constantly at rest and constantly walking.

"Constantly at rest" is *jō-anjū*; *jō* (常) means "constantly" or "permanently." Dōgen says that all of the mountains have two virtues. One is jō-anjū: always abiding, being there. This means peacefully staying; it doesn't move. The other, *jō-unpo*, means "constantly walking." Dōgen says that the mountain has the virtue of always being there and also always walking, changing. These are the two sides.

In the last chapter I discussed time's virtue of coming and going. The virtue of coming and going and the virtue of being there exist together, in each moment. Each moment includes beginningless past and endless future. This seamless moment doesn't move; this seamless time doesn't flow in a linear stream. These are the two sides of the virtues of the mountains.

In 1989, while I lived at Shōrinji in Kyōto, I visited Japanese-American temples and Zen centers in the United States to give Dharma talks. That was my second visit to the United States; the first was when I lived at Valley Zendō in Massachusetts. During the trip, I gave a lecture about *Gakudō-yōjin-shū*, or *Points to Watch in Practicing the Way*, one of Dōgen's writings. In the very first section Dōgen discusses arousing bodhi-mind or awakening mind, the mind that sees the impermanence of all beings and is vital to practicing the Buddha Way:

> The ancestral master Nāgārjuna said that the mind that solely sees the impermanence of this world of constant appearance and disappearance is called bodhi-mind. Therefore, [for now I think it would be appropriate to talk about] bodhi-mind as the mind that sees impermanence.[48]

The year before that trip, I had practiced with Katagiri Rōshi for one month at Daijoji, in Japan. He'd already had some health problems, but I didn't know he had cancer. When I was visiting temples in the United States, I went to Massachusetts. There, one of Katagiri Rōshi's students, Yutaka Ishii, a Japanese-American from Hawaii, was dying of throat cancer. He couldn't speak or eat. He died about ten days after my visit. At other places too I saw and heard about aging, sickness, and death. I had been talking about impermanence, and then I saw the reality of impermanence.

A friend of mine who worked for a Buddhist publisher in Japan asked me to write an essay about my trip to America, so I wrote about impermanence. I wrote about *Gakudō-yōjin-shū* and what I saw and experienced during that trip. Uchiyama Rōshi read my article. He said, "When you talk about *Gakudō-yōjin-shū* it's okay to talk about impermanence; it is important. But impermanence is only half of the Dharma." I was startled.

That became my kōan: What is the other half of Dharma? Of course I understood intellectually, because I had been studying with Uchiyama Rōshi for a long time. He was always saying that the reality of our life is before separation, before any dichotomy, before the distinction between permanence and impermanence. Impermanence is only one side of reality. Theoretically I knew that, but until then I couldn't express or write or consciously think about it. Because I was young, it was difficult for me to see impermanence as my personal experience. When I encountered it, I wasn't able to connect it with the other side: eternity.

Now, twenty-five years later, impermanence is real to me. I am older than Katagiri Rōshi was when he passed away. My eyes are weaker, and things I could once do easily are becoming more difficult. Cross-legged sitting was the most comfortable posture to me for more than forty years, but when I was sixty-three years old I started to need to sit on a chair because of my knee problem. Now I actually feel and face impermanence. When I was young, impermanence was a teaching, something I had to study and investigate. Now it's my body, my life. When we truly see impermanence as our personal reality, we begin to see another half of the Dharma. Until then, either side is simply an idea or theory.

Around the same time as my trip to the United States, Uchiyama Rōshi wrote a collection of poems. He was in his early seventies then and very sick, and we expected he would die any time. But he lived sixteen more years and died when he was eighty-six. I think he expected his own death at the time too, because he wrote a collection of poems about life and death. They are beautiful and profound. They weren't published as a formal book, but Daitsu Tom Wright and I translated them.[49] One of the poems in that collection is as follows:

### SAMĀDHI OF THE TREASURY OF THE RADIANT LIGHT

Though poor, never poor,
Though sick, never sick,
Though aging, never aging,
Though dying, never dying.
Reality prior to division—
Herein lies unlimited depth.

He said that this is the reality of his life. Though his life was very rich, it was a reality that financially he was poor; he never worked for money. He had a regular income for only six months of his life, when he taught philosophy and mathematics at a Catholic seminary. And he lived with tuberculosis for more than fifty years; he married in his early twenties while a university student, and his wife died of tuberculosis after transmitting it to him. He married again and lost his second wife too; she died while she was pregnant. That was one of the reasons he made up his mind to be a Buddhist monk and became Sawaki Rōshi's disciple. He thoroughly experienced impermanence through these sad and painful personal experiences, and when he wrote this poem, he was facing his own life and death.

Physically he was a very weak person. He was sick the last few years that he served as the abbot of Antaiji; often he couldn't sit, and sometimes he vomited blood. Half of his lungs didn't work. That was why he committed to be the abbot for only ten years; he was often sick, and he was aging, and he was dying. That was the undeniable reality of his life. Yet he also said his life was really rich. Because he lived together with the entire universe, he was never sick, he was never aging, and he was never dying. This is the other half of reality for Uchiyama Rōshi.

Intellectually I knew that point of Rōshi's teaching, but it was not my personal reality yet. What is the other side of reality of our life that is never poor, never sick, never aging, never dying, never dead? Is this Buddha's teaching or not? Buddha said, "Everything is impermanent." Then what is this teaching of a reality before any separation of impermanence and permanence? That was my question.

One of the sources of the teaching of eternity is what is written in the *Sūtra on the Buddha's Bequeathed Teaching* (or *The Sūtra on the Final Teaching of the Buddha*, in Japanese, *Butsu-Yuikyō-gyō*. In Japanese temples, this sūtra is recited on the occasion of the Buddha's Parinirvāṇa Day. In this sūtra, after Śākyamuni Buddha gave the final teachings to the monks, right before his death, he said,

> From now on all of my disciples must continuously practice. Then the Thus Come One's Dharma body will always be present and indestructible. You should know, therefore, that everything in the world is impermanent. Meetings necessarily have separations, so do not harbor grief. Every appearance in the world is like this, so you should be vigorous and seek for an early liberation. Destroy the darkness of delusion with the brightness of wisdom. The world is truly dangerous and unstable, without any durability.[50]

When Śākyamuni talked about the impermanence of his own life as he was dying, he said that his Dharma body is manifested in his disciples' practice. Thus, the Buddha's Dharma body will always be present and indestructible, eternal. In the beginning, the "Buddha's Dharma body" referred to the teachings of the Buddha. However, later in Mahāyāna Buddhism, the "Dharma body" is considered to be the reality of all things as they are, rather than the verbal teachings of Śākyamuni Buddha. In the *Avataṃsaka Sūtra*, or *Flower Ornament Sūtra*, and some other Mahāyāna sūtras, the whole universe is itself the Dharma body of the Buddha named Vairocana. In Zen tradition, it is said that each and every phenomenal being is itself a manifestation of the eternal Dharma body.

This is the insight about reality expressed here by Dōgen. Everything is always abiding, always there; at the same time, everything is always changing, always coming and going. That is Dōgen's teaching and Uchiyama Rōshi's understanding about the reality of life. It includes death: even though he is dying he never dies. To me this teaching is central. For now, and for always, this is my kōan: How can I manifest the constant, peacefully abiding reality of life, within the reality of impermanence, which is always changing? How can we live awakening to both sides of reality?

That is Dōgen's charge to us. It didn't become a reality to me until Uchiyama Rōshi and friends who were my own age started to die in the 1990s. Until we see impermanence as personal reality, eternity is also simply a concept. I have to find how I can use the rest of my life to express this reality, the reality before separation of impermanence and eternity.

In the case of our lives, it is easier to see impermanence than eternity. But in the case of mountains, we normally consider them as a symbol of something that does not change. To see the mountains as immovable is very easy for us. But actually they only appear to be stationary. We know that long ago the continents were arranged very differently, that they've moved and shifted and pushed up mountains. I've heard that fossil shells are found in the Himalayas. So now we understand that not only mountains but also continents are walking in a physical way. I don't think Furong and Dōgen knew this. We have more knowledge today than they had. And yet, we have something to learn from them.

> We must devote ourselves to a detailed study of this virtue of
> walking.

As common sense in our daily lives, we assume that mountains never move, and it doesn't cause us a problem. But when we study earth science today, their moving is understood. The same can be said when we study the true reality of all beings as an actual matter in our own lives. We have to study beyond our conventional knowledge. Dōgen wants us to investigate.

> Since the walking of the mountains should be like that of people,
> one ought not doubt that the mountains walk simply because they
> may not appear to stride like humans.

Mountains are walking every moment. And yet each moment, the mountains are also abiding peacefully in their Dharma position. We human beings are the same, walking constantly and yet abiding peacefully. Not only mountains and human beings—all things have these two sides as the nature of time, space, and beings.

## MOUNTAINS' CONSTANT WALKING

> (4) This saying of the buddha and ancestor [Daokai] has pointed
> out walking; it has got what is fundamental, and we should thor-
> oughly investigate this address on "constant walking." It is constant
> because it is walking. Although the walking of the blue mountains
> is faster than "swift as the wind," those in the mountains do not
> sense this, do not know it.

The word Dōgen uses for "constant" is *jō* (常), the opposite of *mujō* (無常, impermanent). Dōgen is saying that the mountain is permanent precisely because it is impermanent. This kind of strange "Buddha is Buddha because Buddha is not Buddha" logic is often used in *prajñāpāramitā* texts such as the *Diamond Sūtra*.

When Dōgen says the mountain is walking fast, he is not talking about the movement of mountains in geologic time. This expression "swift as the wind" is quoted from the third chapter of the *Lotus Sūtra*, entitled "A Parable," in which the Buddha talked about three kinds of carriages and one great white ox carriage. An elder owned a large old house, but it started to burn in a fire. His children were playing in the burning house and refused to come out. In order to persuade them to come out, he told the children that if they would get out of the house he would give them one of three kinds of carriages—goat carriages, deer carriages, or ox carriages—depending upon their preferences. When they came out of the house to gain one of these three kinds of carriages, the elder gave them all the same great white ox carriage. The three kinds of carriage refers to the three vehicles: śrāvaka, pratyekabuddha, and bodhisattva. The great white ox carriage refers to the one vehicle (*eka-yana*) or one-buddha-yana. About the white ox pulling this buddha vehicle, the *Lotus Sūtra*'s third chapter says it was "a handsome, very powerful white ox with a pure hide, capable of walking with a smooth gait and fast as the speed of the wind."[51]

This is the speed of the one-buddha vehicle that carries all living beings to buddhahood. Here Dōgen used this expression from the *Lotus Sūtra* to say that the mountains he is talking about are the one vehicle in which all living beings are already riding: the entire network of interdependent origination. This is what the *Lotus Sūtra* calls the true reality of all beings. And the mountains are walking even faster than "as fast as the wind."

The next part of the sentence is important. "Those in the mountains" are "a person in the mountains," the expression that appears in the verses on Mount Lu by Su Shi, Hongzhi, and Dōgen. Su Shi said that he could not see the mountains' true face because he was in the midst of them. Hongzhi said the mountains were his body, and there was no question of seeing or not. Dōgen followed Hongzhi and added that the body is not a fixed self. Rather, we should love the mountains and live together with all beings coming and going in the mountains; then there is no separation. This expression points out the way all beings are within the network of interdependent origination.

> To be in the mountains is to be "a flower opening within the world."

The same reality is also expressed by the well-known Zen expression "when a flower blooms, the world arises." This expression originally appeared in the transmission verse of the twenty-seventh ancestor Prajñātārā (in Japanese, Hannyatara) to the twenty-eighth ancestor Bodhidharma (Bodaidaruma). The verse is as follows:

> The mind-ground gives birth to various seeds.
> Depending upon phenomenal beings, the principle emerges.
> When the fruits are ripe, the awakening is complete;
> When a flower blooms, the world arises.[52]

Dōgen used this expression, for example, in *Shōbōgenzō* "Baika" ("Plum Blossoms"):

> When flowers suddenly open on the old plum tree, it is exactly like what is said in the expression "when flowers open, the world arises." The expression "when flowers open, the world arises" describes the spring is coming.

When a plum blossom blooms, even though the mountains are still covered with snow, the entire world becomes spring. One tiny phenomenal thing is connected with the entirety of Indra's net; it can change the entire world into spring. This image of plum blossoms in the snow is often used in Dōgen's Dharma discourses on the occasion of the Buddha's Enlightenment Day, December 8.[53]

We are always in the mountains. We are born within this world and we live and die in this world. Where are we going after death? Nowhere! As Uchiyama Rōshi said, we are born with the entire world, live together with the world, and when we die, the entire world dies with us. We are always connected with all beings in this entire world. In this case "the mountains" are the world we live in and at the same time, as Hongzhi and Dōgen said, the mountains are our body.

There's no way to get out of the world or over the mountains. We are always in the mountains. As a Dharma position, the mountain is always abiding peacefully at this moment. Within this moment the entire past and future are reflected. In the next moment it is the same. Something always changes, but as a quality of this moment past and present are included. Moment by moment the mountain is walking; it's changing. Usually we don't think we are changing; we want to believe "I am the same person from the time of birth until death." But nothing continues without changing.

Since we are in the mountains we cannot observe the walking, which could be seen from outside. When we are on a train moving smoothly we don't feel the train moving; we don't feel the wind. Even when we sit quietly in the zendō we are actually moving, because the earth is turning completely around every day. When we sit for a whole day, we turn around the entire earth. We are moving really quickly, faster than riding in a car, but we think we are sitting still because we don't feel the movement of the earth. A person coming and going in the mountains doesn't see the walking of the mountains, but that doesn't mean the mountains don't move.

> Those outside the mountains do not sense this, do not know it. Those without eyes to see the mountains do not sense, do not know, do not see, do not hear the reason for this.

Unless we have eyes, ears, nose, tongue, body, and mind we cannot see, hear, or taste this movement. This condition is called "outside of the mountains." Although we are always in the mountains, we don't usually have the eye to see their walking. Even when we know that the mountain is walking, because we are in the mountains there is no way to see this movement. Yet the mountain moves. How can we believe this? How can Dōgen say such a thing?

This has been a question for me for a long time. For example, in "Jijuyū Zanmai"[54] Dōgen said that many things happen in our zazen—everything in the entire Dharma world becomes Buddhadharma, and all space in the universe completely becomes enlightenment—but we cannot perceive them happening. When we are in samādhi there's no separation between the person sitting and the samādhi, so it is impossible to perceive the samādhi. The person sitting cannot see zazen because the person *is* zazen. Our eyes cannot see our eyes! When we don't have the eyes we don't see, and even when we have them we still don't see because of this nonseparation. No matter what, we don't see.

How did Dōgen know this? How can we understand whether what he says is right or wrong? I am still in the process of searching for this answer. Here is what I think: Even though we can't see with our eyes, somehow from the very bottom of our being we know the mountain's moving. This way of knowing is called the Dharma eye. The Dharma eye, or Buddha's wisdom (*prajñā*), is not a certain way of using our brains. It is what's there when I let go of my thought. It sees both sides of reality. This is zazen, in my experience: zazen itself is Buddha's wisdom. But when I try to explain this, it becomes a concept made by humans, and then it's not reality anymore. To really "see" it we have to practice.

> To doubt the walking of the mountains means that one does not yet know one's own walking.

When we listen to Furong Daokai's teaching that blue mountains are constantly walking, of course we question it. Dōgen says if we react in this way we don't really know even our own walking, our own impermanence. As he said in "Genjōkōan," we are trying to see things moving around us and don't see that "this thing" that sees is moving too.

> It is not that one does not walk but that one does not yet know, has not made clear, this walking.

Even though we are really walking, we don't see our own walking. We don't really understand our own walking, yet we are actually walking. This is an important point. To know or not to know is not essential; in either case we are walking. That is our practice: whether we know it or not we are actually walking. That is what matters. We keep walking. When we don't see, our practice is based on trust or faith in the teachings of our teachers, or Dōgen, or Śākyamuni Buddha. To see that we don't know is the first wisdom. "Not knowing" is an important part of our practice.

"I trust what my teacher says even though I don't really understand it." That was my condition when I started to practice. I knew nothing about Zen or Buddhism, but somehow I trusted my teacher's way of life. I wanted to live like him. That's why I started to practice and that's how I could continue to practice. Now I have a certain understanding of what Dōgen is saying, but more than forty years ago when I began to practice, I knew nothing. Even when I read *Shōbōgenzō* I didn't understand. Nonetheless, this way of life attracted me. It wasn't an intellectual understanding, but maybe trust or faith—I was drawn to it. It's a kind of energy. It's not thinking. I didn't know, but somehow my life knew.

I had a lot of doubts about what Uchiyama Rōshi was saying. But even though I struggled with doubt, even though sometimes I had many good reasons not to practice, somehow I couldn't stop. Something carried me toward practice, past the doubt, much deeper than my personal willpower or intellectual understanding could have. Sometimes it felt terrible; I wanted to do something different. But somehow I could not resist going to the zendō, even when consciously I did not want to.

According to some scientists, walking made human beings different from other anthropoids. Because we started to walk with two legs, our hands were released to do something else. Using our hands helped our brains to develop, and we began to think more and more. (Another side effect of walking with legs is lower back problems!) Walking is very natural for us grownups. However, when we started to walk as babies, it was a lot of work. It's almost a miracle when we watch a baby first stand up and walk. Later walking becomes ordinary, unless we are sick or handicapped. One of the meanings of walking is that it's not something special; it's a very ordinary thing. But Dōgen urged us to carefully study our own walking and notice that we walk together with all beings in the world. When we are walking, the entire world is walking.

Dōgen said:

> Those who would know their own walking must also know the walking of the blue mountains.

If we really know our walking, if we know that our whole life is walking, moving, and changing, then we can see the blue mountains' walking. Dōgen is asking us to clearly see our own selves. Then we can see the world outside of ourselves. Both are walking.

## NEITHER SENTIENT NOR INSENTIENT

> (5) The blue mountains are not sentient; they are not insentient. We ourselves are not sentient; we are not insentient.

"Sentient" is *ujō*, 有情; "insentient" is *mujō*, 無情. Don't confuse this with *mujō*, 無常, which means "impermanent." This *jō* (情) means "sentiment," "feeling," "emotion." A being with emotions is a sentient being, while a being without emotions is insentient. Usually we think a mountain is insentient. But Dōgen says the mountain is neither sentient nor insentient. Not only mountains—we ourselves are neither sentient nor insentient, although we think we are sentient. So is there something in between sentient and insentient? No. There is not a third state.

The reality of our life is connected with mountains; mountains are connected with each of us living within them. Mountains include sentient beings, and sentient beings are included within the mountains.

This one reality of self and the world is neither sentient nor insentient. Or we could say both sentient and insentient. Our lives include both sentient and insentient beings. We are one with the entire mountain. When the mountain is walking, we are also walking. That's why we don't see that the mountain is walking.

> We can have no doubts about these blue mountains walking. We do not know what measure of Dharma realms would be necessary to clarify the blue mountains.

The size of the blue mountains cannot be measured, even using entire Dharma realms or Dharma worlds as the scale, because the mountains are connected to all space and all time. The blue mountains and the Dharma worlds are exactly the same thing. We cannot use a ruler to measure itself.

In my school, after reciting a sūtra we chant a verse that expresses this oneness and boundlessness:

*Ji ho san shi i shi fu;*
*shi son Bussa moko sa;*
*moko ho ja ho ro mi.*

All buddhas, ten directions, three times;
all beings, bodhisattva-mahāsattvas;
wisdom beyond wisdom, mahāprajñāpāramitā.

We are not asking all buddhas in the ten directions and three times to fulfill our desires. This verse is the expression of our awakening that we are one with all buddhas, all bodhisattvas, and all other beings in the ten directions and the three times.

> We should do a clear accounting of the blue mountains' walking and our own walking, including an accounting of both "stepping back and back-stepping."

"Accounting" is a translation of *tenken*, which means to inspect, examine, or overhaul; we have to investigate what this walking of the self and the mountains is. "Stepping back and back-stepping" is a kind of playing with words. The expressions Dōgen uses are *tai ho* and *ho tai*; he just changed the order of the words. *Tai ho* is what we recite in Dōgen's *Fukanzazengi* (*Universal Recommendation of Zazen*): "Take a backward step to turn the light inward and illuminate the self." This *tai ho* is "backward step," "back sliding," or possibly "withdrawing."

Usually *tai ho* is interpreted negatively. However, Dōgen uses it in a positive way; he says our zazen is a backward step to illuminate our selves. Usually we go forward and we think that is a positive action. We try to see, understand, and change things according to our observations and judgments. We don't see this person who is perceiving and evaluating. So "stepping back and back-stepping" means we should study ourselves. That is what Dōgen says in "Genjōkōan": "to study the Buddha Way is to study the self." "To study the self" is a backward step.

> We should do an accounting of the fact that, since the very time "before any subtle sign," since "the other side of the King of Emptiness," walking by stepping forward and back has never stopped for a moment.

"Before any subtle sign" and "since the other side of the King of Emptiness" are the same as the expressions Dōgen used in the introduction: "prior to the kalpa of emptiness" or "before the germination of any subtle sign." It's like before the Big Bang, before anything happens. This time is like chaos. In Dōgen's expression it means beyond thinking, discrimination, and separation. "Since the very time" means since the beginningless beginning. Here he says both "stepping forward" and "stepping back" have never stopped for a moment in all that time.

I have just said that "stepping back" is to inwardly illuminate and study the self. "Stepping forward" is to study myriad external things and to work together with other people in society. Stepping backward is *tai ho*, but it is also called *jō gu Bodai. Jō* (上) means "go high up";

*gu* (求) is "seek"; and *Bodai* is "bodhi," "awakening." So we practice going up higher and higher endlessly to seek awakening, to study Dharma, and to awaken to the reality of all beings; that is stepping backward. Stepping forward is called *ge ke shu jō*. *Ge* is "go down," *ke* (化) means "teach," though its root meaning is "transform"; *shu jō* is "living beings." So we practice coming down and teaching living beings using various skillful means. These are the activities of the Great Compassion Bodhisattva using a thousand eyes and hands.

Thus the two sides of our bodhisattva practice are wisdom and compassion. We take a backward step and clearly see the emptiness of all things; this is the practice of Avalokiteśvara in the *Heart Sūtra*. We also take a forward step to help living beings in need; this is the practice of Avalokiteśvara in the "Kannonkyō" chapter of the *Lotus Sūtra*. The blue mountains are constantly walking both ways.

These two aspects of bodhisattva practice are what Dōgen meant when in the introduction he referred to the virtues of riding on the clouds and of following the wind. We try to go up high and at the same time to go down. These two seem contradictory. We often ask: what is the relationship between practicing in the zendō and working in the world? Dōgen's understanding is that these are not contradictory at all; they are the two aspects of one walking within the blue mountain and of the blue mountains' walking.

## THE *LOTUS SŪTRA* AND THE TRUE REALITY OF ALL BEINGS

One of the sources of Dōgen's idea—that the entire world is walking and the walking of this universe is our practice—is the teaching of the *Lotus Sūtra*, the fundamental sūtra of the Tendai school. Because Dōgen was first ordained as a Tendai monk, he studied Tendai teachings in his early years. So the *Lotus Sūtra* was formative in his understanding of Buddha's teaching. He was the person who decided that when we chant the ten names of Buddha at meals the sixth should be the name of the *Lotus Sūtra*.[55] A few days before he died at the age of fifty-three, he chanted a chapter of the *Lotus Sūtra* and wrote on the pillar of the room, *"Namu myō hō renge kyō an"*: "The hermitage of taking refuge in the *Lotus Sūtra*."

The second section of the *Lotus Sūtra*, entitled "Tactfulness," explains why all buddhas appear in this world.

> This Dharma cannot be well understood through calculation or analysis. Only a buddha can really grasp it. Why is this? Because it is for this great cause alone that buddhas, the world-honored ones, appear in the world.
>
> What do I mean by saying it is for this one great cause alone that buddhas, the world-honored ones, appear in the world? The buddhas, the world-honored ones, appear in the world because they want living beings to open a way to the buddhas' insight.[56]

So buddhas—not only one Buddha but all buddhas—appear in this world because of only one reason: to cause living beings to open their eyes to Buddha-knowledge.

The original Chinese term for Buddha-knowledge is *Butsu chi ken* (佛知見). *Chi* means "to know" or "to understand"; *ken* is "to see" or "to view." These words suggest direct experience combined with understanding. The Sanskrit term is *darshanan*, translated "insight." I think "insight" works better in English to emphasize both the profound and the experiential nature of this knowledge. We make a clear distinction between ordinary human eyes, views, thinking, and knowledge and Buddha's eyes, view, knowledge and insight. So we say Buddha appeared in this world to enable all living beings to open their eyes to the Buddha's insight.

> The buddhas, the world-honored ones, appear in the world because they want living beings to open a way to the buddhas' insight, and thus become pure. They appear in the world because they want to demonstrate the buddhas' insight to living beings. They appear in the world because

they want living beings to apprehend things with the buddhas' insight. They appear in the world because they want living beings to enter into the way of the buddhas' insight.[57]

Repetition is emphasis: there is just this one reason buddhas appear in the world. Buddhas teach us to transform our human views to the Buddha's way: seeing things as they are, and living based on that insight.

It doesn't say here *what* the Buddha's insight is. The beginning of this chapter says:

> The Buddha has fulfilled the whole Dharma—innumerable, unlimited, unprecedented teachings.[58]

So he says, "Stop talking."

> Why? Because what the Buddha has achieved is most rare and difficult to understand.[59]

This sūtra says it is impossible to understand the Law (Dharma) by human thinking, but Buddha wants us to enter that Law. That's why he appeared in this world.

What is this Law or Dharma?

> Only among buddhas can the true character of all things be fathomed.[60]

The older translation of this "only among buddhas" is "only a buddha together with a buddha"—which is the translation of "Yuibutsu-yobutsu," the title of one of the fascicles of *Shōbōgenzō*. And "the true character of all things" is *shohōjissō. Shohō* (諸法) is all dharmas, all things. *Jitsu* is "true" and *sō* is "form," so *jissō* is "true form."

This is the true reality of all beings, all existence. According to the *Lotus Sūtra* this is what the Buddha wanted to transmit to all living beings. Within Zen tradition this is the Dharma that has been transmitted—the true form of all beings, through Buddha to Mahākāśyapa and so forth to us.

What is this true reality of all beings? The sūtra says:

> This is because every existing thing has such characteristics, such a nature, such an embodiment, such powers, such actions, such causes, such conditions, such effects, such rewards and retributions, and yet such a complete fundamental coherence.[61]

In Chinese and Japanese these are called *jū-nyoze,* the ten suchnesses. But the Chinese translation does not match the Sanskrit original at this point. Some scholars think that Kumārajīva, who translated the *Lotus Sūtra* into Chinese, added this point about the ten suchnesses.

*Suchness* is a translation of the Chinese word *nyoze; nyo* is "like" and *ze* means "this." *Jū* means ten. *Nyoze* literally means "like this." D. T. Suzuki's translation of this word is "suchness," "as-it-is-ness," or "thusness." I think Dōgen's understanding is that what buddhas and ancestors transmit is this reality of suchness—not the teaching of suchness but the reality itself.

The ten suchnesses are a very important teaching in the Tendai school.

In this translation *sō* is characteristics (form), *shō* (性) is nature, *tai* is embodiment, *riki* is powers (potency), *sa* is actions (function), *in* is causes (primary cause), *en* is conditions (secondary cause), *ka* is effects, *hō* is rewards and retributions (recompense), and *hon matsu ku kyō tō* is complete fundamental coherence (complete fundamental whole). What follows is my personal understanding of them; I don't know the Tendai understanding because I don't study Tendai teachings in detail.

The first five suchnesses are the uniqueness of each and every being, including human beings. Each being has its own unique characteristics: *sō*, its own appearance or shape. It has its own unique nature: *shō*. It has its own body or substance; *tai* literally means "body," not embodiment.

Each being has its own powers, or energy, *riki*. And it has its own action or influence, *sa*. These are the five elements of one unique being.

The next four suchnesses characterize relationship through time and space. Here Dōgen is talking about Buddhist practice, about expressing a Dharma position. Each one of us has a unique personality and shape, both physically and mentally. Each one of us has some cause, *in*, why we are doing whatever we are doing right now; each one of us has a different motivation, which is related to what we did in the past. The condition, *en*, is the condition we have at this moment in relation to all beings in the universe. There are many things that help us to practice; there are many things that don't. The effect, *ka*, is that perhaps a million years later, as the result of our continuous practice we attain perfect awakening. Then as reward and retribution, *hō*, we become a buddha.

An analogy often used to explain these suchnesses is a flower. A seed is a cause. Conditions, or secondary causes, are humidity, sunlight, temperature, and so on, which are necessary for the plant to sprout and grow. A plant has a relationship with things that happened in the past, with what is happening now, and with things still to happen in the future. A plant's future is a flower or fruit; for us awakening is called a fruit of practice. This connects what we are doing now with the future, but this is not the only result. There is also a reward and retribution, or secondary result, *hō*, of the process. For example, when a flower blooms as a result of the plant's activity, the sprouted seed influences other beings. When we see a flower blooming we become happy, although that is not the flower's purpose in blooming; also the flower offers nectar for bees to make honey.

Taking all of this together, the cause, the conditions, the result, and the secondary results, we have a whole, a complete fundamental coherence. In a similar way, becoming a buddha is not the end of the story. When we become a buddha we have to teach. All beings receive benefit from this person's teaching, which can then be called Buddha's teaching.

This teaching of the ten suchnesses shows us that all beings have their unique nature in body, energy, and work. Yet that uniqueness cannot exist by itself, independent of other beings throughout time and space. The final suchness is most important, *hon matsu ku kyō tō. Hon* means "first one"; *matsu* means "last one"; *ku kyō* means ultimately; *tō* (等) means "equal," "identical," "same." The teaching means this entire process in which we are practicing, this space where we are living, where all beings exist from beginningless beginning to the endless end, the entire universe, all this is one thing. This is what the *Lotus Sūtra* calls the "reality of all beings."

In "Sansuikyō," Dōgen refers to this *hon matsu ku kyō tō* as the mountains; we are within the mountains, we are walking, and the mountains are walking with us. In other words, our practice is not an individual activity to gain something for ourselves. We are part of this entire works, this whole dynamic function, Dōgen's zenki. Even though we are so tiny, so weak, so self-centered, even though our bodhi-mind is not so determined, once we take the bodhisattva vow, we are walking toward buddhahood, we are already in the Way. This entirety is the Buddha Way. We arouse bodhi-mind to practice awakening and enter nirvāṇa or attain buddhahood within the Buddha Way. In each step we are already at the destination.

## THE MOUNTAIN WALKING: JŌSHIN-SAN'S EXAMPLE

We do many things as our practice. From the time we begin, awakening the vow in our body/mind, we continue to practice. We do many different things to fulfill this strange, impossible vow. Sometimes we work in the kitchen, sometimes we give a talk, sometimes we do administrative tasks. Each of us expresses our vow in a unique way.

I would like to introduce one person whose life expression strongly inspired me, a good example of a person coming and going in the mountain. She practiced with and was influenced by many great teachers, and she influenced many practitioners in the United States. Her name is Rev. Jōshin Kasai, or Jōshin-san. Jōshin-san was Kōdō Sawaki

Rōshi's disciple, Uchiyama Rōshi's Dharma sister, a nun, and she was also sewing teacher to Rev. Zenkei Blanche Hartman, the first female abbess of the San Francisco Zen Center.

Once when Jōshin-san was in her early twenties, before she became a nun, she went to a sesshin led by Sogaku Harada Rōshi. Harada Rōshi was the first Sōtō Zen master who practiced at a Rinzai monastery and completed kōan practice, and he introduced kōan practice to the Sōtō school. In his style of practice, attaining kenshō is essential. Jōshin-san attained kenshō in one night. A determined person, she had completely focused on sitting all night and all day. Many years later, when I talked with her about her kenshō experience, she told me that it had nothing to do with enlightenment; it's a matter of "guts." She didn't think that her experience had anything to do with Buddhadharma.

Jōshin-san was ordained first by Ekō Hashimoto Rōshi, who was Katagiri Rōshi's teacher at Eiheiji. Then, when she met Sawaki Rōshi she wanted to be Sawaki Rōshi's disciple. In Japanese culture, to change a teacher is very difficult. She couldn't ask Hashimoto Rōshi if she could leave. What she did was to imitate the second ancestor of Chinese Zen; to show her sincerity she cut off the tip of her little finger. Things like this happen sometimes in Japan. I don't think it is a good tradition; please don't imitate this. But Jōshin-san was that kind of person; she was very determined. Because her personality was like this, some people considered her a troublemaker.

In Sawaki Rōshi's final days, Uchiyama Rōshi and Jōshin-san took care of him, together with several young resident monks at Antaiji. When Sawaki Rōshi died, Jōshin-san asked Uchiyama Rōshi to allow her to stay at Antaiji. Uchiyama Rōshi asked her to be tenzo, monastery cook, during sesshin. She accepted.

I think at that time they didn't expect very many people to come to sesshin, and in the beginning they didn't have many people. But when I first attended a five-day sesshin there were at least sixty or seventy people sitting there. I was amazed. That was 1969, four years after Sawaki Rōshi's death. Jōshin-san prepared meals for all those people by herself. It was really hard work. She cooked with firewood, because we didn't have a gas or electric stove. Of course, whenever we could we helped her, washing and cutting up vegetables before sesshin started and doing dishes after each meal, but still she worked very hard. It was her practice, and she accepted it. The only time she didn't cook for the sesshin was when she was in San Francisco teaching sewing; then the monks took turns cooking.

That was her most important practice, so she really didn't neglect it. The sesshin made her work hard, and she made the sesshin possible. She was a part of the sesshin, and the sesshin was part of her life. In the way she worked as tenzo, her uniqueness was fully expressed. Her practice as tenzo was connected with Harada Rōshi, Hashimoto Rōshi, Sawaki Rōshi, Uchiyama Rōshi, and all other people.

Jōshin-san's other important practice was sewing okesa and rakusu. She sewed many people's okesa when they received priest *tokudo*, and she traveled to teach sewing at San Francisco Zen Center. Because of her teaching, many American Sōtō Zen practitioners sew and wear *nyohōe* (hand-sewn Buddhist robes). Her life was unique, and yet her practice was connected with her teachers and with our current practice in the United States. Through our practice, Jōshin-san is still alive.

Such a life is one way the mountain walks.

## WALKING CONTINUES, WITHOUT LIMIT

> (6) If walking had ever rested, the buddhas and ancestors would never have appeared.

Because everything is moving, changing, and walking in the blue mountains, we can practice, and this practice is also a part of the walking. If we stop walking, the mountains stop walking, no buddhas and ancestors appear. So actually our practice—or the movement of this world—is the mother of all buddhas.

Another way of saying "walking" might be the continuing unfolding of personal karma, life force, and evolution, even when we are not thinking about practice. These are part of the mountains' walking.

Sometimes we feel like we are at a dead end; we can't walk anymore. But the blue mountains' walking has no dead end; there's no limit to the blue mountains' walking. Even when we are dying, the blue mountains still walk; the process of dying is also part of the mountains' walking. So a third meaning of "stepping forward and stepping back" might be birth and death. Arising and perishing could be the two feet of the blue mountains. Birth and death manifest the total function; they are the two feet of one mountain walking.

Next Dōgen says,

> if walking were limited, the Buddhadharma would never have reached us today.

If the mountains' walking were limited to certain places, people, or ages, it would have died away before reaching us. Dōgen did not agree with the idea, popular in the thirteenth century, that Japan was remote from the Buddha's land and their time was the degenerate age of the last Dharma.[62]

> Stepping forward has never ceased; stepping back has never ceased. Stepping forward does not oppose stepping back, nor does stepping back oppose stepping forward.

Working in society does not oppose studying Dharma and practicing zazen, and vice versa. Walking in both directions should never cease. Because our view, capability, energy, and time are limited, sometimes we have to choose this way or that. One person cannot do everything. We need some people who focus on Dharma study, some who focus on sitting practice, and some who focus on working in society. Yet everyone should do a certain amount of each thing. Even monks and scholars have to work outside to help others. Zazen practice and Dharma study can inspire and deepen understanding of the meaning of activity in society.

Without teachers who are thoroughly, deeply sitting, people who are studying or working cannot really understand the profundity of our practice. Not only their instruction but their presence, their practice, and their expression through their zazen benefit the people who are focused on studying or working.

When I practiced at a small zendō in the woods of western Massachusetts, one visitor told me that Americans have too much energy to spend their lives in a quiet place and just sit. I thought the person did not know how much energy it takes to sit still when we want to do many things. Whether we practice in a quiet place or work in a busy society, the important thing is to make the direction of our walking clear and to focus on it. As a bodhisattva, our direction is set by the four bodhisattva vows:

> Beings are numberless; I vow to free them.
> Delusions are inexhaustible; I vow to end them.
> Dharma gates are boundless; I vow to enter them.
> The Buddha Way is unsurpassable; I vow to realize it.

Sometimes we become confused about which way to go: should I go to the zendō or should I study *Shōbōgenzō* or should I do something else? I think the important point is to not lose sight of the direction. Our direction is the same whether we go from this angle or that, this way or that. Backward and forward are the same step, one step in the walking of the mountains. As Nāgārjuna discussed, there is no runner besides the action of running. The person running and the running person are exactly the same thing.

This virtue is called "the mountain flowing, the flowing mountain."

Here Dōgen seems to simply change the order of the words: the mountain flowing and the flowing mountain. But I don't think what Dōgen wants to say is such a simple thing. I think "the mountain flowing" means that "the mountain is flowing"—it's moving, walking, changing. And I think "the flowing mountain" means that "the flowing is mountain": moving, walking, and changing are all mountain. And Dōgen might also have continued, "The mountain is simply mountain," and "the flowing is simply flowing."

This is the same logic that he used in *Shōbōgenzō* "Maka Hannya Haramitsu": "Form is emptiness and emptiness is form; form is form and emptiness is emptiness." He also wrote in *Shōbōgenzō* "Zanmai-ō-zanmai," "Sitting is Buddhadharma and Buddhadharma is sitting, Buddhadharma is simply Buddhadharma, and zazen is simply zazen."

In *Shōbōgenzō* "Yuibutsuyobutsu" ("Only Buddha Together with Buddha"), he writes,

> An ancient buddha who had never spoken once said as follows: "In death, there is the living; in life, there is the dead. There are the dead who are always dead; there are the living who are always living." This is not what is forcibly made by a person; the Dharma is like this.

In these statements, there seem to be opposites: form and emptiness, sitting (a form of our body) and Buddhadharma (which is beyond form), life and death. But Dōgen begins by saying that form is emptiness and emptiness is form; sitting is Buddhadharma, and Buddhadharma is sitting; life is death and death is life. So these two opposite things completely penetrate each other; they are really one. Then he says the opposite: form is simply form, emptiness is simply emptiness, sitting is just sitting, Buddhadharma is just Buddhadharma, life is life and death is death.

Precisely because the two are completely one, they never meet each other. When we say "form," emptiness is already there, and when we say "emptiness," form is already there. We don't need to say "form is emptiness and emptiness is form." When we use this expression, we think there are two opposite concepts, "form" and "emptiness," and then we try to put these two separate concepts into one by putting "is" between them.

In the case of "mountain" and "flowing," in our conventional thinking, mountain does not flow. Mountains are immovable. But here he is saying the mountain is walking, moving, flowing, and changing within time and space. This is possible because there is no such fixed entity called "mountain." Mountains are not fixed as a concept of "mountain that is immovable," therefore they can move and change. Moving and changing are manifested as mountains. And yet, at this present moment, mountains are peacefully dwelling as mountains. Mountains are just mountains. Moving and changing are simply moving and changing; there are no mountains at all.

I think Dōgen's multifaceted and dynamic way of viewing things has something to do with what Nāgārjuna says, for example, in chapter 8 of *Mūlamadhyamakakārikā*, "Examination of the Doer and the Deed." After examining the relation between person and actions, in verses 12 and 13 Nāgārjuna says,

> The doer is dynamically related to the deed and the deed to the doer in order to arise. We cannot perceive any other cause for their establishment or completion.

> Thus, by way of the refutation of the (static concepts of the) doer and the deed, the concept of seizing or clinging (*upādāna*) can be known. And basing the analysis on both the doer and the deed, various other entities (i.e. phenomena) can be understood.[63]

It is clear that when Dōgen talks about mountains' walking, he is talking about our practice. We are in the mountains, we are persons within the mountains, and this entire mountain, including us, is walking. "Mountain" is a name for the entire network of interdependent origination. So "mountain" means the place where we are connected with the myriad things. This walking of the mountains is the walking of each of us. When we walk, the mountain also walks. This walking, this functioning, this activity is our practice. So this entire universe is walking, we are walking within it, and this walking is practice.

## THE ENTIRE WORLD STUDIES ITSELF THROUGH THIS PERSON

(7) The blue mountains devote themselves to the investigation of walking; the East Mountain studies "moving over the water." Hence, this study is the mountains' own study.

When Dōgen says, "moving over the water," he is refering to Yunmen Wenyan's saying that he quotes later.

In these lines Dōgen identifies the subject who does this walking, this studying about mountains and waters. Usually when we read this we think that we are studying Dōgen's teaching about mountains and waters, that he is teaching us, so the subject is us. Whenever we study Dharma or practice zazen, we think, "This person is studying the Dharma" or "This person is trying to find the meaning of our life." But Dōgen says here that a person's inquiry is not simply one's own inquiry: it is mountains studying mountains, and this entire world studying itself through this person's inquiry.

Planet Earth is a tiny product of the evolution of this universe. We human beings are a tiny and relatively new part of nature on this small planet. And yet somehow we have an ability to observe the planet, the solar system, other galaxies, and even the entire universe, and we try to understand what they are, what is really happening, what is the origin of this movement of the universe. We even think about the meaning of all this movement. This is our attempt to see reality, to understand the meaning of our lives and this world. But we can look from another direction and say that because we are a part of the universe, the entire world is using human beings to see itself. In this sense the entire universe is studying itself through us.

We usually don't see it this way. We think we study for the sake of this person. When we see our activity from a broader perspective, we can't be selfish. We can't use things around us as resources or materials simply to make ourselves happy. I think this is an important difference.

I sometimes imagine the universe before sentient beings appeared on this small planet, the universe without any observer. No one sees it, thinks of it, understands it, or evaluates it. No one sees color or hears sound. In this case, is there color or sound at all? To me that is a mysterious world. In the history of the universe from the Big Bang, the universe was without any observer until relatively recently. Things were just happening, without being considered right or wrong, good or bad, well or poorly done. This is an amazing thought to me.

Who is studying? Who is inquiring? In the case of Buddhadharma, Buddha studies Buddha's way through our practice. Or Dharma studies Dharma itself through us, through this person, because this person is part of the Dharma. The term "dharmas" means all beings; "Dharma" with a capital *D* means the way all beings are. But though "Dharma" just means how we are, we usually try to get something from it. That is a kind of distortion. According to Dōgen, when I sit, it is not Shohaku sitting; zazen is sitting Shohaku. Studying other subjects can be the same.

This study or practice is part of the walking of blue mountains.

> The mountains, without altering their own body and mind, with their own mountain countenance, have always been circling back to study [themselves].

The mountains do not alter their own body and mind—mountains are just mountains, with their own mountain countenance. Mountains are just mountains, and they have always been circling back to study themselves.

"Circling back" is a translation of *kai to. Kai* means to circle around, and *to* (途) is path, road, or street. This is an unusual expression. I don't think Dōgen used this expression in any other writings. According to commentaries, this *kai to* means "here and there." "Here" means this present moment, and "there" means the eternal Buddha, prior to anything happening, prior to even the kalpa of emptiness. *Nikon,* this present moment, is here, and eternity is there. In the first sentence of this writing he says that this present moment is one with eternity. That is the meaning of "These mountains and waters of the present are the expression of the old buddhas." This term *kai to* means turning between this present moment and eternity. Mountains turn back and forth between this moment and eternity.

The meaning of this is the same as when Dōgen says in *Tenzo Kyōkun* that when you cook you should invite the Buddha from the buddha hall and make the Buddha into the vegetables.[64] He said to invite a sixteen-foot Buddha body and make it into one stalk of greens. In other words, any vegetables that we chop or cook are actually Buddha's body. The person who is cooking and the activity of cooking must also manifest the sixteen-foot Buddha body. Even though this moment is one with eternity, we also make it one with eternity by cooking in this way.

This particular person is working with particular things. But this particular action can be the practice of turning between this moment and eternity, or between this person and the world. Oneness of this moment and eternity, oneness of the particular and universal: this is what Dōgen is always trying to show us. The phrase "moon in a dewdrop" is an expression of the same reality. We are tiny like a drop of dew, but within this momentary drop the entire universe is reflected. In the *Vimalakīrti Sūtra*, this is expressed as "within a mustard seed, Mount Sumeru is stored; or within a pore of the skin, the great ocean is stored."[65]

This is Dōgen's point. The same point is found in much of Japanese culture: eternity expresses itself within impermanence, the infinite manifests itself within the finite. If you read haiku you can recognize this. A famous example is from Matsuo Bashō:

Old pond,
a frog jumps in,
the sound of water.

Instead of conducting an abstract philosophical discussion, a haiku shows eternity by describing things in one moment.

## BEYOND USUAL UNDERSTANDING

> (8) Do not slander mountains by saying that the blue mountains
> cannot walk, nor the East Mountain move over the water.

In this section Dōgen discusses Furong Daokai's saying "Blue mountains are walking," and here he directly addresses our difficulty with this concept. Maybe most of us have this reaction: "It's not possible for blue mountains to walk." Without thinking, we reject it as nonsense. But rejecting like that is nonsense, too.

Our usual view depends on our understanding, knowledge, and other results of our experience and study. If we hear something that doesn't fit our preconceptions, we just reject it, labeling it as nonsense.

> It is because of the baseness of the common person's point of
> view that we doubt the phrase "the blue mountains walk"; because
> of the crudeness of our limited experience, we are surprised by
> the words "flowing mountain." Without having fully penetrated
> even the term "flowing water," we just remain sunk in our limited
> perception.

I see the process of ordinary education as being like piling up blocks to make a building of knowledge. When that building is completed it becomes our prison. It's difficult to get out. If one is a lawyer, a doctor, or any professional—in my case a Buddhist priest—we accumulate knowledge necessary to our field. A lawyer thinks in legal terms that are not understandable to common people. A doctor speaks in medical jargon; a Buddhist scholar writes using too many Buddhist technical terms. Becoming experts, we close our minds, and we think this is the perfection of our knowledge. We have difficulty opening an entrance or window to get fresh air. This happens not only for elite professionals but for everyone who acquires knowledge. Then when we hear strange things like "mountains are walking," we just say "nonsense" because it is outside of our mental prison. This is only natural. Dōgen says it happens according to baseness and crudeness. These are harsh words, but I think he is right.

When we hear the words "flowing water," we naturally accept the idea without thought or questioning. This is also a problem for us. Dōgen is saying that we need to be free from such ready-made, habitual views created by our karma.

Uchiyama Rōshi said that one aspect of zazen is like doing massage on our heads to make them soft and flexible. It's like opening the window and getting fresh air. That is one of the functions of our zazen: we continue to let go of whatever thinking comes up, and that makes us more flexible.

## THE VITAL ARTERY—THE CENTER OF THE WORLD

> (9) Thus, the accumulated virtues [of the mountain] brought up here represent its very "name and form," its "vital artery."

The life artery of the mountains, that which makes all the buddhas and ancestors possible, is the practice of the mountains or of practitioners.

Dōgen said there are two kinds of virtuous practices: stepping forward to work with others, and stepping back and studying the self. "Accumulated virtues" means that virtues accumulated by such practice are the work of the mountains. As a result of these accumulations, mountains are mountains at this moment; this is their name and form; so we call them mountains. The virtues are also vital arteries, like the "bloodline" of the *kechimyaku*, our lineage chart. They are life itself, the blood circulating in this body. Our practice of stepping forward and stepping back is what gives life to the mountain, gives life to ourselves as mountains. This is what has been transmitted from the Buddha through generations of ancestors.

"To gain merit" is a common expression in Buddhism. It means that our practice or offering brings about some virtue or merit, *kudoku*, which we need to accumulate to become a buddha. Sometimes we offer this merit to all beings. An example of kudoku is in the famous kōan story about Bodhidharma and Emperor Wu. When the emperor asked what merit he had gained from his many good works. Bodhidharma said, "*mukudoku*," or "no merit." His point was that we practice to bring forth the ultimate point of view, rather than practicing for the sake of merit.

> There is a mountain walk and a mountain flow. There is a time when the mountains give birth to a mountain child.

This is about Dharma transmission from teacher to student. Somehow a mountain gives birth to the next mountain. I'll discuss this later, when Dōgen talks about a stone woman giving birth to a child.

> The mountains become the buddhas and ancestors, and it is for this reason that the buddhas and ancestors have thus appeared.

*Mountains* means this entire world, the network of interdependent origination in which we take part. This entire network becomes buddhas and ancestors. This whole network practices.

In Uchiyama Rōshi's life, he was the center of interdependent origination. In my life I am the center. Each and every one of us is the center of our own world.

If we envision our world as flat like a map, there can be only one center. In maps made in Japan, where I learned geography, Japan is the center. Because Japan is so tiny, it is colored red. "Japan is red, so it's a special place": that was my picture of the world. It was difficult to free myself of this view. When I went to Massachusetts, I was going to the edge of the world. Really—the edge of the world. If the center of the world is Japan, the eastern edge is New England.

After I had been at the edge of the world for a few years, I met a Japanese family who were temporarily in the United States while the man was doing research at a hospital in Connecticut. Once I visited his house and saw his children's room. There was an American map, where the United States was the center of the world! I was really surprised.

Even though I was an adult, it had never occurred to me that the center of the world was not fixed.

Actually, since the world is a sphere, wherever we are is the center of the world. This is very important. If I think there is only one center of the world and it's me, that's a problem. If we think there are numberless centers, this means that every one of us is the center of the world. We can respect everyone. The important point is that I see the world from *this* center and you see it from *that*. I cannot see from that side, I can see only from this side. This is why our view is limited and conditioned.

Dōgen is not saying that there is some absolutely right view. He's saying that the right view is to see that our view is limited and conditioned. My point of view is the only way I can see the world. This is not only true for me; it is a human condition. When we hear from others, we can have some understanding of how the world looks from their side. By listening, our views become broader and more flexible. We can learn that "my view" is not always absolutely right. This is how we study the world with a broader perspective; this is the meaning of studying Dharma and teachings. This is very important because our human world has become one society.

Before the twentieth century, Japan had its own territory and we didn't have much interaction. Japanese people could simply be Japanese. We thought the Japanese way was the right way. When we heard views from outside of Japan, we would reject them, or be suspicious or skeptical; sometimes we would try to counterargue or even fight. Then in the twentieth century we met people from different cultural backgrounds. At first we couldn't understand each other, so it was natural to be suspicious, to have fear, to argue or fight. In this century we need to study and listen to each other.

When I worked for the Sōtō Zen Buddhism International Center, there was an idea that I was a Buddhist missionary from Japan. I never liked that idea. I saw my work as making Japanese Buddhism a little more open to the rest of the world. Also, I could help American people come to a broader and more flexible view by studying Buddhism.

When Uchiyama Rōshi was alive, he was the center of the world, and he practiced as a universal self. That is one complete world: the universal self that is Uchiyama Rōshi's expression of the self, connected with everyone, penetrating the entire world. Uchiyama Rōshi was always saying that we are living within the world; we are part of the world and connected with everything. Uchiyama Rōshi called this network *jiko,* or self—the self that includes or is connected with this entire universe. In the same way, I am the center of my world, and you are the center of your world, and we practice as a universal self.

In *Shōbōgenzō* "Zenki," "Total Function," Dōgen said when we are sailing on a boat, this entire world is part of the boat. "I am part of the world and the world is also part of me," is what Uchiyama Rōshi meant when he used the expression "universal self." Another of his sayings was "Everything I encounter is my life." When he was alive, as a disciple I was part of his world. And for me, Uchiyama Rōshi was part of my world as my teacher. You might say "I am this mountain" or "This mountain is me."

Uchiyama Rōshi often said that we think this world is like a stage. When we are born we appear on this stage, we play a certain role for a while, and we exit, but the stage remains—this is our common view. But this is not reality. When I am born this entire world is born with me. I live with this entire world, and its center is me. When I die this world dies with me. Because Uchiyama Rōshi died, his universe is gone. But my universe is here, and in it he is still alive as my teacher.

We think that we have knowledge beyond our personal world. I naturally think the world was there before I was born and the world will be there after my death. This is our common understanding, and as intellectual knowledge it's correct. But as experienced reality, there was no past before I was born. That past consists only of information I got from studying; I create a history of the world from my studies, and that history becomes the part of my present experience that I call "past." Such a past is not real; it is a human fabrication. As a fabrication it might be "correct," which means it may match the histories that other people have created. But it is not a real experience; it is a production of our mind. The real reality of our life is that we are born, live, and die together with our entire universe.

Since my teacher's world is completely his and my world is completely mine, it's kind of strange that Dharma can be transmitted from his world to mine. Maybe it's even a miracle. His experiences, understandings, and expressions are completely his own; there's no way he can give birth to another being or thing. It's like the expression "the stone woman": a woman who is barren and doesn't give birth to anyone or anything. However, his way of life influenced my way of life and my practice is a continuation of his practice. It is a complete oneness.

Somehow this Dharma of complete oneness was transmitted from Bodhidharma to the second ancestor, from the second ancestor to the third ancestor, and from Uchiyama Rōshi to me. It's very strange thing; it's mysterious. "The stone woman gives birth to a child" is an expression of this strangeness. There's no way to transmit the Dharma, but somehow it is transmitted. My teacher's world is only his; his karma is only his and my karma is only mine. Yet somehow his Dharma life and practice continue within my practice. What I am doing here, in a sense, is a reincarnation of his practice. So in that sense Uchiyama Rōshi is still alive.

Each one of us is completely independent and yet we are completely one. Dharma, life, has been transmitted from teacher to student, or from parents to children. I often use the word "strange"; this word is my translation of *myō*, in *Myō hō renge kyō*. *Myō* means "wondrous," "excellent," "beautiful," or "strange"—beyond our thinking, understanding, and grasping. "Wondrous" is how the mountain becomes the mountain and how the mountain gives birth to mountains, how my teacher's life is transmitted to me.

## FOUR VIEWS OF MOUNTAINS, AND OTHER MISTAKES

(10) Even when we have the eyes [to see mountains as] the appearance of grass and trees, earth and stone, fences and walls, this is nothing to doubt, nothing to be moved by: it is not the complete appearance [of the mountains].

In this next section, Dōgen discusses four kinds of views that appear in Buddhist texts about mountains. These are parallel with the four views about waters Dōgen later discusses.

The first view, described above, is a common-sense view, not necessarily a Buddhist one: mountains are a collection of grass and trees, earth and stone, fences and walls. On the mountain there might be Buddhist temples, Shintō shrines, or other buildings and houses. It is nothing to doubt, nothing to be moved by, nothing special; we can accept it easily and naturally. However, Dōgen says this ordinary view is not complete.

The word translated here as "appearance" is *genjō*, as in "Genjōkōan"; another translation could be "manifestation" or "actualization" of the mountains. Such a common view does not get the essential meaning of the mountains. Dōgen urges us to completely penetrate and embody the meaning.

Even when there appears an occasion in which [the mountains] are seen as the splendor of the seven treasures, this is still not the real refuge.

This is the second view about mountains. Some beings see a mountain as something precious, rare, and beautiful. Jewels and precious metals such as gold or silver are found in the mountains. Sometimes we value the beauty of the mountain itself like a jewel, as does a painter, poet, or photographer. By reading poems such as those by Su Shi, or by seeing paintings and photos, we see the beauty of our lives. This is a wonderful thing, but Dōgen says this is still not the real refuge.

The English expression "real refuge" is a translation of *jikki,* or *jitsu-ki. Jitsu* means "true," "real," "genuine." *Ki* means "to return." When *ki* is used as a compound with *e,* it becomes *kie,* which means "taking refuge," as in *Namu kie Butsu,* "I take refuge in Buddha"; *kie* is the Chinese translation of *namu* in Sanskrit. So *jikki* becomes "true things we return to or in which we take refuge." That is the meaning of real refuge: returning to what is genuine. Seeing and praising the beauty of the mountains is not necessarily a Buddhist view.

For Buddhists, we finally return and take refuge not in mountains, beauty, or poetry but in the three treasures. Dōgen Zenji used this term in *Shōbōgenzō* "Kiesanbō" ("Taking Refuge in Three Treasures: Buddha, Dharma, and Saṅgha"). He quotes a text that asks why we take refuge solely in these three treasures. The text's answer:

> Because these three treasures are ultimate places to return and they enable all living beings to depart from life-and-death and to verify the great awakening. Therefore we take refuge in them.

We take refuge in Buddha, Dharma, and saṅgha because these are the final places we return to. In *Shōbōgenzō* "Gyōji" ("Continuous Practice"), Dōgen writes, "Continuous practice is not something worldly people love, but it should be the place all people truly return to." Our continuous, ceaseless practice, coming and going in the mountains, is our real refuge.

> Even when they appear to us as the realm of the practice of the way of the buddhas, this is not necessarily something to be desired.

This is the third view. Some people see the mountain as a sacred place for practice of buddhas, sages, and spiritual practitioners. In any part of the world, in any spiritual tradition, some mountains are considered a sacred sanctuary. In Japan, as I said in the introduction, practitioners of Shugendō worship certain mountains. Women were prohibited from entering some of these mountains, including Mount Hiei, where Dōgen practiced as a novice.

Dōgen objects to the view of mountains as a spiritual place to love. In *Shōbōgenzō* "Raihaitokuzui" ("Getting the Marrow by Doing Obeisance") Dōgen criticized the custom of worshiping mountains, saying this is not necessarily something to be desired. "Something to be desired" is a translation of *aisho—sho* (処) is "place" and *ai* (愛) is "to love," so *aisho* is a place we cling to as something special.

> Even when we attain the crowning appearance of the vision of [the mountains as] the inconceivable virtues of the buddhas, their reality is more than this.

This is the fourth view of the mountains. The "crowning appearance of the vision," the highest vision among Buddhist scholars, is to see this mountain as the "inconceivable virtues of the buddhas." This is what Dōgen said before: the mountain is a result of the accumulation of virtues of practice. Yet he says that the reality of the mountain is even more than this. All these views, including his own view of the mountain, are incomplete.

> Each of these appearances is the particular objective and subjective result [of past karma]; they are not the karma of the way of the buddhas and ancestors but narrow, one-sided views.

"Appearances" is *genjō*. These appearances are views we create when we see the mountains through our karmic consciousness. Even if we see the mountains as the virtues of buddhas and ancestors, still that is our one-sided, karmic view as Buddhists.

The words "objective" and "subjective" are a translation of *ehō* (依報) and *shōhō* (正報). *Hō* is the ninth of the ten suchnesses; it means reward or retribution for past activities. There are two kinds of retribution we receive from our past karma: shōhō, our particular body and mind; and ehō, our environment, our circumstances.

For example, I received DNA transmitted from my parents, was born with this body and mind in 1948 in Osaka, Japan, grew up there within that family, received a certain education, and so forth. This conditioned body and mind is shōhō. *Ehō* means the circumstances in which I was born and lived. Osaka was in a chaotic state three years after World War II. Although as a small child I was not consciously aware of the conditions, through people around me I must have been deeply influenced by the disorder. Shōhō and ehō have been working together to make me into the kind of person I am today. According to both Dōgen and Uchiyama Rōshi, shōhō and ehō make this self into the self. Ehō is this world in which we are living and shōhō is ourselves, this body and mind. Both are retribution from our past karma.

Shōhō is connected to the first five elements of suchness. Ehō is the connection within the past and present. According to Abhidharma, the earliest compilation of Buddhist philosophy and psychology, shōhō—this body and mind with its certain form, nature, strength, and tendency—is my personal retribution. But ehō is shared. During Genzō-e, all participants gather together to study Dōgen because they share the same karma, the same ehō. People share the same zendō, the same meals, the same classroom, and the same lecture on *Shōbōgenzō*. Whatever views we have are produced by collaboration between the self and the myriad dharmas. Our view of mountains might differ depending upon whether we have the karma of a poet, a painter, a hunter, a woodcutter, a mountain climber, or a businessperson in the sightseeing industry.

Our view is created in the relationship between ehō and shōhō. That is what Dōgen is saying here. Depending on the conditions of our body and mind and circumstances, we create different views. Every one of these is just a view created by our karma; therefore it is limited and conditioned. We can't have a view that is not conditioned, because we are inside the world, and to see it we have to take a position. Our view is always only our view. It cannot be the mountains themselves.

"Narrow, one-sided view" is a very common expression in Chinese and Japanese. Literally, it means "a view through a tube or straw." When we see the world through a straw, we see only a tiny part. But we often think this part is the entire world. This way of thinking is widely understood, expressed in terms such as "a frog in a well," "the blind people examining the elephant," the Zen expression "board-carrying fellow," or the English "tunnel vision."

> "Turning the object and turning the mind" is criticized by the Great Sage.

Now Dōgen criticizes certain teachings in Zen Buddhist practice.

"Turning the object and turning the mind" means using our practice to try to change our mind or change the object. Sometimes people think that the goal of meditation is a psychological change: to be enlightened is to reach an extraordinary stage of mind, and only in this stage can we see the truth, whatever it might be. This is a common understanding of practice and Buddhist teaching: if we attain certain conditions we can see objects as they truly are.

Here Dōgen says that this understanding is criticized by the Great Sage—actually, he said "scolded"—because it involves separation between mind and object.

The *Śūraṅgama Sūtra* says,

> "From time without beginning, all beings have mistakenly identified themselves with what they are aware of. Controlled by their experience of perceived objects, they lose track of their fundamental minds. In this state they perceive visual awareness as large or small. But when they're in control of their experience of perceived objects, they are the same as the Thus-Come Ones. Their bodies and minds, unmoving and replete with perfect understanding, become a place for awakening. Then all the lands in the ten directions are contained within the tip of a fine hair."[66]

"Controlled by their experience of perceived objects" is more literally translated as "being turned by things"; "they're in control of their experience of perceived objects" is "they turn things." Here self (mind) and objects (things) seem separate; sometimes the mind is turned by objects and sometimes it turns them. So this sūtra says that people can actually see things as they are.

Dōgen did not like the separation between mind and objects or between turning and being turned. As I said above, our view is created in the relationship between ehō and shōhō—we can't have a view that is not subjective. Although the *Śūraṅgama Sūtra* was valued in Chinese Zen tradition, Dōgen did not appreciate the sūtra. In *Hōkyōki*, Dōgen asked Rujing:

> "Lay people read the *Śūraṅgama Sūtra* and the *Complete Enlightenment Sūtra* and say that these are the ancestral teachings transmitted from India. When I opened up these sūtras and observed their structure and style, I felt they were not as skillful as other Mahayana sūtras. This seemed strange to me. More than this, the teachings of these sūtras seemed to me to be far less than what we find in Mahayana sūtras. They seemed quite similar to the teachings of the six outsider teachers [who lived during the Buddha's time]. How do we determine whether or not these texts are authentic?"
>
> Rujing said, "The authenticity of the *Śūraṅgama Sūtra* has been doubted by some people since ancient times. Some suspect that this sūtra was written by people of a later period, as the early ancestors were definitely not aware of it. But ignorant people in recent times read it and love it. The *Complete Enlightenment Sūtra* is also like this. Its style is similar to the *Śūraṅgama Sūtra*."[67]

In Dharma Hall discourse 383 of *Eihei Kōroku*, Dōgen said,

Therefore we should not look at the words and phrases of Confucius or Laozi, and should not look at the Śūraṅgama or Complete Enlightenment scriptures. [Many contemporary people consider the Śūraṅgama and Complete Enlightenment Sūtras as among those that the Zen tradition relies on. But the teacher Dōgen always disliked them.] We should exclusively study the expressions coming from the activities of buddhas and ancestors from the time of the seven world-honored buddhas[68] to the present. If we are not concerned with the activities of the Buddha ancestors, and vainly make our efforts in the evil path of fame and profit, how could this be study of the way? Among the World-Honored Tathāgata, the ancestral teacher Mahākāśyapa, the twenty-eight ancestors in India, the six generations [of ancestors] in China, Qingyuan, and Nanyue [Huairang], which of these ancestral teachers ever used the Śūraṅgama or Complete Enlightenment Sūtra and considered them as the true Dharma eye treasury, wondrous mind of nirvāṇa?[69]

The two sentences between brackets are a note by the compiler of the volume. From these quotes, it is clear that Dōgen was consistent in criticizing the *Śūraṅgama Sūtra*, from the time he was in China studying with Rujing until two years before his death when he gave this lecture from *Eihei Kōroku*.

> "[E]xplaining the mind and explaining the nature" is not affirmed by the buddhas and ancestors; "seeing the mind and seeing the nature" is the business of non-Buddhists.

"Explaining the mind nature" and "seeing the nature" are essential points in the *Śūraṅgama Sūtra*. In "explaining the mind and explaining the nature," mind is *shin* (心) and nature is *shō* (性).[70] The nature of mind is sometimes called true self, original face, true face, or even buddha nature. Some people have thought that mind-nature (*shinshō*, 心性) is within ourselves, hidden in this body and mind, and that discovering such mind-nature is seeing true nature or enlightenment.

But Dōgen said that such an idea is not affirmed by buddhas and ancestors. The expressions "seeing the mind" (*kenshin*, 見心) and "seeing the nature" (*kenshō*, 見性) actually mean the same thing. Dōgen Zenji didn't like the term *kenshō*: it implies that our self (our body and mind, the five aggregates) is separate from nature and that our (nonphysical) eyes can see it. In reality the nature cannot be seen; it cannot be the object of the subject, because the nature is ourselves. We cannot see ourselves; our eyes cannot see our eyes. There's no way we can see the nature; that is Dōgen's point.

This word *kenshō* is important in Rinzai Zen and is the source of the long discussion between Sōtō and Rinzai. In Rinzai practice kenshō, "seeing the nature," is identical with satori. But for Dōgen, satori is exactly this mountain self. The walking of the mountain is great realization, or satori. Satori is not something we can see as an object, and it's not something we can attain.[71] This actually does not disagree with genuine Rinzai teaching, only with superficial ideas of Rinzai teaching. I'll talk about this later when Dōgen discusses incomprehensible enlightenment in the section about Yunmen Wenyan.

> "Sticking to words and sticking to phrases" are not the words of liberation.

This is a very common saying in Zen. "Words and phrases" means conceptual and dualistic thinking.

> There are [words] that are free from such realms: they are "the blue mountains constantly walking" and "the East Mountain moving over the water." We should give them detailed investigation.

We should go beyond words and phrases, and there actually are words that are free from words and phrases. Those words are "the blue mountains constantly walking" and "the East Mountain moving over the water." These are Dōgen's words beyond words. For him, realization means coming and going within the mountains as our body, which means living with all beings within the network of interdependent origination.

Sometimes we study Dōgen's writing, grasp his teaching, and make it a concept that we can hold on to. This is like trying to make the mountains stand still. But the blue mountains are constantly walking and they do not stand still. If we try to make them stand still, if we try to make the teaching a concept, we completely miss the teaching.

What Dōgen wrote was words, and I am still writing words. It is essential to understand that if we grasp this teaching as words or concepts, then we miss it. Dōgen teaches by deconstructing our views. If we turn his words into another view, thinking this new view is Dōgen's teaching, then we miss the point completely. That's why he tells us to continue with detailed investigation. The teaching is penetrated only in the walking of the mountains—only in our life and practice.

## THE STONE WOMAN GIVES BIRTH IN THE NIGHT

(11) "The stone woman gives birth to a child in the night."

Now Dōgen comments on the second part of Furong Daokai's saying. Dōgen's comments above on the mountain's walking are long; his comment on the stone woman's giving birth is very short. The meaning of the two expressions is similar: mountains do not walk, and a stone woman does not give birth. Mountains are immovable and a stone woman is lifeless. This is common sense. Furong's saying challenges this habitual, common-sense way of viewing things. Both Furong and Dōgen point out that these immovable and lifeless things are actually moving dynamically and living vigorously, even to the extent of giving birth.

The Chinese expression "a stone woman" can mean two things. One is a barren woman. Another is a stone statue of a woman. Because

Furong is talking about "giving birth," it sounds like "a stone woman" refers to a barren woman. We can investigate this by looking at other places where the expression is used.

Here is the expression "stone woman" in "Hōkyōzanmai" ("The Song of Precious Mirror Samādhi"), a well-known long poem written by Dongshan Liangjie (in Japanese, Tōzan Ryōkai):

> The wooden man starts to sing,
> the stone woman gets up dancing.
> It is not reached by feelings or consciousness;
> how could it involve deliberation?[72]

Here "the stone woman" is used together with "the wooden man." "A wooden man" means a wooden figure or a puppet.

I think it is clear that in "Hōkyōzanmai," "the stone woman" does not mean a barren woman but a stone statue of a woman, like the wooden puppet of a man. In this case, "wood and stone" (*bokuseki*) tells us that the wooden man and stone woman do not have human sentiment. They are free from human feeling, consciousness, discriminating mind. Without being moved by such karmic consciousness, the wooden man and the stone woman freely sing and dance, living vigorously.

In this way, we can read these lines from "Hōkyōzanmai" as showing how the reality of all beings, which is without any discrimination, can reveal itself as a man or a woman—in other words, as each and every phenomenal being, in the middle of discrimination.

> This means that the time when "a stone woman gives birth to a child" is "the night."

"Night" is the same as the "darkness" in "Sandōkai," or "Merging of Difference and Unity," a poem written by Shitou Xiqian (in Japanese, Sekitō Kisen). He writes, "the branching streams flow in the darkness." This darkness or night means the realm beyond discrimination. Both "stone woman" and "the night" refer to the ultimate reality beyond discrimination and karmic consciousness.

In *Shōbōgenzō* "Kannon," Dōgen discusses a dialogue between Yunyan Tansheng (in Japanese, Ungan Donjō) and his Dharma brother Daowu Yuanzhi (Dōgo Enchi). Both are Dharma grandsons of Shitou, and Yunyan was Dongshan's teacher. All these masters are connected; they are the headstreams of Sōtō Zen tradition. In the dialogue, Yunyan asked, "What does the Great Compassion Bodhisattva do with innumerable hands and eyes?" Daowu replied, "[The bodhisattva] is like a person who is reaching his hand behind, groping for the pillow in the night." In his comment on this reply, Dōgen says,

> "In the night" is an expression of darkness. It is rather like the expression "seeing mountains in the daytime". . . . We should investigate "thinking of the nighttime from daytime," and "being nighttime within nighttime." We should investigate the time that is neither daytime nor nighttime.[73]

What Dōgen is saying here is identical to what is said in "Sandōkai":

> Right in light there is darkness, but don't confront it
>     as darkness;
> Right in darkness there is light, but don't see it as light.
> Light and dark are relative to one another
> Like forward and backward steps.[74]

Light and darkness, or nighttime and daytime—that is, the ultimate reality without discrimination and conventional reality—are opposite each other and yet always together.

Daokai and Dōgen express this insight: The ultimate reality beyond duality is not barren or stagnant but full of life. Without any arising and perishing, it gives birth to the phenomenal beings that are arising and perishing, being born and dying.

There are male stones, female stones, and stones neither male nor female. They repair heaven, and they repair earth. There are stones of heaven, and there are stones of earth. Though this is said in the secular world, it is rarely understood. We should understand the reason behind this "giving birth to a child."

These are all quotes from the Chinese classics about stones having gender, life, and functions. I think it is clear by now that "the stone woman" means a stone statue of a woman, not a barren woman. Dōgen is elaborating on the image above: stone woman, stone man, stone without gender, all in the dark beyond discrimination give birth, in heaven or earth or any world. They give birth to practice, give birth to a life, give birth to the life of student and teacher, give life to the universe.

At the time of birth, are parent and child transformed together? We should not only study that birth is realized in the child becoming the parent; we should also study and fully understand that the practice and verification of birth is realized when the parent becomes the child.

This is not only about parent and child but also about Dharma transmission. I think "parent and child" corresponds to eternity and present, bodhisattvas and living beings, and buddhas and practitioners. Within our practice, within the walking of the mountains, we grow, mature, and become parents. That is the process of our practice. First we are a baby, just learning, completely absorbed in the excitement of our discovery of Dharma. While we are beginners, we receive support from so many people, including teachers, copractitioners, and other friends. We make an effort to deepen our understanding, become wise, and finally become a bodhisattva, with parental mind taking care of all beings, completely entering the world, teaching our students, giving birth to something in our students. This is one way of understanding the process of our practice.

He's also saying that each step of our practice is a Dharma position.

The parents appear; parents manifest within each practice. In that sense parent becomes child, newly born within each step. Or Buddha becomes a bodhisattva, teaching and helping all beings. There is a mutual interaction between living beings and buddhas, a walking together of this particular moment and eternal reality. This moment, this Dharma position, is an intersection of phenomenal beings (mountains and waters) and eternal Buddha. So eternal Buddha comes to us and allows us to practice, to manifest Buddha's life. Through our day-to-day practice we invoke Buddha and manifest Buddha's life.

Even though our day-to-day activity is incomplete, without it there's no Buddha's mind, no Buddha's enlightenment. If we don't practice, Buddha's enlightenment ended twenty-five hundred years ago. Because of our incomplete practice, right here at this Dharma position, Buddha's enlightenment is here. Otherwise Buddha's enlightenment is only recorded in the sūtras. Our practice is very important. This is what Dōgen says in *Shōbōgenzō* "Gyōji":

> Therefore, because of the buddhas' and ancestors' continuous practice, our continuous practice is actualized, and our own great Way is penetrated. Because of our own continuous practice, the continuous practice of all buddhas is actualized, and the great Way of buddhas is penetrated. Because of our own continuous practice, there is the virtue of the circle of the Way. Because of this, each and every one of the buddhas and ancestors dwells as Buddha, goes beyond Buddha, upholds Buddha mind and complete buddhahood without interruption.

Our practice is actually Buddha's life. That practice is the walking of mountains.

There's an interesting discourse by Dōgen, the second in *Eihei Kōroku*, about our karmic views and activity and eternal truth. Dōgen is discussing how, no matter what way we view the Dharma world, our view is still limited.

How can we consider the universe of many worlds large; how can we consider an atom small? Both are not true. How can you get it right with a single phrase? Smashing our old nest [of views held] of the whole universe until now, dropping off our old sandals [worn to enter and leave] an atom until now, how will you speak of it?[75]

He's discussing our view from the largest perspective, the entire Dharma world, to the smallest thing, atoms: "how will you speak of it?" How do you express this reality, which is beyond our karmic tunnel vision?

The next sentence, also the last, is his answer.

A frog on the ocean bottom eats gruel; the jeweled rabbit in the heaven washes the bowl.[76]

This sentence uses ōryōki meals as a poetic image of our practice. We are the frog on the ocean bottom; the jeweled rabbit is the moon. The common expression is "a frog in a well"—such a frog has only a limited view. Here Dōgen places the frog in the ocean; the view is not so narrow. Of course there is no such frog in the ocean, but this is a very beautiful image of a bodhisattva. We are not in a well; we are in the ocean, the saṅgha, and it is a boundless place. We are still a frog, a tiny creature, yet we live in the vastness of the ocean and eat gruel. Eating gruel means our practice; it takes place at the bottom of the ocean, not some elevated place. When the frog eats the gruel, the rabbit in the moon washes the bowls. Within this practice, within each and every tiny, ordinary activity, the moon rabbit is washing the bowl in the highest place. For me this is a beautiful image. The parent (eternal truth) gives birth to the child (our practice at the present moment), and at the same time, the child (our practice right here and now) gives birth to the parent and enables the eternal truth being revealed.

There might be another meaning in this expression: that discontinuity and continuity interpenetrate each other. As Dōgen discusses in "Genjōkōan," the moment when firewood dwells in the Dharma position of firewood is a perfect moment. The before and after of the moment is cut off, and both past and future are reflected in that moment. The next moment is the same. Each moment is an absolute and independent moment, is discontinuous and disconnected like a stone woman. And yet, the stone woman gives birth, the discontinuous moment brings about the next moment.

In the same way, each master in the lineage was completely independent from every other. They lived and practiced only for themselves. They did not practice for the previous generations or the future generations. Sawaki Rōshi practiced only by himself and for himself, and Uchiyama Rōshi was the same. Sawaki Rōshi's practice is "self selfing the self." He said that we cannot exchange even a fart with others.[77] Each is completely independent. No one can rely on others. And yet, the Dharma is transmitted and continued through them. Because of Uchiyama Rōshi's practice for himself, I began to practice. When stone woman gives birth to the child, the child is always a stone. A child stone receives Dharma transmission from the stone woman.

## 2-2 East Mountains Walking in the Water

### WHERE IS THE BUDDHA WALKING RIGHT NOW?

(12) The Great Master Yunmen Kuangzhen has said, "The East Mountain moves over the water."

Yunmen's "The East Mountain moves over the water" is a reply to a question from a monk. This dialogue is from Yunmen's *Record*. In Urs App's translation:

> Someone asked, "What is the place from whence all the Buddhas come?"
>
> Master Yunmen said, "[Where] the East Mountains walk on the river."[78]

I have a problem with this translation of the monk's question. In Japanese, the monk's question is "Where is the *shobutsu shusshin no tokoro* (如何是諸仏出身処)?" *Shobutsu* is "all buddhas"; *tokoro* is "the place." My concern is the meaning of *shusshin*. *Shutsu* means "to exit or get out." *Shin* (身) is "body." In this translation *shusshin* is translated as a "place where someone is from," as in "Where is the place from whence all the buddhas come?" It implies that buddhas are now teaching in their buddha lands here and there, and yet they all came from somewhere else. In this understanding, the monk is asking what the original source is of all buddhas.

In modern Japanese *shusshin* means "where you are from," so as a literal translation the excerpt above is not mistaken. For example, I am from Osaka and so I say, "My *shusshin-chi* is Osaka." However, I don't think that is what Yunmen and the monk meant.

When we study Dōgen we have to interpret words according to his understanding. To understand this word *shusshin*, I looked at how Dōgen used it in *Fukanzazengi*. In the end of the first paragraph, Dōgen says,

> Suppose you are confident in your understanding and rich in enlightenment, gaining the wisdom that glimpses the ground [of buddhahood], attaining the way and clarifying the mind, arousing an aspiration to reach for the heavens. You are playing in the entranceway, but you still are short of the vital path of emancipation.[79]

In the last sentence "entranceway" is a translation of *nitto no hennryō*. *Ni* means "to enter," *tō* (頭) is "head," and *hennryō* means "edge or border." So a literal translation of this might be "put the head into." "Vital path of emancipation" is a translation of *shusshin no katsuro*. "Vital path" is *katsuro*, and "emancipation" is a translation of this word *shusshin*. *Nitto*, or "put the head into," corresponds with *shusshin*, which could be translated as "get the body out." These words describe someone who has almost reached enlightenment. Dōgen says such a person is still "playing in the entranceway"; only their head begins to enter buddhahood.

The "vital path of emancipation" means our entire body should transcend the Buddha Way, freeing ourselves even from buddhahood. This is what Dōgen calls *Butsu kō jyōji*, "the matter of going beyond Buddha." We cannot abide in buddhahood; we have to go beyond it as a bodhisattva working in this world. This is how Buddha continues to walk.

I think this is the meaning of *shusshin*: going beyond Buddha. In my understanding, the monk's question is not "Where is the Buddha from?" but "What is the place where all buddhas walk free from buddhahood?" How do all buddhas work in the world? How does Buddha continue to practice in the world of saṃsāra, with all living beings?

Because I translate the question differently from App, my understanding about Unmon's answer is different, actually opposite from his. If the question is "What is the place from whence all the buddhas come?" then the answer is somewhere else, and it sounds like some mysterious place where mountains walk on rivers. But I believe the monk is asking "Where are all buddhas walking right now?" At this moment right now, right here (*nikon*), they are walking liberated from buddhahood.

The first words of "Sansuikyō" are "These mountains and waters of the present." This writing is about this moment. Yunmen said, "[Where] the East Mountains walk on the river." The mountain is Buddha, and the mountain is walking. Buddhahood is not a goal; it is right now, right here, within the mountains' walking. Buddha walks as rivers and mountains together with all living beings.

According to Urs App, Yunmen's answer is from a verse by Layman Fu, a Chinese lay Zen adept, who lectured Emperor Wu without saying a word.[80] According to *Jingde Chuandeng Lu* (*Record of Transmission of the Lamp*, or in Japanese, *Keitoku Dentoroku*), Layman Fu was a contemporary of Bodhidharma. His verse:

東山水上浮。西山行不住。北斗下閻浮。是眞解脱處。

[Where] the East Mountains float on the river and the West Mountains wander on and on, in the realm [of this world] beneath the Great Dipper: just there is the place of genuine emancipation.[81]

This world right here, in which all mountains in the East and West are walking, is the place of genuine emancipation.

In this verse, "in the realm of this world beneath the Great Dipper" (北斗下閻浮) needs some explanation. The Great Dipper in the original verse is *Hokuto*. *Hoku* means "north" and *to* (斗) means a "dipper," so Hokuto means "north dipper." "The realm of this world" is a translation of *embu*, an abbreviation of *Nanembudai* (南閻浮提), which is the Japanese term for *Jambudvīpa*, or our continent according to Indian Buddhist cosmology. In this name *nan* means "south." Thus, in his verse Layman Fu is talking about all four directions: east, west, north, and south. Wherever we walk in this ten-direction world, we are in the place of genuine emancipation. This place is not somewhere else; it is right here in our walking in this world of saṃsāra.

When the monk asked the question, "What is the place where all buddhas walk free from buddhahood?" Yunmen answered, quoting Layman Fu's verse, "That is everywhere in the east, west, north, and south."

When Dōgen comments on this in the next paragraph, he says, "The import of this expression is that all mountains are the East Mountain." There's no such fixed place as east. We say Asia is east, and America and Europe are west, but actually America is east of Japan if you go the shortest way. Wherever we are, we are the center of the world. So when Yunmen talks about the East Mountains he means all mountains: all mountains are walking over the water.[82]

This is the way buddhas express their emancipation. If a buddha (or a mountain) has to stay in one place on the Lotus Seat, then he (or she or it) is not really liberated from buddhahood. So a buddha should stand up from the Lotus Seat and start to walk. The way Buddha walks is the way the mountains are walking and the way we are walking and practicing within the mountains.

## PRACTICE AND VERIFICATION

> (13) The import of this expression is that all mountains are the East Mountain, and all these East Mountains are "moving over the water." Therefore, Mount Sumeru and the other nine mountains are all appearing, are all practicing and verifying [the Buddhadharma]. This is called "the East Mountain."

In Indian Buddhist cosmology, Mount Sumeru is the center of this entire universe. According to Vasubandhu's *Abhidharmakośa* our world is flat, with Mount Sumeru like a cylinder in the center, nine mountains, like a square of mountains, around it, and seven mountain ranges around that in concentric squares. Our continent, Jambudvīpa, is south of Mount Sumeru. Underneath this ocean and earth that we know there is a golden circle layer. Below the earth there is a water circle, and below that is a wind circle.[83]

According to *Abhidharmakośa,* the world is supported by the wind circle. Later in this writing Dōgen talks about these water and wind circles. He says that all the mountains in this universe are the East Mountain. All mountains, without any exceptions, are practicing, and we are the mountains. The walking of the mountains is practice and verification.

This "practice and verification" is a translation of *shu shō* (修証). Dōgen's fundamental teaching is that shu and shō are one, shu shō. All mountains are manifesting (genjō) themselves as their practice, and this manifestation is verification of the Buddhadharma. The colors of the mountains are Buddha's body.

The common understanding of Buddhism is different from this teaching of Dōgen. In that understanding, shu and shō are separate: shu is a cause and shō is the result. As a bodhisattva we arouse bodhi mind and start to practice; through our practice we attain enlightenment, and millions of years later we become a buddha. This becoming a buddha is shō; awakening is shō. But Dōgen says shu, our practice, and shō, the result of practice, are one. Within our practice in this moment, shō, or the result, is already here. This is because shō is the seed of the lotus; within the flower (shu) the seed is already there. This is one of the meanings of the lotus flower as a metaphor for wondrous Dharma: because within the flower the seed is already there, within practice the result is already there.

> But how could Yunmen himself be liberated from the "skin, flesh, bones, and marrow" of the East Mountain and its life of practice and verification?

The expression "skin, flesh, bones, and marrow" comes from the story of Dharma transmission from Bodhidharma to the second ancestor, Huike. Bodhidharma said to his four disciples that the first attained his skin, the second his flesh, the third his bones, and finally Huike attained his marrow. Commonly these four are interpreted as progressing from shallowness to depth, and therefore, only Huike attained the essence of his teacher and became the second ancestor. However, in *Shōbōgenzō* "Kattō" ("Entanglement") Dōgen interprets these four as equal.[84] Here the "skin, flesh, bones, and marrow" of the East Mountain means each and every aspect of practice and movement within the network of interdependent origination. Not only Yunmen—no one can be liberated from the walking of the East Mountain, because the mountain's walking is itself the vital path of liberation. Practice-verification is the path of liberation.

## DŌGEN CRITICIZES

> (14) At the present time in the land of the great Song there is a certain bunch of illiterates who have formed such a crowd that they cannot be overcome by the few real [students].

This is one of the places Dōgen criticizes other people with harsh or even violent words. Some people think that he even violated the Buddhist precept of right speech. Here, Dōgen is finding fault with his contemporaries for their understanding of Yunmen's saying; "the land of the great Song" refers to China under the Song Dynasty, meaning the China of Dōgen's time.

In considering Dōgen's sharp criticisms, I'd like to begin by discussing one of his informal talks at Kōshōji, spoken before "Sansuikyō" and recorded in *Shōbōgenzō Zuimonki*, section 5-7.

> There is an old saying which goes, "Although the power of a wise man exceeds that of an ox, he does not fight with the ox." Now, students, even if you think that your wisdom and knowledge is superior to others, you should not be fond of arguing with them.[85]

This is Dōgen's teaching to his students: "Don't argue." And he repeats it; he shares a story from Zen Master Zhenjing Kenwen about one of his friends, Xuefeng Daoyuan, who was arguing with others, and goes on to comment:

> Students of the Way, you also should consider this thoroughly. As long as you aspire to make diligent effort in learning the Way, you must be begrudging with your time. When do you have time to argue with others? Ultimately, it brings about no benefit to you or to others. This is so even in the case of arguing about the Dharma, much more about worldly affairs. Even though the power of a wise man is stronger than that of an ox, he does not fight with the ox.
>
> Even if you think that you understand the Dharma more deeply than others, do not argue, criticize, or try to defeat them.
>
> If there is a sincere student who asks you about the Dharma, you should not begrudge telling him about it. You should explain it to him. However, even in such a case, before responding wait until you have been asked three times. Neither speak too much nor talk about meaningless matters.
>
> After reading these words of Zhenjing, I thought that I myself had this fault, and that he was admonishing me. I have subsequently never argued about the Dharma with others.[86]

This is what he said when he was about thirty-six years old. When he wrote the critical words in "Sansuikyō" he was forty. Dōgen was highly intellectual and I think also very argumentative his whole life. Keizan's *Denkōroku*, or *Record of Transmitting the Light*, includes a story about Dōgen's visit to Chinese Zen master Ruyan of Mount Jing. During their conversation, the master commented, "What a talkative fellow." Dōgen replied, "It's not that I'm not a talkative fellow, but why am I not correct?" Then Ruyan said, "Sit a while and have some tea."[87] Dōgen as a youth would argue even with the abbot of a prestigious monastery in China.

Although he advised his students not to waste time arguing or criticizing, and he himself tried not to argue, he was not able to follow his own advice. I rather like his inconsistency on this point. I feel like he was an actual human being.

> They maintain that sayings such as this "East Mountain moving over the water" or Nanquan's "sickle" are incomprehensible talk. Their idea is that any saying that is involved with thought is not a Zen saying of the buddhas and ancestors; it is incomprehensible sayings that are the sayings of the buddhas and ancestors. Consequently, they hold that Huangbo's "stick" and Linji's "roar," because they are difficult to comprehend and cannot be grasped by thought, represent the great awakening preceding the time "before the germination of any subtle sign." The "tangle-cutting phrases" often used as devices by earlier worthies are [they say] incomprehensible.

We need to think carefully about why Dōgen thought he had to criticize people. Many scholars think such criticism was actually directed toward his own students, not people in China or in the Rinzai tradition.

Many of Dōgen's students came from one of the early Zen movements in Japan, called Nihon Daruma-shū, the school of Japan named after Bodhidharma. Its founder, Dainichi Nōnin, was a contemporary of Eisai. Eisai was the first Japanese master to enter China, return, and transmit Zen to Japan. He established Kenninji, where Dōgen later practiced with his teacher Myōzen. But Dainichi Nōnin simply practiced Zen by himself, attained enlightenment, and started to teach. He was very popular. Eventually he sent two of his students to China with a letter expressing his understanding of Dharma. Those disciples visited Zhuoan Deguang (in Japanese, Setsuan Tokkō), a Linji (in Japanese, Rinzai) Zen master, who recognized Dainichi Nōnin's enlightenment and gave him a letter of transmission. Some people criticized him because he had not received face-to-face transmission, but he had many students. He gave transmission to his disciple Bucchi Kakuan. Kakuan had many students, including Koun Ejo, who became Dōgen's Dharma successor, and Ekan, who joined Dōgen's assembly in 1241 and brought his disciples. These people became a major part of Dōgen's sangha, and after Dōgen's death, they formed the early Sōtō Zen tradition.

When Ekan and his disciples became Dōgen's students, they already had a certain understanding and style of practice, transmitted from Dainichi Nōnin and Kakuan. According to the conversation between Ejo and Dōgen when they first met, the practice of Daruma-shū was the Zen of *kenshō jōbutsu* (becoming Buddha by seeing nature) transmitted from Chinese Linji Zen. Dōgen's criticism in "Sansuikyō" paragraph 10 regarding "turning the object and turning the mind," "explaining the mind and explaining the nature," and "seeing the mind and seeing the nature," and also his complaint in paragraph 14 about people who preferred "incomprehensible talk," are all pointing toward the teaching of this particular lineage. Their basic idea is that kenshō—seeing the mind-nature that is hidden inside ourselves—is enlightenment. To see the mind-nature, we need to stop thinking with words and concepts; incomprehensible expressions are the only tool to accomplish this.

(15) Those who talk in this way have never met a true teacher and lack the eye of study; they are worthless little fools. There have been many such "sons of Māra" and "gang of six" shavepates in the land of Song for the last two or three hundred years. This is truly regrettable, for it represents the decline of the great way of the buddhas and ancestors. Their understanding is inferior to that of the hīnayāna śrāvakas, more foolish that that even of non-Buddhists. They are not laymen; they are not monks. They are not humans; they are not gods. They are dumber than beasts that study the way of the buddha. What you shavelings call "incomprehensible sayings" is incomprehensible only to you, not to the buddhas and ancestors. Simply because you yourself do not comprehend [the sayings] is no reason for you not to study the path comprehended

by the buddhas and ancestors. Even granted that [Zen teachings] were in the end incomprehensible, this comprehension of yours would also be wrong. Such types are common throughout all quarters of the state of Song; I have seen them with my own eyes. They are to be pitied.

"Shavepates" means people who become monks but have no idea of the Dharma. "Gang of six" refers to a group of the Buddha's disciples that appear in the Vinaya texts who did outrageous things such as manipulating people to give them money and persuading other monks to commit suicide.

Dōgen used these very strong statements to persuade Daruma-shū monks to change their understanding and practice into the way he was teaching. I agree with those who think Dōgen's criticism of Chinese Zen was not for the sake of argument but was intended as a caution to his own students.

Now I'd like to talk about the point of Dōgen's criticism. Here is an example: the kōan about Nanquan's sickle. Nanquan was working on the mountain, cutting grass with a sickle. A traveling monk passed by and asked, "Which path should I take to go to Nanquan?" Nanquan was the name of the mountain where this Zen master's monastery was located, and also the abbot's name, so Nanquan could mean either the place or this master himself. Nanquan said, "I bought this sickle for three cents. I bought this cheap." And the monk said, "I don't ask about the price of the sickle. I want to know how to go to Nanquan." Nanquan then said, "This sickle is very sharp." That's the end of the story. It seems to make no sense.

Zen kōans are full of stories like this. People assume their point is to interrupt discriminating thought. Since the reality of all beings is beyond discriminating thought, people believe that to see this reality we have to cut off all thoughts. So masters used kōans and other extreme methods: Huangbo hit students with a staff and Linji shouted unexpectedly. This would mean that when we study kōans we should stop logical, conceptual thinking. We are deluded because of our thinking, so when we cut off our thinking, then we see reality. This is one understanding of Zen practice: no-mind, no-thought is enlightenment.

Dōgen is critical of this approach.

## BEYOND ELIMINATING THOUGHT

Personally, my practice is not to eliminate my thoughts. I have never done kōan practice; my only understanding of it comes from a time when I needed a job.

One year before I came to this country in 1993, I lived in a Catholic nunnery in Kyōto, and I had to support my family. A friend who was working for a Buddhist publisher gave me work transcribing the *teishō* (lectures) of a Japanese lay Rinzai master, Sōmei Tsuji. I transcribed twenty-four hour-long tapes in which Sōmei explained his practice. He said in Rinzai practice, especially in the beginning, the teacher doesn't recommend that the students read Buddhist texts because, he said, they are merely obstacles until one attains kenshō. In fact, all knowledge before attaining kenshō is considered as just an obstacle in the tradition.

Beginners in Rinzai practice are usually requested to work with the kōan *mu* or with the sound of one hand clapping.[88] A friend who was a Rinzai practitioner described to me his own experience of practice, focusing on mu or counting breaths. Whatever miscellaneous distracting thoughts came up, he would just stop them and focus on his kōan, or on counting his breath. It took a long time, many years, but when he really, completely focused on that mu, no thought arose, and he was free. He said that after attaining such an experience one is able to understand Zen teaching and Buddhist texts.

But the teacher Sōmei Tsuji said that kenshō is not the goal of Rinzai practice but a starting point, the beginning of practice and study. After experiencing kenshō practitioners have to study many other kōans by not only sitting but also reading texts and understanding Buddhist teachings. By the time they complete kōan practice, they have both the experience of going beyond thought and also an understanding of the teachings. Then they need to use this experience and understanding to help others. But novice or careless Rinzai practitioners might think that kenshō, or eliminating thought, is the purpose of their practice.

Some people think that when we eliminate all thought and experience enlightenment we are liberated; we don't have to do anything else and can be happy for the rest of our lives. I think this is a misunderstanding or even a superstition. Dōgen tried to caution his students that the point is to let go of thoughts and just be as you are. No-thinking is not enlightenment; that is not our goal.

I have been practicing for more than forty years so I have experienced many conditions during zazen. Sometimes I have had the experience of no thought, of simply being there. It was very pleasant. But from the beginning of my practice I was taught that any condition is merely the scenery of zazen, so I don't consider it a special or "good" part of zazen. Sometimes my mind is very busy and distracted, but still that is part of my zazen. When my mind is busy I try to sit upright and breathe deeply and smoothly and keep my eyes open. When I find that I am interacting with thoughts, I try to let go.

In our zazen we are like the blue sky; many thoughts and emotions come and go, like the way clouds somehow appear, stay for a while, and go away. We don't control clouds because it is neither possible nor necessary. Sometimes my mind is like a cloudy day; the entire sky is covered with clouds. Sometimes I have beautiful, fluffy clouds as in spring. Sometimes my mind is a completely clear, blue sky. Depending on our internal and external condition, different scenery comes and goes. We don't control anything. Even when our mind is completely covered with clouds or we have a storm, the important point is that above the clouds the sky is blue and the sun shines.

If we think that *this* condition is favorable and *that* one is unfavorable, then we create saṃsāra in our zazen: "I want to get there; I want to experience this more often, or longer." When we are successful, we are happy, and otherwise we are sad. Any condition of our mind is the scenery of our zazen, or the scenery of our life. So we don't cling to any condition. Even in Rinzai practice, eliminating thought is not the goal, but a preparation to study Dharma without discriminating thought. I think that is Dōgen's point.

I learned from my teacher that any condition, whether mental or physical, is just a condition. In my practice the most important thing is just to keep the upright posture, breathe deeply from my abdomen, keep my eyes open, and let go of whatever comes up from my consciousness. That's all I do. I try to keep this posture under any condition. To create certain conditions of our mind is not the purpose of our sitting.

Sawaki Rōshi quoted a dialogue between Zen Master Longya Judun (Ryuge Kyoton, 835–923) and a monk:

> The monk asked, "How did the ancient master finally cease doing things and completely settle down?" Longya replied, "It was like a thief slipping into a vacant house."

Sawaki Rōshi commented,

> A burglar breaks into an empty house. He can't steal anything. There's no need to escape. Nobody chases him. It's nothing. Understand: It's nothing.[89]

The point of this sitting practice is to keep the upright posture and awareness of whatever is going on, within and without our life. We are already in the mountain. And yet we cannot live above the clouds. We are always conditioned. If we notice only what happens below the clouds, we are overwhelmed by each condition we experience. We need faith that the blue sky and sunlight are always there above the clouds even though we cannot see them. When we take an airplane or climb a high mountain, we can see that even when there is stormy weather, above the clouds the sun is always shining and the sky is always blue. However, we don't live above the clouds. We have to go through all the different weather on the earth. The essence of our practice is to weather all our earthly conditions with an upright posture of body and mind.

Dōgen tells us here that eliminating thought is not our practice and is not enlightenment. Cutting off our human ability to think does not make us healthy. Instead, we need to understand how to use this ability as a tool to perceive reality more deeply and intimately, and not be controlled by our thoughts. I think—and this is only a thought—our thought is an incomplete copy of reality, like a map. If we think our thoughts are reality itself, as we usually do, then we are deluded about the reality beyond our thinking. Our map is always incomplete, because reality has three dimensions, but our map has only two: like or dislike, right or wrong.

In the physical world, however we make a map or atlas, something is distorted. The center of the map is usually our country. Parts of the map near the center are relatively accurate. The edges of the world are distorted—for example, on some maps Greenland is bigger than the United States. In our personal maps as well, things we love and hate seem bigger than they are, and things we don't care about seem much smaller than they are.

The most important thing is to see how our map is distorted. Then we are free from our map. Zazen is not a method to correct the distortion of our map, nor a way to throw the map away. Rather, our zazen places our entire body on the earth, on the ground of reality, not on the map. We sit with the distorted map. All different kinds of thoughts and feelings arise as a result of our karma. When we see that this map is not perfect but distorted, we are liberated from our own system of opinions. This small liberation transforms our way of life.

I think this is a very important point. Our zazen, as Sawaki Rōshi said, is good for nothing. Our map is still distorted. As Dōgen said, even though we are on the ocean bottom instead of a well, we are still a frog. We have to practice as this frog, limited and conditioned. In zazen we settle our entire being in the ocean, not in the well. We use our karmic consciousness, our distorted map, for the sake of the Dharma, this entire, interpenetrated reality of life.

Many students think Zen is a method to stop thoughts. This is a kind of extreme. One extreme is grasping our thoughts, opinions, or understanding (as we usually do in ordinary life), and another extreme is thinking we have to give up all opinions and all understanding. Dōgen wants to show the middle path between those two.

> They do not know that thought is words.

That is, words come from our discriminating thoughts, our distorted map. And yet:

> [T]hey do not know that words are liberated from thought.

I think this is a very wonderful teaching. Even though words come from thought, they are at the same time liberated from thought. How can we express a word liberated from thought? Knowing that those thoughts are distorted, we are liberated, and our words can be liberated as well. Our words can be an expression of Dharma, not merely an expression of one person's karmic consciousness, our desire.

> When I was in the Song, I made fun of them, but they never had an explanation, never a word to say for themselves—just this false notion of theirs about "incomprehensibility." Who could have taught you this? Though you have no natural teacher, you are natural little non-Buddhists.

Dōgen expresses himself again.

## BONES AND MARROW, MOUNTAINS AND WATERS

> (16) We should realize that this [teaching of] "the East Mountain moving over the water" is the very "bones and marrow" of the buddhas and ancestors.

Dōgen continues to comment on Yunmen's saying from paragraph 12. This saying is vital—indeed the very bones and marrow of the buddhas and ancestors. Rather than incomprehensible sayings, as so many people mistakenly think, Yunmen's teaching is actually the essential teaching of the buddhas and ancestors.

> All the waters are appearing at the foot of the East Mountain, and therefore the mountains mount the clouds and stride through the heavens. The mountains are the peaks of the waters, and in both ascending and descending their walk is "over the water." The tips of the mountains' feet walk across the waters, setting them dancing.

Here, Dōgen is talking about the relation between mountains and waters. In ordinary reality, we think of mountains as solid, quiet, and immovable, while water is soft, musical, and always moving. In Su Shi's poem, water is the voice of Buddha and the colors of mountains his body. Water evaporates. When it cools, it condenses within clouds. Then as rain or snow it falls again to the earth, humidifying plants and sustaining all living beings. Water forms ponds, lakes, and rivers, returning to the ocean. Water is always circulating, changing its form. In contrast, mountains seem immovable and eternal.

Dōgen, as usual, has another perspective. Earlier he said mountains have the two virtues of peacefully abiding and constantly walking. Later he says that water also has two virtues: flowing and not flowing. When frozen, water is as solid as diamond and as immovable as mountains. Dōgen says here that mountains and waters both have the same virtues as Dharma. Because of the water, a mountain can ride on a cloud and go up to the heavens and down to the ocean. Moving and not moving, impermanence and eternity, support each other. That is why, within our practice, the process of growing, maturing, and aging is a manifestation of the eternal Dharma body of the Buddha at each moment.

> Therefore, their walking is "seven high and eight across" and their "practice and verification are not nonexistent."

The expression "seven high and eight across" means "with complete freedom": mountains walk freely and reach everywhere.

"Their practice and verification are not nonexistent" comes from the dialogue between Huineng, the Sixth Ancestor, and his disciple Nanyue:

> When Nanyue first visited Huineng, the master asked, "Where do you come from?"
>
> Nanyue replied, "I came from Mount Sung."
>
> Huineng asked, "What is it that thus comes?"
>
> Nanyue could not understand the question and practiced with the master for eight years. Then Nanyue said to Huineng, "I finally understand what you asked when I first visited you."
>
> Huineng asked, "How do you understand?"
>
> Nanyue said, "If I say anything, I miss it."
>
> Huineng asked, "Then is there practice and verification?"
>
> Nanyue said, "It is not that practice and verification are nonexistent. But they cannot be defiled."
>
> Huineng said, "This nondefilement is what all buddhas have been protecting and maintaining. You are thus and I am thus. Ancestors in India were also thus."

"It is not that practice and verification are nonexistent" means that mountains and all beings including ourselves carry out practice and verification. This is not to say that we don't need to practice; we need to be free from the defilement of the three poisons: greed, anger, and ignorance. Mountains and waters have no defilement. Mountains are simply being mountains and accepting all beings within them. Oceans do not reject water from any river.

This paragraph of "Sansuikyō" is a bridge between the mountains section and the waters section.

## THE *SUTTANIPĀTA* ON CAUSE AND EFFECT, DEPENDENT ARISING, AND *NĀMARŪPA*

I'd like to introduce a section from *Suttanipāta*, one of the oldest Buddhist scriptures, recorded in Pāli. The name of this sutta is *Kalahavivāda Sutta* (Sn IV, 11), or *Disputes and Contentions*, and I think it's very important for understanding Buddha's teaching of interdependent origination.

In early Buddhism the correct expression is "dependent origination" or "dependent arising," not "interdependent origination." The idea of interdependent origination is from Mahāyāna Buddhism, from Nāgārjuna, and the meaning is slightly different. Here is the text from *Suttanipāta*:

> 1. "Sir," said a questioner, "Whenever there are arguments and quarrels there are tears and anguish, arrogance and pride and grudges and insults to go with them. Can you explain how these things come about? Where do they all come from?"[90]

Twenty-five hundred years ago, this person was asking the cause of a certain human problem, which we still have today. In the final form of the teaching of dependent origination, called the twelve links of causation, the main point is that karma continues from the past life through the present life to the future life, based on ignorance. In this older version of the teaching, the point is how we can be released from difficulties we have in this lifetime.

> 2. "The tears and anguish that follow arguments and quarrels," said the Buddha, "the arrogance and pride and the grudges and insults that go with them are all the result of one thing. They come from having preferences, from holding things precious and dear. Insults are born out of arguments, and grudges are inseparable from quarrels."

This *preference* is the same as the ninth of the twelve links: in Pāli *upādāna* and in Chinese *qu* or 取. Other English translations are "craving" or "attachment." The only cause of arguments and quarrels is the preference, craving, or attachment we have toward pleasant things.

Then the person asked:

> 3. "But why, Sir, do we have these preferences, these special things? Why do we have so much greed? And all the aspirations and achievements that we base our lives on, Where do we get them from?"

I think this is a very important question for us too. What is the cause of preferences and attachments? What makes certain things so important to us that we compete or fight with others to acquire or protect them?

> 4. "The preferences, the precious things," said the Buddha, "come from the impulse of desire. So too does the greed and so too do the aspirations and achievements that make up peoples' lives."

In other words, the aspirations that drive our lives originate in desires. This is the eighth link: in Pāli *taṇhā* and in Chinese *ai* or 愛. Another English translation is "thirst."

What is the cause of this impulse of desire?

> 5. "From where, Sir, comes this impulse of desire? From where do we derive our theories and opinions? And what about all the other things that you, the Wanderer, have named—such as anger, dishonesty, and confusion?"

> 6. "The impulse of desire arises when people think of one thing as pleasant and another as unpleasant: that is the source of desire. It is when people see that material things are subject both to becoming and to disintegration that they form their theories about the world.

7. "Anger, confusion, and dishonesty arise when things are set in pairs as opposites. The person with perplexity must train himself in the path of knowledge. The recluse has declared the Truth after realization."

"Pleasant" and "unpleasant" refer to the seventh link: in Pāli *vedanā* and in Chinese *shou* or 受. Another English translation is "sensation." No sensation lasts forever; it comes and goes as its cause arises and disappears. We see impermanent things arising and perishing; we interpret events positively or negatively; then based on these positive and negative experiences we gradually create our own picture of the world, our system of values, our philosophy.

8. "But why, Sir, is it that we find some things pleasant and some unpleasant? What could we do to stop that? And this idea of becoming and disintegration, could you explain where that comes from?"

What is the cause of pleasant and unpleasant sensations? If we could stop interpreting sensations in this way, we would be released from desire and craving, and thus also freed from arguments and quarrels, tears and anguish.

9. "It is the action of contact, of mental impression, that leads to feelings of pleasant and unpleasant. Without the contact they would not exist. And as I see it, the idea of becoming and disintegration also comes from this source, from the action of contact."

Contact between the six sense organs and their objects is the sixth link: in Pāli *phassa* and in Chinese *chu* or 触. The Buddha points out that the actions of contact between self and other things and people is the origin of all our problems. This is a strictly logical approach. The Buddha does not talk about any gods or demons, any myth at all as the source of human conditions. Therefore in his teaching we can find the path of liberation within the relation between self and others.

> 10. "So what, Sir, does this contact come from? And the grasping habit, what's the reason for that? Is there anything that can be done to get rid of possessiveness and anything that could be eliminated so that there would no more contact?"

How can we avoid contact? It's a very good and important question. Is it possible to live without contact with others as objects of our sense organs? If not, the Buddha's teaching does not make any sense. And this has something to do with what Dōgen is discussing here in "Sansuikyō."

The Buddha says:

> 11. "Contact exists because the compound of mind and matter exists. The habit of grasping is based on wanting things. If there were no wanting there would be no possessiveness. Similarly, without the element of form, of matter, there would be no contact."

"Name and form" here is the same as the fourth link: in Pāli, *nāmarūpa*, and, in Chinese, *mingse* or 名色. But in the twelve links, *nāmarūpa* is translated into English as "mentality-materiality" and refers to a certain stage during gestation in the mother's womb before mind and body separate, whereas in *Suttanipāta* and other older texts, according to the great twentieth-century Buddhist scholar Hajime Nakamura, nāmarūpa refers to the objects of the sense organs.

If the habit of grasping in our mentality ceases, and if nāmarūpa, or the object of our desire, ceases, there is no contact. I think this is a very logical teaching. Here our desire and our objects of desire are interdependent with each other. When one is there, the other is there. If either ceases to be, the other does too. They arise together and contact arises with them.

12. "What pursuit leads a person to get rid of form? And how can suffering and pleasure cease to exist? This is what I want to know about."

How can we be released from being hooked between our desires and their objects? If such a thing is possible, we will be released from both suffering and pleasure. Usually we want to be released from suffering and keep pleasure. Unfortunately what the Buddha teaches is nirvāṇa as the cessation of the dichotomy between suffering and pleasure.

13. "There is a state where form ceases to exist," said the Buddha. "It is a state without ordinary perception and without disordered perception and without no perception and without any annihilation of perception. It is perception, consciousness, that is the source of all the basic obstacles." (874)

The Buddha clearly says that there is a state where form (nāmarūpa) ceases to exist: we can be released from bondage. What kind of state is it? I think this is the most important point. The Buddha describes the state: without ordinary perception and without disordered perception and without no perception and without any annihilation of perception. And he continues, "It is perception, consciousness, that is the source of all the basic obstacles." (Perception is not named in the twelve links, but consciousness is the second link.)

This sutta mentions six links of causation—consciousness/perception, nāmarūpa/name-form, contact, sensation, desire/thirst, craving/preference—and the resulting arguments, quarrels, tears, and anguish. This is one of the older forms of the teaching of dependent origination. According to Buddhist scholars, the twelve links we know are a final version of various older versions. We need to pay attention to the fact that the Buddha says that perception or consciousness is the source of the problems, but annihilation of perception is not the resolution of the problems.

How can we be free from this contact between the sense organ, our mind, and the object of mind? There are many different answers to this question, from early Buddhism to Mahāyāna and Zen Buddhism.

In Yogācāra teaching, the way is to negate the object and see only consciousness. The way in early Buddhism is to eliminate mind and acknowledge only form. A third way is to go beyond the dichotomy of self and other, sense organ and object. This is our approach, following Dōgen. Nāgārjuna showed us that the two sides of every pair negate each other. By negating both sides he points to the reality that is there before our mind creates these dichotomies. Dōgen does the same.

This short section in *Suttanipāta* concerns the middle path between thinking and no-thinking—without ordinary perception, without mistaken or disordered perception, without no perception, and without any annihilation of perception. This is our zazen. We let go of both ordinary and distorted perceptions. They still happen, but we don't believe or act on them; this is freedom from our perceptions. We also don't negate or eliminate perceptions. In zazen we just sit. This "just sitting" is free from ordinary and disordered perceptions, yet the perceptions are still there, not annihilated. This is freedom from contact, like and dislike, and our preferences.

Dōgen's verse about Mount Lu from the *Eihei Koroku*:

A person in the mountains should love the mountains.
With going and coming, the mountains are his body.
The mountains are the body, but the body is not the self
So where can one find any senses or their objects?

In the section of *Suttanipāta* above, Buddha diagnosed the action of contact as the fundamental cause of arguments and quarrels, tears and anguish, arrogance and pride, and grudges and insult. In the compounds of mind and object, self and all beings, subject and object, if one or both are missing, no contact is made. On hearing this, some people fled society to live in caves, forests, or mountains. This is one way to try to avoid contact. A second way is to try not to think anything and to live without perceptions, concepts, or value judgments.

These ways don't work very well. Priests or monks who live in forests or monasteries and try to avoid contact with society don't work to teach and help others. Benefiting others is one of the points of Mahāyāna Buddhism. Yet when we meet people, situations, and conditions, naturally something happens in our minds. We cannot stop thoughts and emotions from welling up.

How then can we avoid this problem of contact? This is the essence of our practice and the teaching of Mahāyāna. In *Mūlamadhya-makakārikā* Nāgārjuna writes, "I pay homage to the Fully Awakened One, the Supreme Teacher who has taught the doctrine of relational origination, the blissful cessation of all phenomenal thought constructions."[91]

One of the major themes of Nāgārjuna's writings is to refrain from grasping phenomenal thought constructions. "Phenomenal thought construction" is *keron* in Japanese or *vikalpa* in Sanskrit, meaning "idle argument." What Nāgārjuna tried to do, using logic, was to deconstruct any logical statement to show us the reality preceding any view. Nāgārjuna is very logical in showing us the reality of interdependent origination beyond logic, concepts, conditioned ideas, and tunnel views. This gives us a way to be free of the problems that arise from contact. Instead of creating views and grasping them, we deconstruct our own views. This is an essential point in Buddhism from Śākyamuni to Dōgen and beyond.

I would like to introduce one example in Chinese Zen, from Zen master Linji's *Linji Lu*. The basic teaching of Rinzai (Linji) Zen is the same as what we are discussing here: how the self and myriad dharmas can meet without the flame of the three poisons. For example, in the beginning of part 2, "Instructing the Group," there is a saying, later considered a very important kōan in Rinzai tradition, called "Four Procedures." Linji says,

> At times one takes away the person but does not take away the environment. At times one takes away the environment but does not take away the person. At times one takes away

both the person and the environment. At times one takes away neither the person nor the environment.[92]

He's talking about how the self can relate or connect with things without creating problems such as like and dislike, preferences, attachment or detachment, pursuing or escaping, and greed or hatred. Linji asks that his students sometimes negate the self and see only the myriad things, sometimes negate the myriad things and see the self, sometimes negate both, and sometimes see both self and myriad things as they are.

Linji's fundamental teaching is "Don't seek anything outside." He says,

> When students today fail to make progress where is the fault? The fault lies in the fact that they don't have faith in themselves! If you don't have faith in yourself, then you'll be forever in a hurry trying to keep up with everything around you, you'll be twisted and turned by whatever environment you are in and you can never move freely. But if you can just stop this mind that goes rushing around moment by moment looking for something, then you will be no different from the patriarchs and buddhas.[93]

We need faith in ourselves. To teach this Linji used shouting or hitting—a very direct, violent, and dynamic way.

What Dōgen taught through poetry, using the image of mountains and waters, is the same as what the Buddha taught in *Suttanipāta*, what Nāgārjuna taught through logic, and what Linji taught through shouting and hitting. These teachings aim to avoid the poison caused by contact between self and myriad things. We do this by letting go of thought in our sitting practice and also by examining our views for distortions and fixed foundations.

Dōgen maintains there is no fixed foundation. When we take a close look at how our views are conditioned, then we can be liberated from our own preferences and cravings. In this practice, we discover that each of us is connected with all beings in the network of interdependent origination. We are living as the person in the mountain whose body is all the mountains.

Although I have been studying this difficult and yet beautiful writing for many years, I have sometimes been overwhelmed. I often wanted to give up. But if we can follow the thread of the teachings from Buddha through Mahāyāna Buddhism and Zen until Dōgen, we can discover the meaning of this wondrous writing for ourselves. We will completely miss the point if we simply read Dōgen and create a fixed philosophy based on our understanding of his writings. If we do that, we create another system of views—another problem. Instead, when we read Dōgen we have to apply his words in our lives, studying the relationship between our self and the myriad things.

This is the end of the questions and answers on dependent origination in the *Suttanipāta*. But there is another question regarding the stage of purification.

14. "Sir, you have explained to us everything we have asked you about. There is one more question we would like you to answer for us: Do the learned scholars of the world say that this is the highest purification of the individual being or do they say that there is some other kind of goal?"

15. "There are scholars and authorities," replied the Buddha, "who say that this is the highest and the purification of the individual. There are others who maintain that the highest purity is to be found in the complete eradication of the five components of the person."

16. "And there is also the *muni*, the wise man. He has realized which things are dependencies and he knows that these

are only crutches and props. And when he has realized this, he has become free. He does not enter into argument and so does not enter the round of endless becomings."[94]

The Buddha does not answer whether purification is the ultimate goal or whether there are higher stages. He said that such discussion is only crutches and props; such arguments again create desire to attain or to compete with others, resulting in tears and anguish within spiritual practice. So we should avoid them.

I think this teaching of the Buddha is the source of Dōgen's saying that the mountains always rest at the Dharma position of this moment and yet are also always walking. We rest peacefully here and now, yet we practice going up and going down, stepping forward and backward, ceaselessly and endlessly. Of course Dōgen never studied *Suttanipāta*, but I think we can see a thread that connects these two teachings.

I N THIS SECTION Dōgen discusses water, but this water is not simply the water flowing in the river or the water we drink every day. He talks about water as a metaphor of Buddhadharma. As we have studied, "the mountains" is the metaphor of the network of inter-dependent origination in which we are coming and going.

In the commentaries on "Sansuikyō" by Sōtō Zen scholar-monks, this water is called *hosshō-sui*, or Dharma-nature water. *Hosshō* (Dharma nature) is a translation of the Sanskrit word *dharmatā*, the way all beings really are, and is used as a synonym of *tathatā* (thus-ness), *buddhata* (buddha-nature), and *dharmakāya* (Dharma body). In *Zoagon-kyō* (one of the earliest Buddhist scriptures), it is said, "Whether the Tathāgata appears in the world or does not appear in the world, the Dharma nature is always abiding." Dharma nature refers to the truth the Buddha awakened to. But even if the Buddha did not awaken, the truth or reality, the dharmatā, is always there. That is why the Buddha said that he did not fabricate the dharmatā but he simply discovered it, as if someone had discovered an abandoned palace hidden in the deep forest, which no one knew was there.

In his commentary on *Mahāprajñāpāramitā Sūtra*, Nāgārjuna said,

> Dharma nature is the true reality of all things (*shohōjissō*). When the ignorance and delusions in our mind are replaced

and we see things with undefiled genuine insight, we can see the true nature of all things. This is called Dharma nature (dharmatā). The "nature" refers to truth. All living beings are bound because of mistaken view and liberated by true insight.

Dōgen wrote in a fascicle of *Shōbōgenzō* entitled "Hosshō" that Dharma nature is not something abstract but our concrete practice, and all things we encounter in our practice:

> Clarifying the great way of Dharma nature by following the scriptures and teachers is clarifyiing the Dharma nature by the self. The scriptures are Dharma nature, and are the self. Teachers are Dharma nature and are the self. Because it is the self as the Dharma nature, it is not the mistakenly conceived "self" by non-Buddhists or demons. In the Dharma nature, there is no non-Buddhists or demons. Dharma nature is simply eating morning gruel, eating noon rice, and drinking tea.

In the Sōtō Zen tradition, in the *jukai* (receiving of precepts) ceremony, before a master gives the precepts, he purifies the recipient by sprinkling water on the person's head (*shasui*). That water, which comes from the top of the master's head, is called *hosshō-sui*; this Dharma-water refers to the wisdom that sees all beings as they are.

In the following discussion, the water is Dharma nature that is the self, the masters, the scriptures, and all other things we are living and working together. The point is, how can we live and practice together with other people and things without making them into nāmarūpa?

## Beyond Dichotomy

First Dōgen says that the water as Dharma nature is beyond conceptual dichotomies:

(17) Water is neither strong nor weak, neither wet nor dry, neither moving nor still, neither cold nor hot, neither being nor nonbeing, neither delusion nor enlightenment. Frozen, it is harder than diamond; who could break it? Melted, it is softer than milk; who could break it?

Dōgen is discussing the reality of our life beyond the dualities that are a product of our mind, of the "contact" between our sense organs and their objects. Water doesn't have any fixed self-nature, so it changes in many ways: sometimes it is wet, of course, but sometimes it's very dry. When the temperature is very low, for instance, snow is not wet at all—it is more like flour. Sometimes water moves, sometimes it doesn't. The ice at the North and South Poles might lie millions of years without moving, and yet it might melt if the global weather changes.

"Neither being nor nonbeing" refers to form and emptiness. There's actually no such thing as what we call "water"; it is merely a collection of two atoms of hydrogen and one of oxygen. When electrolyzed it becomes a vapor of hydrogen and oxygen. Just as a bubble is an event within the interaction between air and water, water is an event in which hydrogen and oxygen are connected. There is no fixed entity called water. And yet, we cannot say a bubble is not there, or water is not there. As an event, each of them is actually there. This is what "emptiness" means.

"Neither delusion nor enlightenment," of course, is not only about water but ourselves. We are beyond these dichotomies too. Dōgen shows the middle way beyond duality. This is expressed in the *Heart Sūtra*: "All dharmas are marked by emptiness; they neither arise nor cease, are neither defiled nor pure, neither increase nor decrease."

"Diamond" here, as in the title of the *Diamond Sūtra*, refers to prajñā, wisdom that is not destroyed by anything and can cut through all things. On the other hand, water can be softer than milk, nurturing all beings as compassion.

## WATER STUDIES WATER

> (18) This being the case, we cannot doubt the many virtues realized
> [by water]. We should study the occasion when the water of the
> ten directions is seen in the ten directions.

As water is beyond these dichotomies, it is beyond the dichotomy of self and other, subject and object, or self and the myriad dharmas. "When the water of the ten directions is seen in the ten directions" means that we see water not only from our tunnel vision but beyond our particular karmic point of view.

We naturally see each thing from *my* point of view, from this side; otherwise we cannot see it at all. This is the origin of dichotomy. And then we create even more separations. We separate things we want from things we don't, the desirable from the undesirable and the valuable from the worthless. Then we want to get this side and push away that side. That's how we create saṃsāra: we try to live on one side alone. Sometimes we succeed and are temporarily happy, but more often we fail, and then we suffer. There are many things we don't want or value, so we try to escape them. But even though we escape temporarily they follow us somehow. Thus, our life becomes chasing and escaping things. This is saṃsāra.

When we see with karmic consciousness, we are the subject and things are objects (nāmarūpa). Naturally then, we have contact between subject and object, and we have preferences. But when Dōgen says "the water of the ten directions is seen in the ten directions," he means not seeing from our particular position. Seeing in the ten directions, there's no separation between the person who is seeing and the water that is seen. Water is seeing water. This is a completely different perspective.

When we have a drought, we want to have rain. In ancient times, people prayed to the dragon gods for rain. And yet, if the rain continues for many days with flooding, we hate rain and pray for it to end. Rain is simply rain. Depending on conditions, sometimes we love it and sometimes we hate it. But rain itself has nothing to do with the dichotomy of our like and dislike.

What we see is our self. A monk asked Dongshan, "Among the three bodies of Buddha, which one does not fall into any category?" Dongshan said, "I am always close to this."[95] "Close to this," often translated as "intimacy," means self and object are one. In other words, when we let go of our views and perceptions, the self and all beings are one. From the very beginning we are actually part of the myriad dharmas. In perception it seems that there is contact between two separate things, subject and object, and thoughts arise, and we create various views. When we take action based on these views, this person and all myriad things appear separately. But when we let go, we are part of the universe, simply five aggregates, the same as all other things. In this way, when we let go of views and perceptions, we are connected with all beings. This is when Avalokiteśvara Bodhisattva clearly sees that all five aggregates are empty and thus relieves all suffering. This is what interdependent origination means.

> This is not a study only of the time when humans or gods see water: there is a study of water seeing water.

*Water* means the self—the self that includes self and others: one mind is all things and all things are one mind. This is the self Dōgen is discussing. When we study the virtues of water, actually the water itself is seeing, studying, practicing, verifying the water. This is the same as he said in *Shōbōgenzō* "Hosshō": to study following scriptures and teachers is to study the self. We are a drop of water that is studying the entire ocean in which we are a tiny part.

This writing is about the true reality of all beings, as discussed in the *Lotus Sūtra*. Wet or dry, soft or hard, being or nonbeing, still or moving, and enlightened or deluded are all, according to Dōgen, "virtues realized by water." So water has these virtues, the same virtues mountains have.

> Water practices and verifies water; hence, there is a study of water
> telling of water.

Dōgen says there's no separation between the human or divine point of view and the things viewed. Here is a paradox: How can water see water? This is difficult to convey if we see things from "my" point of view.

We are part of the universe, right? Even though we as human beings imagine ourselves as separate, we are part of the universe. Our actions, our efforts to understand, actually *are* the world. They are this universe trying to understand itself. Thus, when Dōgen says that water sees the water, that means this universe sees itself through us. I think that is what Dōgen means by "Water practices and verifies water; hence, there is a study of water telling of water."

So there is only water: no dichotomy, no separation between observer and observed. That is how water practices and verifies water, the self practices and verifies the self, the entire world practices and verifies the world.

In *Shōbōgenzō Zuimonki*, Dōgen talks about the kōan of Nanquan cutting a cat into two. He says if he were Nanquan, he would cut the cat into one. Here he is saying the same.

> We must bring to realization the road on which the self encounters
> the self; we move back and forth along, and spring off from, the
> vital path on which the other studies and fully comprehends the
> other.

There is a way we can comprehend ourselves, and others can comprehend others, by just sitting, by letting go of any thought or dichotomy. The self is just being the self, the frog is just being the frog, the wind is just being the wind, water is just being water, and this universe is just being the universe. Nāmarūpa ceases to be. That is the way we go beyond, even beyond Buddha. This reality of going beyond even the Buddha Way is the Buddha Way.

In my case, I found out who I am by studying with my teacher. That's transmission. I didn't actually receive anything, but I found that I am one with all beings. That was what he taught by his way of life. The human convention that we are all different and independent is a very strange thing, a wondrous thing. We are educated in that convention. As a result we must search to find what has been true from the very beginning, before we have questions, even before we learn that we are different and independent. Even though everything has its own uniqueness, these things cannot exist without relations with others.

We are nothing other than the relation of billions of things. Somehow we have to find this truth. This is the process of study and practice. Mountains see mountains and waters see waters.

## WAYS OF SEEING

When we clearly see nāmarūpa as nāmarūpa, we are released from the bondage between perception and nāmarūpa. When we see delusion as delusion, we are not deceived by delusions; then they cease to be delusions and we can even enjoy them.

> (19) In general, then, the way of seeing mountains and waters differs according to the type of being [that sees them]. In seeing water, there are beings who see it as a jeweled necklace. This does not mean, however, that they see a jeweled necklace as water. How, then, do we see what they consider water? Their jeweled necklace is what we see as water.

Dōgen introduces an example used in Yogācāra called "the four views on one and the same water." The Yogācāra text says human beings see water as water, heavenly beings see water as a jeweled necklace, and hungry ghosts see water as raging flames or as pus and blood. Dragons and fish see it as their palace or dwelling. Thus, depending upon our karmic consciousness we see the thing called water as many different things.[96]

Heavenly beings see what we call water as a jeweled necklace. Do they view our jeweled necklaces as water? We are not sure, but probably not. How do we see their water? We don't know that either. So how can human and heavenly beings communicate and understand each other, with such different pictures of the world?

Not only between human and heavenly beings but among the beings in each of the six realms of saṃsāra, is it possible to share the same concepts, understanding, and values? Of course, when they ask these questions, Yogācāra philosophers and Dōgen are not actually talking about beings in different realms—they are talking about different human beings.

Within the human realm, does everyone perceive things the same? We might assume that all human beings share the same perceptions, but actually we often experience that we see the same thing in a subtly different way, or a very different way—even between spouses, parents and children, siblings, or close friends. It is apparent that people from different countries, races, and cultural and religious backgrounds have different views. We can even wonder: is there any such "same thing"?

> Some see water as miraculous flowers, though it does not follow that they use flowers as water.

We create perceptions and views, we make judgments, and we try to choose what is good for us. Within human society we have certain conventions. We think that water should be seen this or that way. Paper is used for this or that sake. We share some things, but if we take a closer look at what we see it might be completely different.

For example, one of my friends has a problem with his eyes and cannot distinguish between orange and brown. He cannot read the sign in the subway station in Kyōto because it is written in brown on an orange background. When only a few people have such a condition, we think they have a problem. We assume there is actually a distinction between orange and brown. But it is worth asking whether brown and orange really exist for him. If more people in this society had eyes like his, people who could see the difference would be very special, or even strange. We would think that they were the ones with a problem because they see what does not exist. It's simply a matter of numbers.

In fact all human eyes see only a certain range of wavelengths between ultraviolet and infrared. We perceive a certain range of color and sound, but some animals can see and hear a wider range. Even when we think it's quiet, for those animals it may be very noisy because of their range of hearing. If our eyes could see ultraviolet or infrared, this world would be completely different for us. Because none of us sees it we think this is normal. Actually we don't know whether what we see is reality or not. All color and sound is a human convention; we create our picture of the world based on this convention. Yet many human beings have certain extraordinary capabilities of sight, hearing, or taste. Actually nothing is fixed as we commonly think. This is another way of explaining the meaning of emptiness. Based on our ability to see between the range of ultraviolet and infrared, we name each color. If we had more accurate eyes there would be many more shades between orange and brown.

We don't know how heavenly beings or any other beings see this world. Yet because we have consensus as human beings, we see the world in *this* way. We also have values: this is important and that is not. This is how we live as members of human society. That's fine, but still it is a karmic way of life. It's not absolute truth.

In this section Dōgen is discussing the reality that we can see things only based on our karmic consciousness. Our view is limited and conditioned. We don't know how hungry ghosts see the water; we don't even know whether hungry ghosts exist. This is one perspective. Dōgen tries to go beyond. How can we be released from this karmic view?

> Hungry ghosts see water as raging flames or as pus and blood. Dragons and fish see it as a palace or a tower, or as the seven treasures or the *mani* gem. [Others] see it as woods and walls, or as the Dharma nature of immaculate liberation, or as the true human body, or as the physical form and mental nature.

When we refer to things we see as "Dharma nature," "immaculate liberation," or "true human body," these are Zen expressions based on the way we view and understand things in the Zen Buddhist tradition. The full expression behind the "true human body" is "the entire ten-direction world is the true human body." "The ten-direction world" means east, west, south, north, between each of them, and up and down. The entire universe is the "true human body." In Buddhism, we view things using the concepts such as "physical form" and "mental nature." These are all views whether they are right or wrong, useful or not useful.

> Humans see these as water. And these [different ways of seeing] are the conditions under which [water] is killed or given life.

This expression "conditions under which water is killed or given life" is a little difficult. Perhaps it should be "water is affirmed as water and negated as not water." According to Menzan and some other commentators, it means there are many different ways of viewing water, and these ways are as different from each other as killing is different from giving life. There is an expression regarding Mañjuśrī's wisdom sword: "the sword which kills or gives life." I believe that here "killing" means to negate everything completely to show emptiness. "Giving birth" means affirming everything as abiding at its Dharma position. In this case "killing" is not so different from "giving life."

## QUESTIONING OUR VIEWS

> (20) Given that what different types of beings see is different, we should have some doubts about this.

Although "doubts" is a standard translation, I think "questions" would be better. We need to get closer to clearly see and investigate the thing or person; Dōgen is recommending taking a closer look at our karmic views.

*Is it that there are various ways of seeing one object?*

If so, that would mean that there is one fixed object and different beings see it from different perspectives. How can we know that, if our view is simply one of the conditioned views? The question here is whether our ideas exist outside of our minds, in reality. Is there one thing that different beings view in different ways, for example, water viewed as water, a jeweled necklace, or blood? Or is water really several different things? This is a good question, I think. Dōgen is good at asking questions. He asks us to find the answers.

*Or is it that we have mistaken various images for one object?*

Our views are various, but there is one object. Is this true or not? How can we know there's only one thing? If our view is only karmic and limited, how can we know there is one thing called water?

Dōgen is talking not only about water here but about everything, including this being Shohaku. Whether such a being is called Shohaku or human or Buddhist priest or deluded or enlightened—do any of these things really exist? It's a good question, and we don't know how to respond. To know that we don't know is an important wisdom. We should remember the example of Socrates: "I know that I know nothing."

Dōgen's purpose here is to confuse us, to deconstruct our ready-made, fixed views. He's not trying to offer another fixed view; he is trying to destroy our views, our clinging to our conditioned narrow views. That's how we become released from our fixed perspective. Still we can say this is merely Dōgen's view. He doesn't say his view is absolutely true. His view is his view; that is the only view he could see. But it is not necessarily true. That is his point. Nāgārjuna is like this too. Both negate fixed ideas while affirming that these ideas are the way we see. This process of simultaneous negation and assertion is how we are liberated from grasping our views as the right way and not listening to other perspectives.

At the peak of our concentrated effort on this, we should concentrate still more. Therefore, our practice and verification, our pursuit of the way, must also be not merely of one or two kinds, and the ultimate realm must also have a thousand types and ten thousand kinds.

We usually practice with the goal of becoming buddha, and the assumption that all buddhas are the same. But Dōgen says our practices are different; even after we become buddhas we are different. In Mahāyāna Buddhism there are many different buddhas, different depending on their vows, and each buddha land has its own characteristics. What he is saying is true within Mahāyāna Buddhism. We cannot say there is one fixed way of true practice; we cannot say ours is the only true practice.

## LIBERATION OF WATER

(21) If we reflect further on the real import of this [question], although we say there is water of the various types, it would seem there is no original water, no water of various types.

Which is real: the water before being perceived by beings, or the various perceptions of water by various beings? Is there an original water that is the true thing, while our views are illusory? How can we know whether there is such a fixed, original water? How can we go beyond our perceptions and see it? And if there is no original water, then what?

This is the same as the question of whether we can see the true face of Mount Lu from our point of view within the mountains. Su Shi says it is not possible. Hongzhi and Dōgen said the point isn't whether we can see it or not; the mountains are simply our body, and we live together with all beings in them.

Nevertheless, the various waters in accordance with the types [of beings] do not depend on the mind, do not depend on the body

[of these beings]; they do not arise from [different types of] karma;
they are not dependent on self; they are not dependent on other.

Here Dōgen is saying something different, even opposite from what
he said before. Depending on the mind and body means depending on
our karmic conditions. The various waters are seen differently depending upon our karmic views, and also on the situation of self and others;
that is what he said previously. Here he clearly negates it, saying the
waters are not dependent on our views.

They are liberated dependent on water.

Dōgen says that water is liberated, any kind of viewed water is liberated, even our view of water is liberated.

"Liberated" is a translation of the Zen expression *tōdatsu*, which was
used before in this text with *genjō* (manifestation). As a Zen expression this means "freely penetrating," "going through any barriers," and
"totally liberated." Here it means water is simply water, completely free
of its relationship with observers and any other causes and conditions.
"Dependent on water" means that water depends only on itself, nothing else. Water is simply being water, and this is its complete liberation.
Not only water but everything is liberated from everything.

In the example of a baby, of course a baby is a baby, but also a baby is
not a baby because it has a life power that negates babyhood. That's how
a baby becomes a child. Within babyhood there is some energy that is
free from being a baby. That's why a baby cannot be a baby forever. At
this moment a baby is one hundred percent a baby, but this hundred-
percent baby is liberated from babyhood. And a buddha is liberated
from buddhahood. The power of things to negate themselves is what
enables change.

This is Dōgen's expression of emptiness, with no fixed and permanent self-nature. Everything is completely interdependent origination;
nothing is fixed. This is the reality of all beings according to Dōgen.
Everything dwells in its Dharma position at this moment. But even

though we dwell in this Dharma position, at the same time we are liberated from this position. We cannot stay here; in the next moment we go somewhere else. This constant flowing, according to Dōgen, is the reality of our life.

We are deluded human beings and yet we are not deluded human beings; a buddha is not a buddha. Everything is free; everything is liberated from itself. It is an incredible view. It allows us to release our fixed concept of ourselves, our idea of human life, our point of view, and our system of values.

> Therefore, water is not [the water of] earth, water, fire, wind, space, or consciousness; it is not blue, yellow, red, white, or black; it is not form, sound, smell, taste, touch, or idea.

*Idea*, the last in this list of the six sense-objects, means "object of mind."

> Nevertheless, the waters of earth, water, fire, wind, space, and the rest have been spontaneously appearing as such.

Water is appearing simply as water and yet water is completely liberated. Although water is completely liberated, water is appearing one hundred percent as water.

"Appearing" in the last sentence is a translation of *genjō* in *Genjōkōan*. Both sides of being—manifestation (*genjō*) and liberation (*tōdatsu*)—are constantly at rest and constantly walking. This is the true virtue of the mountain and water.

In the very beginning of *Shōbōgenzō* "Zenki, "Total Function," written three years after "Sansuikyō," Dōgen writes,

> The great Way of all buddhas, when it is completely penetrated, is liberation and is manifestation. Liberation means that life liberates itself from life and also death liberates

itself from death. Therefore, there is leaving life-and-death, there is entering life-and-death; both are the great Way that is completely penetrated. There is abandoning life-and-death; there is crossing over life-and-death; both are the great Way that is completely penetrated. Manifestation is life; life is manifestation. At the time of the manifestation, there is nothing but the total manifestation of life; there is nothing but the total manifestation of death.

Dōgen always sees the reality of all beings from the two sides of liberation (tōdatsu) and manifestation (genjō) at once. In *Shōbōgenzō* "Kenbutsu" ("Seeing Buddha") he says, "Seeing all forms (*shosō*) and no-form (*hisō*) is seeing Tathāgata."[97]

## LIBERATION OF ALL THINGS IS LIKE THIS

(22) This being the case, it becomes difficult to explain by what and of what the present land and palace are made. To say that they rest on the wheel of space and the wheel of wind is true neither for oneself nor for others; it is just speculating on the basis of the suppositions of an inferior view and is said only out of fear that, without such a resting place, they could not abide.

The first sentence refers to asking, who created the land, water, palace, and so on, and also what are these creations? In Buddhism, we don't talk about an original creator. We try to see the world just as we see and experience it.

The wheel of space and the wheel of wind are the foundations of this world, according to the cosmology of Buddhism in *Abhidharmakośa*.[98] We want a safe, steady, fixed foundation; otherwise we feel unsafe. Dōgen says that this idea is a fiction. Everything is moving, everything is liberated, nothing is fixed. When we read this teaching it frightens us. I was frightened when I read the *Heart Sūtra*. No eyes, no ears, no nose, no tongue, nothing: what is this? Dōgen and the *Heart Sūtra* are saying nothing is fixed, and this is liberation. But we are afraid of this kind of liberation. We want to have a secure foundation.

(23) The Buddha has said, "All things are ultimately liberated; they have no abode."

According to commentaries, this is a quote from *Daihōshakukyō* (*Mahāratnakūṭa Sūtra*), but I cannot find exactly the same sentence. There are many similar statements in the prajñāpāramitā sūtras. They mean that everything is coming and going—arising, staying for a while, changing, and disappearing. Everything is free from self-nature. The baby is liberated from babyhood, buddhas are liberated from buddha-hood, and everything is walking everywhere within the mountains and waters. And mountains and waters are also walking without any resting place. This is the reality of impermanence.

(24) We should realize that, although they are liberated, without any bonds, all things are abiding in [their own particular] state.

Again he uses liberation (tōdatsu) and manifestation (genjō) together. The expression "their own particular state" is the same expression Dōgen uses in "Genjōkōan": "Firewood dwells in the Dharma position of firewood."

Although a baby is not fixed as a baby, it is dwelling in the Dharma position of a baby at this moment. Everything is always changing, but still, at this moment, a baby is completely a baby. A child is a child; a middle-aged person looks middle-aged and an aged person like I am seems like an aged person. We have to live in our Dharma position here and now; we have to practice in the same way that a baby practices as a baby.

Practice is the manifestation of our life force at this moment. Through this practice right now, we negate this stage, and this practice allows us to grow and go to the next stage. We are completely right now, right here, and we take care of this moment. My responsibility here and now is to write about Dōgen's "Sansuikyō" in English. It is very difficult and I don't always like it, but I try. By doing this I discover and experience new things, which allows me to grow.

What we do is completely this moment, as a function of this Dharma position. This allows us to "go somewhere else." That is life force. Simply walking, moving, or changing, as Uchiyama Rōshi says, is half of the true reality. Impermanence is half of reality. The other side is that everything is always abiding peacefully in its Dharma position where nothing arises and nothing changes. Everything is there at this moment. It is a strange thing; that is why it is called "wondrous Dharma." We cannot grasp it by thinking, so we try not to grasp. We open our hand and trust everything in this moment, in this body/ mind. That is our practice in zazen.

In the *Heart Sūtra* these two sides are expressed as "Form is emptiness and emptiness is form." There is nothing called "form"; that is the meaning of "emptiness." But emptiness is nothing other than form, this form as Shohaku at this moment. Everything is liberated from itself and yet everything manifests itself just as it is. So we have to take care of this Dharma position.

> However, when humans look at water, they have the one way that sees it only as flowing without rest.

This is the common view for human beings; water flowing in a stream is the common image of water.

> This "flow" takes many forms, of which the human view is but one.

Our idea that water flows from higher to lower places is only one way of viewing the movement of water. There are many other ways that water moves.

> [Water] flows over the earth; it flows across the sky.

"[Water] flows over the earth" is what we see commonly. Water flows from high mountains to lower places through rivers, lakes, ponds, waterfalls, and wetlands, changing its conditions: snow meltwater, pure, clear spring water, muddy stream water, stagnant swamp water, and so forth. Water flows even within plants, animals, and humans. Then finally it flows into the ocean.

"It flows across the sky" as different kinds of clouds that influence our lives as weather. Fog and mist also float in the air.

> It flows up; it flows down. [Water] flows around bends and into deep abysses. It mounts up to form clouds; it descends to form pools.

Evaporated water from the ocean becomes clouds. When the clouds hit high mountains, the evaporated water goes higher up. When it reaches a certain height, it cools and falls as rain or snow. On the earth it then starts another journey toward the ocean. Water circles ceaselessly, transforming its shape in numberless ways.

> (25) The *Wen Tzu* says, "The tao of water, ascending to heaven, becomes rain and dew, descending to earth, becomes rivers and streams."

*Wen Tzu* is a Chinese classic. For us today the statement is common sense, but a thousand years ago it might have been an unusual view.

> (26) Such is said even in the secular world; it would be shameful indeed if those who call themselves descendants of the buddhas and ancestors were more stupid than the secular.

In modern times lay people are better educated and have a greater range of knowledge than Buddhist priests. In Dōgen's time, Buddhist monks were the educated; only monks and aristocrats could read and write.

[This passage] says that although the way of water is unknown to water, water actually functions [as water]; although the way of water is not unknown to water, water actually functions [as water].

Whether knowing or not knowing, water is simply water and functions as such. Zen Master Nanquan said, "The Way is not concerned with knowing or not knowing."[99] Our actual function, activity, and practice is more important than whether we know it or not. This is a critical point in Dōgen's teaching.

## PRACTICE-BUDDHA: WATER PERMEATES EVERYWHERE

Dōgen often uses the expression *gyō-butsu*. *Gyō* means "practice," "action," or "activity." *Butsu* means "buddha." One fascicle of *Shōbōgenzō*, for instance, is titled "Gyōbutsu-Igi." *Igi* means "dignified forms," "conduct," or "decorum": the actions of buddhas. The common reading of this phrase is "practicing Buddha's dignified decorum." We should practice the way all the buddhas did. But Dōgen reads this *gyō-butsu* as one word: *gyōbutsu*, or "practice-buddha." Here again he ignored Chinese grammar to change the meaning of a word or phrase. He uses this *gyōbutsu* as the name of a buddha; his interpretation of the phrase "Gyōbutsu-Igi" is "dignified form of Practice Buddha." That is how he defines our daily activity in the zendō, Dharma hall, and other places. Each form is a dignified form of Gyōbutsu Buddha. In a sense, Dōgen creates the fourth body of Buddha: dharmakāya, saṃbhogakāya, nirmāṇakāya, and practice-kāya. This is a unique way of thinking. It considers our every action a manifestation of the Buddhadharma.

The biography of Śākyamuni Buddha says that when Buddha was born he stood up, walked seven steps in the four directions, and in each step a lotus flower bloomed. Gyōbutsu, Practice Buddha, is like that. When we do things as a practice or form of Gyōbutsu, the lotus flower, the Dharma flower, blooms in each step. According to Dōgen that is the meaning of our formal practice. We are ordinary human beings, and yet our wholehearted practice following the Buddha's teachings is Buddha.

What he is saying here is that to know or to not know is not most important. To do, to practice, to work is important. In "Genjōkōan," Dōgen writes, "When buddhas are truly buddhas they don't need to perceive they are buddhas; however they are enlightened buddhas and they continue actualizing buddha."[100]

> (27) "Ascending to heaven, it becomes rain and dew." We should realize that water climbs to the very highest heavens in the highest quarters and becomes rain and dew. Rain and dew is of various kinds, in accordance with the various worlds.

"Various worlds" here means the conditions, situations, involvements, or circumstances of each being. We become like heavenly beings, hungry ghosts, fishes, or human beings, just as the form of water varies between the tropics and the poles. The forms and conditions vary, but water goes everywhere. Here it seems that Dōgen is talking not simply about $H_2O$ but also hosshō-sui, the water of Dharma nature that permeates everywhere in the triple world (the world of desire, material, and nonmaterial) and the ten realms (hell, hungry ghost, animal, fighting spirit, human, heavenly being, śrāvaka, pratyekabuddha, bodhisattva, and buddha).

> To say that there are places to which water does not reach is the teaching of the hīnayāna śrāvaka or the false teaching of the non-Buddhist.

Within the Mahāyāna Buddhist community, śrāvakas and pratyekabuddhas are considered to be hīnayāna, smaller vehicle. However, no Buddhist groups think of themselves as hīnayāna. We don't use this word anymore to refer to groups or schools of Buddhism. And we cannot say non-Buddhist teachings are mistaken or people who follow other ways are wrong. Today we live with people from other Buddhist traditions and other religions as our neighbors. We should eliminate notions based on discrimination against other spiritual traditions, within or without Buddhism. Dōgen's statement here is simply a vigorous denial that there is any place that water (in all its meanings) does not reach.

In *Abhidharmakośa*, it is said that there are some places water does not reach, but those places are not relevant here. Dōgen says the water of Dharma nature penetrates all realms.

> Water extends into flames; it extends into thought, reasoning, and discrimination; it extends into awareness and the buddha nature.

Here Dōgen is not talking about water in nature but water as buddha nature, which is the same as Dharma nature. Thought, reasoning, and discrimination are how our minds function. "Awareness" is a translation of *kakuchi*, which means "awareness" or "awakening." We conditioned human beings see in a different way from the way awakened beings see. Nevertheless, in our discriminating way of thinking, water is there; in Buddha's awakening, water is there. Even in buddha nature water is there, because water is buddha nature, as all things are.

> (28) "Descending to earth, it becomes rivers and streams." We should realize that, when water descends to earth, it becomes rivers and streams, and that the essence of rivers and streams becomes sages.

As Dōgen says in "Genjōkōan," the wind of the Buddha's family transforms water into cream. It is the water that becomes sages, not individual people. It is buddha nature that becomes a sage, even though the sage looks like a person.

> The foolish common folk think that water is always in rivers, streams, and seas, but this is not so: [water] makes rivers and seas within water.

Common sense tells us that water is in a river, ocean, lake, or bowl, and that it comes out when we tip the bowl. Dōgen says that wherever water goes, that place becomes a river; where water stays becomes a lake; where water becomes large and rests becomes an ocean. There is no ocean, river, or lake before the movement of water. Water is first; names follow. Each of these conditions is simply one Dharma position of this movement of water.

> Therefore, water is in places that are not rivers and seas; it is just that, when water descends to earth, it works as rivers and seas.

This is the same as our life force: it works in certain ways. To be a writer is not my essence. It is simply a part within the stream of my life force. As a Dharma position at this moment I can be a writer, a lecturer, an abbot, a customer, a client, and so on. I am a teacher only when I am teaching. When I am at home with my family I am not a teacher. If I try to teach they become angry and don't listen, so I try not to teach and I don't say much about Dōgen. To be a Buddhist priest is only one condition of the water flowing, the water of my life.

Often we make a certain self-image and define ourselves: I am a teacher; I am a Buddhist priest; I am a husband; I am a father. We invent an identity with these concepts. The forms of water seem more real to us than its movement. This is what Nāgārjuna called "phenomenal mind construction." The movement of water is the real thing. But the names of the condition of the moment—a river, a lake, an ocean, rain, dew; a teacher, a father, a student—are the concepts fixed in our mind. There are so many different conditions of water, but we grasp the names of each as if they were real. What actually is working there is water, is life force.

## BUDDHA LAND IS EVERYWHERE

> (29) Moreover, we should not study that, when water has become rivers and seas, there is then no world and no buddha land [within water]: incalculable buddha lands are realized even within a single drop of water.

The example Dōgen used in "Genjōkōan" is dew: this tiny being that appears and stays less than a second and disappears. But within this tiny drop of dew, boundless moonlight, eternity, is completely reflected. This reflection of the boundless in a tiny, impermanent drop of water is the appearance of the buddha land.[101]

> Consequently, it is not that water exists within the buddha land, nor that the buddha land exists within water: the existence of water has nothing whatever to do with the three times or the Dharma realm.

The water Dōgen is talking about is not conditioned. In each moment water is conditioned, but flowing water is not conditioned and has "nothing to do with the three times." "Three times" means past, present, and future. "Dharma realm" here means every place within time and space. That is, the flowing movement of water is not limited to a certain time or place. Each and every moment is where water exists; each and every moment is where the buddha land is created.

This water contains both form and emptiness. It is not on the side of emptiness and it is not on the side of form. Rather, in the same way as Dōgen says that mountains are both constantly at rest and constantly walking, form and emptiness are two virtues of the water. We cannot say that water exists within the buddha land because water is itself the buddha land.

> Nevertheless, though it is like this, it is the kōan of the actualization of water.

"Actualization" is a translation of *genjō*. This is the Genjōkōan of water. From the beginningless past to the endless future, moment by moment, water dwells in each Dharma position in each moment and creates the Dharma world, or buddha land. Dōgen discusses this in "Genjōkōan": in each moment of change or movement, the reality of all beings is manifested. "Sansuikyō" is like a commentary on "Genjōkōan," using mountains and waters as examples of genjō and kōan. Genjō is right now, at this present moment. Kōan is beyond time and space; together they invoke timeless reality functioning here and now. The reality of our life is the intersection of the present moment and eternity.

## "GENJŌKŌAN": PRESENT BECOMING PRESENT, WHAT WE HAVE TO DO

> (30) Wherever the buddhas and ancestors are, water is always there; wherever water is, there the buddhas and ancestors always appear.

"Appear" is another translation of *genjō*. In the first sentence of "Sansuikyō"—"these mountains and waters of this present are the expression of the old buddhas"—"expression" is also *genjō*, but I think it's not the best translation. *Genjō* is one of the key words in Dōgen's teachings, and "expression" doesn't convey its full power. In fact, Dōgen used an alternative Chinese character (公按), so the meaning is a little different, even though the pronunciation is the same as the usual characters (公案).

*Gen* (現) means "appear" when used as a verb; as an adjective it means "present." Other possible meanings are "real" or "true"; "actual" is best. *Jō* (成) means "to become," "to accomplish," "to achieve," or "to complete." Moment by moment, things become something. As Buddha said in *Suttanipāta,* our perception and experience of becoming and disintegration (arising and ceasing) is the basis for our interpretation of the world. *Genjōkōan* refers to the process of becoming and disintegration/disappearance—the way things become something and change again, moment by moment. *Genjō* means this process happening at this moment, the actual reality of this moment. Uchiyama Rōshi paraphrased *gen-jo* as "the present moment becoming the present moment."

*Kōan* is the same expression as in kōan stories. This word is used in China to mean a public document in a government office. In ancient China all government documents were issued in the name of the emperor and had absolute power and authority. No one could question them or complain. From this meaning the word evolved to mean the absolute truth expressed by Chinese Zen masters. That is one of the meanings of *kōan* in Zen literature—the expression of absolute reality with absolute authority. We have to study and master this teaching, and try to live based on it.

For kōan, Dōgen used (公按) instead of the usual Chinese character (公案). The usual character for *an* (案) means "paper" or "desk." Within 案, 木 means "wood" and 安 means "to place," so the combination means to put something on something made of wood: a desk, or a document placed on the desk. And it also means "to think"—what we do at a desk. So the usual *an* has these three meanings. However, in the character Dōgen used for *an* (按), the left side (手) means "hand" and the right (安), "to place hand on something." This *an* has the connotation of doing something to solve a problem, such as healing in *anma*, massage.

Dōgen's disciple Senne, who wrote the first commentary on *Shōbō-genzō*, interpreted *kōan* with this kanji: 公按. According to Senne, kōan means a public work: the way public officers should work. This is one meaning of kōan in Dōgen's writing. Not simply an absolute truth or authority but something we have to do using our body to help others or improve a situation. In this case kōan is also a function. Putting the characters together, *Genjōkōan* is a manifestation of universal, eternal reality at this moment within time, space, and function, in oneness with all beings.[102]

> Therefore, the buddhas and ancestors have always taken up water as their own body and mind, their own thinking.

This is about the genjō (manifestation) of buddhas and ancestors within our practice at this moment. Waters are the bodies of all buddhas and ancestors. When buddhas and ancestors or bodhisattvas think, they think based on this water, which is Dharma nature, instead of thinking based on preferences caused by karmic consciousness. In other words, bodhisattvas use their karmic consciousness as water of Dharma nature. This means they use their karmic consciousness as a manifestation of eternal reality.

## "Up and Down" of the Buddha Way

> (31) In this way, then, [the idea] that water does not climb up is to be found in neither Buddhist nor non-Buddhist writings. The way of water penetrates everywhere, above and below, vertically and horizontally.

Right before the Genzō-e retreat in 2002, I read in an online Japanese newspaper that a Japanese scientist found there is five times as much water below the earth's surface as in the ocean. We cannot imagine water in such a hot place, stored inside the earth. We don't know the conditions of that water. The water we see in the ocean is just a tiny part of the entire water of our planet. Earth is sometimes called a planet of water, and up to seventy percent of the human body is water. The metaphor of water as buddha nature is very appropriate. In a sense, living beings are various embodiments of water.

> Still, in the sūtras it is said that fire and wind go up, while earth and water go down.

Fire, earth, wind, and water are called the four great elements. These are not actual fire, earth, wind, and water but the elements comprising everything. For example, in our body, heat is the fire; movement is the wind; bones and fingernails are the earth; and blood and other body fluids are the water.

A sūtra says that fire and wind elements ascend while earth and water elements descend.[103] Dōgen found that there is a contradiction between what is said in the sūtra and what he says, so he tried to make an interpretation:

> But this "up and down" bears some study—the study of the up and down of the way of the buddha.

As mentioned before, in Mahāyāna Buddhism, "going up" is studying and practicing Dharma for oneself, and "going down" is helping others. This "up" and "down" do not necessarily refer to altitude on the Earth nor to the heaven and hell of Buddhist cosmology.

> [In the way of the buddha], where earth and water go is considered "down"; but "down" here does not mean some place to which earth and water go.

In other words, if water rises to the heavens or sky, the sky is "down." When we talk about up and down or this way or that, within our mind we are making the origin and the coordinate axes of a graph. Without this framework, there is no way to judge up or down. If we are to measure or decide where something locates and moves, there must be a fixed origin for reference. Dōgen asks us to question whether such a fixed origin exists.

The idea that there is some immovable, absolute origin from which to measure things, not only in space but also in value, is a mental construction. We often make a value judgment based on a certain origin, with one axis plotting my desires or preferences and the other, my responsibilities or obligations. "This is something I want to do and I should do." "This is something I want to do and yet I should not do." "This is something I don't want to do but I should do." "This is something I don't want to do and I should not do." We categorize things based on our karmically fixed system of values, desires, preferences, obligations, responsibilities, possibilities, capabilities, and so on. The problem is that the origin also changes. What I wanted to do in my twenties is not interesting at all in my sixties.

Dōgen is saying that there is no fixed origin and thus no way to measure the movement of water. The water exists prior to any attempt to grasp it with our intellect. We cannot fit this timeless, spaceless movement within our thinking. It is the opposite: our thought is part of this movement. Naturally we cannot contain this entire movement within our thought. The impossibility is obvious, but we try anyway. That is a basic delusion.

What we have to see is that we cannot evaluate life using a starting point and measuring standard that are part of life. We don't need to eliminate our systems of measurement, but we need to know they are only part of the universal flow of water, which cannot be contained within our system of values. That is what Buddha, Nāgārjuna, Linji, and Dōgen are saying. We need to be free from our attachments to our measurements and views. This is how we can avoid the poisonous contact between the self and the myriad dharmas. This spaciousness makes our life more peaceful, harmonious, compassionate, and flexible.

> Where fire and wind go is "up."

Actually everywhere is up and everywhere is down. There is no origin and no viewer to observe this movement. Everywhere is connected with everywhere as one seamless space—that's all we can say.

> While the Dharma realm has no necessary connection with up and down or the four directions, simply on the basis of the function of the four, five, or six elements, we provisionally set up a Dharma realm with directions.

The four elements are fire, earth, wind, and water. The five elements add space. The six include consciousness. The four elements were used since early Indian Buddhism. Space or emptiness was added by Mahāyāna Buddhism, and consciousness by Vajrayāna Buddhism.

Based on the movement of these elements, we invent an origin and axes and then try to gauge location, quality, and value. Dōgen points out that every such judgment is tentative.

> It is not that the "heaven of nonconception" is above and the "*Avīci* hell" is below: *Avīci* is the entire Dharma realm; the heaven of non-conception is the entire Dharma realm.

Once again, the three worlds are desire, material or form, and no form. The world of desire is where we live. The other worlds are realms of meditation, or samādhi. The highest layer of these samādhis is called the "heaven of nonconception" (*musō-ten*). This is a realm of samādhi that Śākyamuni Buddha achieved when he studied with his Indian meditation teacher Ārāḷa Kālāma, right after he left his father's palace.

Avīci is the lowest place in Indian Buddhist cosmology, the most painful part of hell. Here Dōgen says the heaven of no-conception is not a higher place and Avīci hell is not a lower; both are the entire Dharma realm. Each condition of our lives within the six realms where we are transmigrating is the entire Dharma realm. It seems to me that Dōgen doesn't really believe the theory of transmigration within the six realms from past to present to next life in the way we commonly understand. I think he is saying that the six realms exist right now, within our life. We are always transmigrating within them. Our condition at this moment is the entire Dharma realm. This is the same as when he says in "Genjōkōan" that both big birds and small birds are flying in the entire sky.

## LIBERATING OUR STUDY

> (32) Nevertheless, when dragons and fish see water as a palace, just as when humans see palaces, they do not view it as flowing.

For dragons and fish, the water is their palace, and they don't think their dwelling is flowing, just as we don't think our houses move.

And, if some onlooker were to explain to them that their palace was flowing water, they would surely be just as amazed as we are now to hear it said that mountains flow. Still, there would undoubtedly be some [dragons and fish] who would accept such an explanation of the railings, stairs, and columns of palaces and pavilions.

Dōgen is saying to his students that we should see the mountains are walking when we are taught by an onlooker like himself. However, this is extremely difficult, because we are bound to our karmic views. Our practice of letting go of thought helps us release our fixed views and become a little more flexible.

We should calmly consider, over and over, the reason for this.

By thoroughly thinking and calmly considering, we are liberated from ourselves. This study of Dōgen's writing resembles kōan practice with a Rinzai teacher; whatever you say, she negates. So we have to try again and again until we tire of thinking and give up. Dōgen's method is to become free from our habitual way of thinking by thoroughly thinking. In Zen this is called "taking the wedge out by using the wedge." When we split wood we hit a wedge. Sometimes this wedge can neither come out nor go farther into the wood. So we use another wedge to widen the space; then we can remove the first wedge. Similarly, we use our thinking to liberate ourselves from our thinking.

If our study is not liberated from these confines, we have not freed ourselves from the body and mind of the commoner, we have not fully comprehended the land of the buddhas and ancestors, we have not fully comprehended the land of the commoner, we have not fully comprehended the palace of the commoner.

Until we are liberated (tōdatsu) from the fixed thinking created by our karma, we don't really see the reality of our lives. We must break free of the prison we built with blocks of concepts and knowledge.

## The Water of the Buddha Way

(33) Although humans have deeply understood what is in seas and rivers as water, just what kind of thing dragons, fish, and other beings understand and use as water we do not yet know. Do not foolishly assume that all kinds of beings must use as water what we understand as water.

We know the liquid of oceans, rivers, lakes, wells, and so on is water: $H_2O$. We know it is one of the essential elements of our lives. We know how to use it. We have extensive knowledge of water. Yet Dōgen requests us to open our hands, hearts, and minds, to free ourselves from clinging to our conditioned knowledge, and not to assume that our views are true for all beings. In "Genjōkōan" he says:

> Within the dusty world and beyond, there are innumerable aspects and characteristics; we only see or grasp as far as the power of our eye of study and practice can see. When we listen to the reality of myriad things, we must know that there are inexhaustible charactaristics in both ocean and mountains, and there are many other worlds in the four directions. This is true not only in the external world but also right under our feet or within a single drop of water.[104]

(34) When those who study Buddhism seek to learn about water, they should not stick to [the water of] humans; they should go on to study the water of the way of the buddhas. We should study how we see the water used by the buddhas and ancestors.

Dōgen says there are many different views and virtues of water. For human beings water is water, of course. For heavenly beings water is like a jeweled necklace, for hungry ghosts water is pus and blood, and for dragons and fish water is their dwelling. Now he says all these views are still based on the human concept of water, and he asks us to study the buddhas' water.

The *Lotus Sūtra* says that all buddhas appear in this world for only one reason: to show us the true reality of all beings and allow us to live in accordance with that reality. This means we don't know the true reality of all beings; we know only the forms (nāmarūpa) seen by human eyes. We see only the human water. We use that human water as water, but for buddhas and ancestors it is something else. This is what Dōgen has been discussing: "What is the reality of water?"

Dōgen is saying that we should see water as a true reality of all beings. This means to see water just as it is. Then we need to ask if there is such a thing as "water as it is" before being seen by beings. Even if there is "water as it is," how can we see it? How can we make certain that what we see is the true reality of water, instead of another, new nāmarūpa? When we reach this point, all we can do is open the hand of thought and just sit.

We see water as an object of our desire. Of course we need water to drink when we are thirsty. Water is the majority of our body, so without it we cannot live; we need water to become ourselves. We also use water beyond our needs, however. As a result we pollute it, and because of this pollution many living beings die. This pollution also harms us. This happens because we see water only as an object of our desire. Fulfilling our desires can hurt us.

> We should study whether within the rooms of the buddhas and ancestors there is or is not water.

We see water as the object of our perception, and at the same time, we see that our perception is not necessarily the reality of water. That is how genjō (manifestation) and tōdatsu (liberation) work within our practice in our daily lives.

To see the true reality of all beings means that we live together with all beings; we feel connected with all beings. When we don't see this, we kill part of this network of interdependent origination; actually then we are killing ourselves. Keeping this entire network as healthy as possible is one of the most important issues in this century. How can we see water "as it is" or as the buddhas see it? How can we live together with water? If we apply Dōgen's teaching here, we can study the mountains and waters from the buddhas' point of view, and we can study how we use our own lives. This is a very important point of our practice, not only as Buddhists or Zen practitioners but simply as human beings.

We have to accept the current situation. And we need to examine how we have been harming the planet. Without acceptance and investigation, we can't work with it. Accepting doesn't mean we say, "It's okay. Nothing is wrong." Through our hard work to make our lives materially rich and convenient, we have been destroying nature. And by destroying nature we are destroying ourselves.

Until about 1960, when I became a teenager, we were taught that this world was advancing by the development of scientific knowledge and technology. In the part of Japan where I grew up especially, rice paddies, woods, and even mountains were destroyed and rivers were polluted to build houses, factories, highways, railways, and so forth. We thought that such materialistic development was the true development of human civilization. That was how we had been taught and how we acted. But now we know that material development doesn't really make our lives healthy, enjoyable, and peaceful. So we need to change the direction of our civilization. To do so, we need to be free from anthropocentrism, to learn to view things beyond our human self-centeredness. I think that is what Dōgen means by buddhas' views. To accept where we are is important. Otherwise, we will just be in denial while conditions worsen.

Traditional Buddhist teachings do not give us specific instructions for changing the direction of human civilization. We need to use all our available spiritual wisdom, scientific knowledge, and technology to find a way to change our direction. Still, we might learn something from Dōgen's teaching on how to purify our body, mind, and entire life. Within the collection of *Shōbōgenzō*, there are two fascicles—"Senmen" or "Washing Face," and "Senjō" or "Washing and Purifying"—in which Dōgen gives instruction on how to wash our face, brush our teeth, and use the toilet. Dōgen says we should wash our face every morning right after waking up, in a certain way. He prescribes forms and procedures of washing in detail. In some traditional monasteries, parts of the procedure are still maintained. They help the monks stay aware of purifying their lives.

Still, purification is not necessarily some kind of mysterious, spiritual ceremony but should be our day-to-day way of life. When we make a mess, we just clean up. That is purification. That is what we need to do with our whole civilization.

# Mountains and Waters Are Dwelling Places for Sages

## THE MOUNTAIN WAY OF LIFE

> (35) From the distant past to the distant present, mountains have been the dwelling place of the great sages.

THE PHRASE "distant past to the distant present" is a translation of *chō ko chō kon* (超古超今). *Ko* is the *ko* in *kobutsu* or "old buddhas"; it means "old" or "ancient." *Kon* is as in *nikon*, "the present." *Chō* means "to transcend," "to go beyond"; the expression "distant past to the distant present" is meant to convey going beyond the past and present. Dōgen is talking here about transcending the distinction between this present moment and the eternal buddha, between this moment and eternity. These two become one at this moment; that is *Genjōkōan*. This intersection of the present moment and eternity is where all buddhas and ancestors dwell. This is the mountains and waters.

> Wise men and sages have all made the mountains their own chambers, their own body and mind.

For buddhas and ancestors, mountains are their dwellings and also their own bodies and minds. The sages *are* the mountains.

And through these wise men and sages the mountains have appeared.

"Appeared" is *genjō* again, but "appeared" doesn't adequately convey the meaning. Genjō is eternal truth manifested at this moment in concrete forms. Buddhas and ancestors have been dwelling within the mountains and manifesting the true reality of the mountains through their practice. By saying "the mountains have appeared," Dōgen is talking about the way people actualize the virtues of mountains and waters through their lives.

> However many great sages and wise men we suppose have assembled in the mountains, ever since they entered the mountains no one has met a single one of them. There is only the expression of the mountain way of life; not a single trace of their having entered remains.

People disappear and become the mountain; that is the background of this sentence. In the early history of Zen Buddhism, all well-known Chinese Zen masters established their own monasteries in the mountains. Masters like Guishan (in Japanese, Isan) or Dongshan are known by the name of the mountains where they dwelled. But Dōgen is saying more here than that. Once those sages and buddhas enter the mountains they disappear by becoming one with the mountains—and "the mountains" refers to the entire network of interdependent origination. Those masters completely become knots in Indra's net. Then the knots disappear, the masters disappear, and only the net remains. This is the meaning of becoming the mountain.

"Trace" is a translation of the expression *shōseki*. Shōseki is like a footprint. When we see the footprint we know that someone walked on this path. That is the meaning of "trace" here. When there is a particular style (*igi*) of footprint, it is the trace of a person who walked in that style. Dōgen talks about sages who did not leave any such trace;

they had so completely entered the mountains that they became completely one with the mountains. Their footprints are nothing other than the mountains themselves.

When Dōgen says, "Not a single trace of their having entered remained," he also refers to what Dongshan said about the way of birds. Migratory birds know where they are going every year, but humans can't see their path. Although we don't see their flyway, the birds know it, even though the traces don't last. The masters are like birds: with no trace we can see, nonetheless the birds can find the path. If we love the mountain's way of life, even without footprints, still we see the traces of the masters' way of life.

When the Zen masters who entered the mountains became the mountains, their self-centered way of life and karmic consciousness disappeared as they merged with the mountains. Only a traceless trace of their mountain way of life remains.

"Mountain way of life," being one with buddhas, is nothing abstract but simply daily activities, like a household. A buddha carries water and collects firewood. A buddha prepares meals; a buddha receives the meals with ōryōki; a buddha washes the ōryōki bowls—that is the mountain style of life. These are activities of Gyōbutsu, Practice Buddha.

In *Chiji Shingi, Pure Standards for the Temple Administrators*, Dōgen says, "After all, not to sell cheaply or debase the worth of the ordinary tea and rice of the Buddha ancestors' house is exactly the mind of the Way."[105]

> The "crown and eyes" [of the mountains] are completely different when we are in the world gazing off at the mountains and when we are in the mountains meeting the mountains.

Here Dōgen is talking about the difference between seeing the mountains from the city and seeing them from within the mountains. In *Shōbōgenzō* "Uji," he says we should directly enter the mountains and see the thousand peaks from inside.[106] And in the beginning of "Sansuikyō," he says that there is no such place as outside the mountains. We are all within the mountains. And yet, until we awaken that truth, we are blind to being the person in the mountains, and we imagine we are observers from outside.

Dōgen says if we don't have the "eye" to see the mountains, we are outside. This doesn't mean that we are actually outside the mountains. There is no border between the mountains and the world; the world is part of the mountains. However, unless we really enter the mountains, enter that reality of life, we cannot really see the reality of life. Entering the mountains means starting to practice, arousing bodhi mind, taking bodhisattva vows, studying Buddha's teaching, practicing zazen, and performing day-to-day activities. Then we are seeing the mountains from inside.

Dōgen asks us to directly enter the mountains and live there. When he wrote this fascicle he was not literally in the mountains, but three years later he entered into the mountains to establish Eiheiji. From then on he often talked about mountain dwelling and wrote many poems about the mountain way of life.

There is nothing special about practice, nothing special about living in the mountains. When people first come to a Zen community it seems strange, something special or unique. It's beyond their common sense. Once you are inside the mountains, they are nothing special. But the mountains you see are completely different.

> Our concept of not-flowing and our understanding of not-flowing should not be the same as the dragon's understanding.

When we are in the mountains we don't see the mountains' walking. When we are in the water we don't see the water not-moving in the way the dragons or fish see water not-moving or not-flowing. When we are in the mountains, even though we are in the mountains, we see both flowing and not-flowing. Seeing only not-flowing is seeing only half of reality. Seeing both is the mountain way of life.

Humans and gods reside in their own worlds, and other beings may
have their doubts [about this], or, then again, they may not.

We are the same; we still have doubts, or maybe not. But this having
a doubt or not having a doubt is our condition. We should practice
with this condition. We should inquire how we can live within the
mountains. This question gives us energy. When we lose questions and
doubts, then we lose the energy to inquire ever more deeply into the
way of mountains.

As Dōgen said in "Genjōkōan," when we are sailing, the ocean looks
like a circle, but this circle is not the entire form or virtue of the ocean.
We should investigate the virtues of the ocean, one by one. He said
when we encounter one thing, one dharma, we closely perceive one
dharma. When we practice one dharma we penetrate one dharma.[107]
When we meet one thing at a time we understand each one. And we see
that what we do as our practice is connected with everyone's practice in
the community. Whatever we do, we have to do it with our whole body
and mind. This is how, action by action, we deepen our understanding
of the mountain, of the true reality of all beings. Each concrete practice
is like this.

## TEACHER AND STUDENT

(36) Therefore, without giving way to our surprise and doubt, we
should study the words "mountains flow" with the buddhas and
ancestors.

Our teachers are buddhas and ancestors. We encounter our teacher as
a buddha and an ancestor even though our teacher is just an ordinary
human being. Uchiyama Rōshi often said, "No human being can be a
true teacher. Only Buddha and zazen are our true teachers." Human
beings are just ordinary human beings. Yet the teacher who teaches us
that only buddhas and zazen are the teacher *is* a true teacher. If we meet
a person who says, "I'm a true teacher. I make no mistakes, so you have

to believe and follow me," we should take this with a grain of salt. It is better to question.

Uchiyama Rōshi also said, "I never face my students. If you want to be my student you should face the same direction." He was always facing the Buddha. So we faced Buddha, and we saw Uchiyama Rōshi's back, not his face. He never took care of his students; he just carried out his own practice wholeheartedly. If I wanted to be his disciple, I had to follow his direction. I had to walk with my own legs. He often said, "The teacher is not a caretaker or a babysitter."

My father visited the temple to attend my tokudo ceremony. When he greeted my teacher before the ceremony, my father asked Uchiyama Rōshi, "Please take care of my son." The next day Uchiyama Rōshi said to me, "Although your father asked me, I cannot take care of you. You have to practice on your own." That was my first teaching as his disciple. I accepted it. I relied on my teacher by walking with my own legs, as he instructed. Actually he helped a lot; he always pointed out which way I should go. But once I started to walk in a direction, he didn't say, "You shouldn't do this or that." He really trusted his disciples, and he sent three of us to America on our own.

Uchiyama Rōshi's teacher Sawaki Rōshi didn't have his own monastery, so his disciples had to practice by themselves. Sawaki Rōshi was always traveling all over Japan to teach. Sawaki Rōshi said that his method of training his disciples was like pasturage. When farmers raise cattle they send them to the mountains and leave them there to grow by themselves until the winter comes. That was Sawaki Rōshi's way to educate his disciples, and it was Uchiyama Rōshi's style too. When he retired Uchiyama Rōshi was sixty-three. As a Zen teacher, he was still young. But he had to retire because he was physically very weak. He could not do sesshin anymore. When he retired I was twenty-six, and in that same year I came to America. It was 1975. I was very young, almost too young to practice without my teacher's guidance. But the way to be his student was to go and grow by myself; that was his guidance. It is a very kind way of training but also very difficult.

Dōgen says we should study the words "mountains flow" with our teacher as buddha-ancestor and as a concrete example of how to live in the mountains.

> Taking up one [view], there is flowing; taking up another, there is not-flowing. At one turn, there is flowing; at another, not-flowing. If our study is not like this, it is not "the true Dharma wheel of the Thus Come One."

"The Thus Come One" is Tathāgata, the Buddha. The expression of these two sentences is kind of strange, but it is like Dōgen said before. The mountain has two virtues: dwelling peacefully and constantly walking. These are the two sides of the mountains. In a sense they are opposites. If we study only one side, just walking or just being still, our practice is not the true Dharma wheel of the Tathāgata. The Buddha's teaching always has two sides: peacefully being still and always walking vigorously.

## TWO VIRTUES: PEACEFUL DWELLING AND CONSTANT WALKING

> (37) An old buddha has said, "If you wish to avoid the karma of *Avīci* hell, do not slander the true Dharma wheel of the Thus Come One."

This is a quotation from "Shōdōka" ("The Song of Enlightenment") by Yongjia Xuanjue (in Japanese, Yōka Gengaku, 665–713), a famous and beautiful poem. We should not slander the true Dharma wheel of the Tathāgata. This Dharma wheel has two sides: peacefully abiding and constantly walking—going higher and deeper each moment.

Uchiyama Rōshi wrote a book titled *Susumi to Yasurai*. *Susumi* means "progress" or "improvement." *Yasurai* means "peacefulness." Rōshi studied Western philosophy in undergraduate and graduate school at Waseda University in Tōkyō, majoring in German philosophy, especially Hegel. After finishing the master's-level course, he became a teacher at a Catholic seminary. He taught philosophy and mathematics, and he studied Catholic theology. After that he became a Buddhist monk. When he was a student, in the beginning of the twentieth century, he had the thought that he was living at an intersection of Western civilization and Eastern tradition. Since the nineteenth century Japan had been very influenced by the West. The Japanese government wanted to make its nation as civilized and as powerful militarily and economically as Europe, so the government adopted the European school system. Students were educated in Western sciences and humanities.

As a boy Uchiyama Rōshi was educated in the Western method, yet culturally and mentally he still belonged to the East. He saw the main characteristic of Western civilization as progress: improvement through hard work. And he saw the main feature of Asian culture as pursuing peacefulness, stillness, and harmony with nature. That was why material civilization was not very developed in the East. He thought he would like to discover the best way to integrate these two approaches. That was the central theme of his life, even before he became a Buddhist monk.

I think Uchiyama Rōshi was right. And it's more than that. His life in early twentieth-century Japan was at the intersection of Eastern and Western civilizations, and in our lives in twenty-first-century America, cultures from all over the world meet each other, not only East and West. For him it was like an intersection with two streets crossing, but for us it is like a big public square where many streets meet, with crowds of people walking from various places and going to different places. People from very different cultural, racial, and spiritual backgrounds need to live together as neighbors in one integrated human society. This entire world becomes one society.

We have to study each other; otherwise we cannot live in peace and harmony, understanding, trusting, and supporting each other. In this situation, Buddhism can be a very important and meaningful element of the mix of cultures. The main point of Buddhism is to find peace of mind by studying the self and living in a harmonious way with others. The main emphasis of Western culture is progress toward a goal.

For Uchiyama Rōshi, one source of his idea of "progress" and "peace" is this teaching of Dōgen to study both: being still and at peace while we walk toward the future. Not only Zen practitioners but all of us living in the twenty-first century need to discover how to live with peace of mind without ignoring progress.

## ENGRAVING THESE WORDS ON OURSELVES AND THE WORLD

> (38) These words should be engraved on skin, flesh, bones, and marrow, engraved on interior and exterior of body and mind, engraved on emptiness and on form; they are engraved on trees and rocks, engraved on fields and villages.

"These words" means the expression of the mountains. Mountains are always peacefully abiding and walking and flowing. These are their expressions. Resting within the Dharma position at each moment and yet constantly walking: these virtues should be inscribed on our skin, flesh, bones, and marrow—our entire being. We should embody the mountains and practice as the mountains.

"Interior and exterior of body and mind" is a translation of *shinjin eshō*. *Shinjin* is "body and mind." *E* or "exterior" means the environment or circumstance we are living in. *Shō* (正) or "interior" is a retribution of karma as our own body and mind. We should engrave these words "constantly in peace and constantly walking" both inside and outside ourselves—on our body and mind and environment. We should care for ourselves and our circumstances and keep the whole (*e-shō*, interior and exterior as one thing) healthy.

"Engraved on emptiness and on form" means we should see both sides as one. In the *Heart Sūtra* we read that form is emptiness and emptiness is form; Dōgen adds in *Shōbōgenzō* "Maka Hannya Haramitsu" that form is form and emptiness is emptiness. This peace and progress should be engraved, inscribed, on both emptiness and form.

"They are engraved on trees and rocks" is from a story in the *Mahā-parinirvāṇa Sūtra* about one of Śākyamuni Buddha's previous lives. He was a practitioner named Sessan Doji (Snow Mountain Boy) living in the Himalaya Mountains. He encountered a monster (*rākṣasa*) reciting the first two lines of a verse.

> *Shogyō mujō*
> *zeshomeppo*
>
> 諸行無常
> 是生滅法
>
> All beings are impermanent.
> These are the beings of arising and perishing.

The boy thought it was a beautiful verse that precisely expressed the truth he was looking for, yet he also thought it was only half of the Buddha's teaching. He asked the monster to recite the second half of the verse. But the monster said, "I'm too hungry to recite the rest of the verse!"

Then the bodhisattva said, "After you chant the rest of the verse you can eat me. I offer my body to you. So please recite the second half of the verse."

The monster recited:

> *Shōmetsu metsui*
> *Jakumetsu iraku*
>
> 生滅滅已
> 寂滅為楽
>
> Arising and perishing cease;
> Calm extinction is nirvāṇa.

This expresses the other half of reality: the perishing of arising and perishing. Hearing the entire verse, the bodhisattva Snow Mountain Boy inscribed it on the trees and stones to share the Dharma with all beings. Then he jumped from a large rock to offer his body to the monster. But actually the monster was Indra, the guardian god of Dharma. Indra had appeared in the form of a monster to test the boy's determination. He then changed his form to appear as the god, and caught the boy's body to save him.

This is the source of this expression "inscribed on trees and rocks." But it does not mean literally inscribed on trees and rocks. Trees, rocks, and everything else are the reality of both arising and perishing and the cessation of arising and perishing. The true reality of all beings is engraved on each and every thing. When we see anything in nature with the Dharma eye, we see the reality of all beings everywhere.

When Sawaki Rōshi was a teenager, he lived in very difficult conditions with his stepparents. After hearing a Buddhist priest discuss this story, he was inspired to seek the Dharma. Later he said that was one of the reasons he became a Buddhist monk.

"Fields and villages" comes from the eighteenth chapter of the *Lotus Sūtra*, "The Benefits of Responding with Joy." The Buddha encourages people to expound the *Lotus Sūtra* everywhere, including temples, solitary places, cities, towns, fields, and villages. Not only things in nature such as trees and rocks but also human activity in cities, villages, fields, and so on can express the Dharma of peacefully dwelling and yet constantly moving.

All these are examples of the numberless places where the wondrous Dharma should be expounded. Not only in nature, not only in the mountains but also where human beings are living and working, the true reality of all beings is engraved.

## LOVING THE MOUNTAINS

(39) Although we say that mountains belong to the country, actually they belong to those who love them.

In our ordinary understanding, mountains belong to the country in which they sit. Dōgen says mountains really belong to the people who love them. And for practitioners it is not only mountains but this whole world, this reality, our entire lives including self and environment—all this belongs to us, those who love it, who practice.

Usually the word "love" or *ai* (愛) is not used in a positive way in Buddhism; it is usually used as "attachment," a negative thing. *Ai* is the translation for the negative qualities of thirst or impulse of desire (*taṇhā*) in the twelve links of causation. In Shitou Xiqian's poem "Sō An Ka" ("The Song of the Grass Hut") he said, "I don't love what mundane people love." Here the original expression of what mundane people love is *aisho* (愛処), so again this *ai* is negative. But the common Chinese word also has a positive meaning: to love and take care of things. When Dōgen uses this word *ai* here, it is positive. When Japanese people translated the Bible, *ai* was used as an equivalent of God's love.

> When the mountains love their owners . . .

I don't like this word "owners." People who live in the mountains are not owners. The word Dōgen used here is *shu* (主), "owner" or "lord." But *shu* also means "host," as in the Zen expression "host and guest" in Dongshan's "Hōkyōzanmai." A master living in a monastery is the host, and the training monks are guests. That is the meaning of *shu*. Just as the abbot is not the owner of the monastery, mountain lovers have no desire to "own" the mountain. But the mountains may love the people who live in the mountain, who become one with the mountain, who become the host. Though mountains belong to the people who love them, people also belong to the mountains. There is no ownership, only intimacy. In the mountains, people disappear and only the mountains remain: people and mountains are one.

> . . . the wise and virtuous inevitably enter the mountains.

Because the reality of life loves us, we inevitably are being drawn into the mountains, where mountain lovers live as our teachers.

> And when sages and wise men live in the mountains, because the mountains belong to them, trees and rocks flourish and abound, and the birds and beasts take on a supernatural excellence.

I don't know about "supernatural." Another possible translation is "spiritual." I think "spiritual" is better. The mountains belong to people who love them; when such people enter and live in the mountains, the mountains start to radiate a spiritual light. The beauty of this light attracts more way-seekers. Again Dōgen talks about a person and environment working together, influencing and supporting each other.

The structure of what Dōgen is saying here is exactly the same as his description of zazen practice as *jijuyū zanmai*, or self-receiving and self-employing samādhi, in *Bendōwa*. Each person's zazen influences everything in the world, everything reveals its own original realization, and the realization of all beings influences the person in zazen. The person sitting works together with everything in the world to turn the Dharma wheel everywhere. The self and the myriad dharmas work together without separation between perception and nāmarūpa (objects). There is no action of contact that creates saṃsāra here.

> This is because the sages and wise men have covered them with their virtue.

Even if a Zen temple is located in a city, each temple has its own mountain name; temples and the community of the temples are also mountains. This is the virtue of practice, insight, and true reality of all beings or reality of life. Our lives become ever more vital and vigorous. Our environment flourishes and becomes more wholesome. A saṅgha is a mountain. Whether or not the practice community is vital depends on the teacher (host) and students (guests). The condition of the saṅgha changes depending on its members. When we have a really good teacher and sincere practitioners, wherever we are becomes great mountains.

> We should realize that the mountains actually take delight in wise men, actually take delight in sages.

The mountains love practitioners, and practitioners love mountains.

## MOUNTAINS AND SAGES HAVE AUTHORITY OVER THE MUNDANE WORLD

> (40) Throughout the ages, we have excellent examples of emperors who have gone to the mountains to pay homage to wise men and seek instruction from great sages. At such times [the emperors] respected [the sages] as teachers and honored them without standing on worldly forms.

I am not sure whether historically this is true or not, but there are many such stories in Chinese classics. Dōgen introduces one of them below to discuss the relation between the mundane way of life and the mountain way of life.

> For the imperial authority has no authority over the mountain sage, and [the emperors] knew that the mountains are beyond the mundane world.

I am also not sure if this is literally true. Here Dōgen says the worldly system of value and the mountain way of life are different, and the authority of the world doesn't influence the mountain. This is not actually speaking of mountains or Buddhist practitioners in relation to political authority but about these two authorities within ourselves. Even when we are practicing in the saṅgha, we have to follow conventional rules, ethics, and laws. We should not confuse these conventional ways with the mountain way of life. We have to find a way to interrelate these two, yet basically we have to honor the mountain way more than mundane, conventional ways. Otherwise we lose the genuine spirit of the mountains of Dharma. In *Bendōwa*, Dōgen says, "People who think secular duties interfere with buddha-dharma only know that there is no buddha-dharma in the secular realm, and do not yet realize that there is nothing secular in the realm of buddha."[108]

The next sentence is one of the stories about an emperor going to the mountain:

> In ancient times we have [the cases of] Kongtong and the Hua Guard: when the Yellow Emperor made his visit, he went on his knees, prostrated himself, and begged instruction.

This story appears in chapter 11 of *Chuang-tzu*, entitled "Leaving the World Open." The Yellow Emperor was the legendary emperor of China who invented Chinese characters, the calendar, music, and medicine. At the time of the story the emperor had been on the throne for nineteen years. One day, when he heard that Guangchengzi (Koseishi, 広成子) was living in the Kongtong Mountains, he went to ask him about the essence of perfect Dao.

Guangchengzi refused to teach him, saying, "How can I discuss perfect Dao with a narrow-minded man like you!" Upon hearing this, the Yellow Emperor gave up the throne and lived by himself in a grass hermitage for three months. Then he revisited the mountain hermit.

Guangchengzi was lying on the bed with his head facing south. In a humble manner, the Yellow Emperor crept toward him and bowed twice before he asked the same question about the perfect Dao. Then the hermit began to talk about Dao. In China, when an emperor met with his retainers, the emperor always sat facing south while his retainers stood facing north. In their meeting, the Yellow Emperor behaved like one of his retainers, treating the hermit like an emperor.

Dōgen discusses another example, Buddha's father:

Again, the Buddha Shakyamuni left his royal father's palace and
went into the mountains; yet his royal father felt no resentment
toward the mountains nor distrust of those in the mountains who
instructed the prince.

After the Buddha left the palace he did different kinds of spiritual
practices, including some meditation, and some ascetic practices. I am
not sure if the Buddha practiced these in the mountains or not. In Zen
tradition, it is said that Śākyamuni Buddha practiced on the mountain
called Dantaloka (in Japanese, Dantokusan). For example, in Keizan's
*Denkōroku*, the Buddha's practice before he attained awakening is
described as follows.

Shakyamuni Buddha was of the Sun Race in India. At
the age of nineteen he leaped over the palace walls in the
dead of night, and at Mount Dantaloka, he cut off his hair.
Subsequently he practiced austerities for six years. Later, he
sat on the Adamantine Seat, where spiders spun webs in
his eyebrows and magpies built a nest on top of his head.
Reeds grew up between his legs as he sat tranquilly and
erect without movement for six years. At the age of thirty,
on the eighth day of the twelfth month, as the morning star
appeared, he was suddenly enlightened.[109]

In *Jingde Chuandeng Lu*, it is also said that the Buddha practiced
in Mount Dantaloka. This may not be historically true.[110] Anyway,
Dōgen's point here is that after Śākyamuni left his father's palace and
practiced in the mountains, the king did not have negative feelings
toward the mountains and the spiritual teachers in the mountains.

[The prince's] twelve years of cultivating the way were largely spent
in the mountains, and it was in the mountains that the Dharma
King's auspicious event occurred.

"Auspicious event" means enlightenment. Actually Bodhgayā, where the Buddha achieved enlightenment, is flat, but Dōgen speaks based on the story of Śākyamuni in the Zen tradition. He is talking about the metaphoric mountains we have been discussing, not physical mountains.

> Truly, even a "wheel-turning king" does not wield authority over the mountains.

It is important in a spiritual community that the "emperor" doesn't wield authority over the Dharma practice. Even though this refers to the Buddha's father, King Śuddhodana, "king" here can mean our worldly thinking.

> (41) We should understand that the mountains are not within the limits of the human realm or the limits of the heavens above. They are not to be viewed with the calculations of human thought. If only we did not compare them with flowing in the human realm, who would have any doubts about such things as the mountains' flowing or not flowing?

Spiritual practice should not be viewed with the calculations of human sentiments based on like, dislike, or gain. We should not evaluate the virtues of the mountains, the true reality of life. If we don't cling to our human sentiments, if we directly see mountains and waters, which means to see each thing in its reality as the network of interdependent origination, then we cannot possibly have doubts about mountains flowing or not flowing.

## LIVING BY THE WATER

> (42) Again, since ancient times, wise men and sages have also lived by the water. When they live by the water they hook fish. Or they

> hook people, or they hook the way. These are all "water styles" of
> old. And going further, there must be hooking the self, hooking the
> hook, being hooked by the hook, and being hooked by the way.

Starting with this paragraph Dōgen talks about people who live by
the water, or about the water as dwelling place of sages, buddhas, and
ancestors. In this section he also talks about the transmission of the
way from teacher to student.

"Living by the water" means hooking or fishing people. This is an
interesting kind of fishing. There is neither bait nor bite, and it is very
difficult to fish without bait. There are not many fish who come up by
themselves without bait.

There was a Zen master who used to be a fisherman before he became
a monk. His name was Xuansha Shibei (Gensha Shibi, 835–908). He
was the person who said, "The entire ten-direction world is one bright
jewel," an expression Dōgen discussed in *Shōbōgenzō* "Ikka-no-Myōju"
("One Bright Jewel"). In the beginning of that fascicle Dōgen said,

> While he was a lay person, he loved fishing. He fished on his
> boat, mingling with other fishermen on the Nantai River.
> He might not have been waiting even for the golden-scaled
> fish that comes up by itself without being fished.

To live by the water and hook fish means to hook people who would
be able to become a Dharma successor and transmit Dharma. Zen masters hook the Way to keep the practice of the Way; that is how this
Dharma has been transmitted from the Buddha to us. All Zen masters,
in that sense, are living by the water and fishing without bait. We can
say that they are hooking themselves, to live their own water style of
life. Or they are hooking the hook—just enjoying hooking, with no
object to be hooked. This means they simply enjoy practice for their
own sake, not for catching something valuable.

> These are all "water styles" of old.

"Old" means the ancient people or buddhas; "water styles" is their way of life, similar to the mountain way.

> And going further, there must be hooking the self. . . .

In a sense these Zen masters are not hooking someone else as a disciple; they are hooking themselves. When I asked to become his disciple, Uchiyama Rōshi said that he never encouraged people to be a priest/ monk. He was not fishing; he was just practicing for himself, just fishing himself. Somehow I wanted to be hooked. He didn't hook me, so I had to hook myself. We are hooking the self in the way we practice within the saṅgha; we are fishing the self.

> . . . hooking the hook, being hooked by the hook, and being hooked by the way.

It's not "me" hooking myself. There is no person who is hooking and no self that is hooked; this is the entire world of hooking. Hooking is the hook, or the hook is hooking the hook. There is no separation between subject and object. This is similar to Dōgen's expression in "Genjōkōan":

> "Conveying oneself toward all things to carry out practice-enlightenment is delusion. All things coming and carrying out practice-enlightenment through the self is realization."[111]

When this person (Shohaku) is hooking something called Dharma or truth, that is not real practice. Those masters were hooked by hooking and they could not stop hooking. Ultimately they were hooked by the Way. They hooked the Way and at the same time they were hooked by the Way. The Way hooked the Way; or hooking hooked hooking itself. Sawaki Rōshi said, "In zazen, the self does the self with the self by the self for the self." Zazen sits zazen. Shohaku is doing Shohaku. Subject and object are one in this wondrous Dharma.

## BOATMAN DECHENG

Dōgen next gives the example of a Zen master who lived by the water, Chuanzi Decheng (Sensu Tokujō, 780–850). *Chuanzi* means "boatman."

> (43) Long ago, when the Preceptor Decheng suddenly left Yaoshan and went to live on the river, he got the sage of Huating River.

"Preceptor" is a translation of *oshō*, which is a transliteration of the Sanskrit *upādhyāya*. In China and Japan *oshō* is used not specifically for a person who can give precepts but is a very common word for Buddhist priests/monks. Here, even though "preceptor" is a literal translation, it leads to confusion, because in the story Decheng was a boatman who had no intention to ordain anyone.

The story of Boatman Decheng is connected with "Sansuikyō," with Dōgen's personal life, and with the *Suttanipāta.* Boatman Decheng was a disciple of Yaoshan Weiyan (Yakusan Igen, 751–834), who was a disciple of Shitou Xiqian. Dōgen says Decheng left "suddenly," but I don't think his departure was sudden—he left because his teacher died. When Yaoshan died, his three eminent disciples, Daowu Yuanzhi, Yunyan Tansheng, and Decheng, discussed how to continue Yaoshan's Dharma and practice. (Yunyan and Daowu are the Zen masters in the kōan of the thousand hands and eyes of Avalokiteśvara I discussed before.)

Decheng said to his Dharma brothers:

> "You two must each go into the world your separate ways and uphold the essence of our teacher's path. My own nature is undisciplined. I delight in nature and in doing as I please. I'm not fit [to be head of a monastery]. But remember where I reside. And if you come upon persons of great ability, send one of them to me. Let me teach him and I'll pass on to him

everything I've learned in life. In this way I can repay the kindness of our late teacher."[112]

Decheng urged them to find good locations to establish monasteries, teach students, and continue the Dharma of Yaoshan. He himself had no intention to establish his own monastery. He wanted to hook a disciple without having a monastery. This is like hooking a fish not only without bait but also without a rod and line.

After that he went to the river and lived as a boatman. He ferried people across the river. This is an archetype of bodhisattva practice: not to live in a monastery but to live in the world and ferry people between this shore and the other.

Yunyan and Daowu traveled to find mountains to establish their own monasteries to continue their teacher's Dharma.

Later Daowu went to Jingkao, where he happened to see Jiashan Shanhui (Kassan Zenne, 805–81), who later became a great Zen master. When Daowu met Jiashan, Jiashan was not a Zen monk; he was already a teacher, possibly in the Tiantai (Tendai) school. When Daowu visited his temple, Jiashan was giving a lecture.

A monk attending the talk asked Jiashan, "What is the dharmakāya?"

Jiashan said, "The dharmakāya is formless."

*Dharmakāya* means the Buddha's body as Dharma, true reality itself. As dharmakāya, the myriad dharmas (all phenomenal beings) are formless.

The monk asked, "What is the Dharma eye?"

How can we see that formless Dharma body? Only with the Dharma eye. Then what is the true Dharma eye? Because true reality is formless, it cannot be the object of our six sense organs: eyes, ears, nose, tongue, body, or mind. That means it cannot be nāmarūpa. What is this formless reality? How can we see this formless reality?

Jiashan said, "The Dharma eye is without defect."

This answer relates to the expression *kūge* (空華), or "cataract." The literal meaning of *kūge* is "empty flower" or "sky flower." When we have a cataract, we see something like a flower, even when nothing is there. In *Shōbōgenzō* "Kūge," Dōgen read this as the flower of emptiness and used this expression with a very positive meaning. Here Jiashan says that because his Dharma eye has no defect or cataract, he clearly sees dharmakāya: everything as it is.

> When he heard this, Daowu laughed loudly in spite of himself.
> Jiashan got down off the lecture platform and said to Daowu, "Something I said in my answer to that monk was not correct and it caused you to laugh out loud! Please don't withhold your compassionate instruction about this!"

Jiashan knew there was something lacking in himself, even though he was already a teacher. This feeling of lack is important, as Dōgen says in "Genjōkōan";[113] it's a sign of a person filled with Dharma.

There are many stories of this sort in Zen texts. It seems as though these stories record things that actually happened. But actually, we find many versions of the same story. When we read different versions of the same story in the order in which they were written, we find that many stories develop, becoming more interesting and meaningful over time. Chinese Zen practitioners liked telling stories instead of writing about their philosophy in a logical way. So we don't need to worry about whether these stories are historically true or not.

> Daowu said, "You have gone into the world to teach, but have you not had a teacher?"

Daowu is telling Jiashan that he understands Buddhist teachings in the scriptures quite well, but he hasn't yet experienced what it means through practice with a genuine teacher.

> Jiashan said, "I've had none. May I ask you to clarify these matters?"
>
> Daowu said, "I cannot speak of it. I invite you to go see the Boat Monk at Huating."

Thus Daowu fulfilled Decheng's request to send him a person of great ability.

> Jiashan said "Who is he?"
>
> Daowu said, "Above him there is not a single roof tile, below him there's no ground to plant a hoe. If you want to see him you must change into your traveling clothes.

Decheng was a real home leaver without any property. There were no roof tiles above him and no inch of land underneath his feet. He was truly a mountain person, who lost not only his possessions but even himself within the mountains and waters.

> After the meeting was over, Jiashan packed his bag and set out for Huating.
>
> When Decheng saw Jiashan coming he said, "Your Reverence! In what temple do you reside?"
>
> Jiashan said, "I don't abide in a temple. Where I abide is not like...."

He says that he gave up having a temple to live in. Jiashan has begun to resemble Decheng. This conversation relates to the original question and answer: "What is the dharmakāya?" "What is Dharma eye?" No-abiding is one side of the dharmakāya; there is nowhere to abide so everything is empty and moving like mountains' walking.

Decheng said, "It's not like? It's not like what?"

"It's not like" refers to nothing being fixed.

Then Jiashan said, "It's not like the Dharma that meets the eye."

Jiashan is referring to our usual experience: an object meets our eyes, and the object becomes nāmarūpa. This has something to do with Śākyamuni Buddha's teaching of dependent origination in *Suttanipāta*. The action of contact is a source of problems that makes our life suffering and our world burn with the flame of the three poisons. This dialogue is about a different way of meeting objects. How can we meet all things and people without creating nāmarūpa? This is one of the fundamental aims of Buddhist teaching from the Buddha to Dōgen, throughout many different theories, philosophies, approaches, and practices.

What Jiashan says here is that there is nothing in front of his eye. There is no separation between his eye and objects; therefore there is no nāmarūpa and no action of contact. When nāmarūpa ceases to be, dharmakāya appears. This means he sees the emptiness of all beings.

Then Decheng said, "Where did you learn this teaching?"
Then Jiashan said, "Not in a place which the ears or eyes can perceive."

He did not study this from a certain teacher; he sees this where the eyes and ears cannot perceive. This means there's no dichotomy between eyes and objects of eyes, ears and objects of ears. This is transcending the dichotomy of subject and object as the *Heart Sūtra* said with no eyes, no ears, no nose, no tongue; no color, no sound, no taste, and so on. That was Jiashan's answer.

Then Decheng uttered an expression famous in Zen:

Decheng said, "A single phrase and you fall into the path of principle. Then you're like a donkey tethered to a post for countless eons."

This expression is *ikku gattō no go, mangō no kero ketsu* (一句合頭語、萬劫繫驢橛). *Ikku* means "one phrase," "one word"; *ga* is "to meet" or "to join"; *tō* (頭) means "head"; and *go* (語) is "word." So this means a phrase that hits the mark: an accurate expression of the true reality. *Man* is "ten thousand," *gō* (劫) is "kalpa"—ten thousand kalpas. *Ke* (繫) means "to tie," *ro* is "donkey," and *ketsu* is a "stake" or "pole." In ancient China, farmers tied donkeys on stakes. The donkey could walk as much as it wanted, but no matter how far it walked, it was simply walking around the post.

Decheng is simply saying, "One phrase that really hits the mark might become a post to which a donkey is bound for ten thousand kalpas." He is saying that Jiashan's expression really hit the mark, but if it became the post around which he walked for the rest of his life, he would never be free from that understanding.

Decheng's caution is the same as what Daowu said to Jiashan when they met: What you say is not a mistake, but you have not yet been released from your conceptual thinking. Dharma eye and dharmakāya without separation between subject and object are still what you are "thinking." Therefore, it is still nāmarūpa of your thinking mind. You are still caught in the action of "contact" between your mind and its object.

Usually we start to study or practice because of some problem or question. When we are lucky we find some answers, some way we think we can solve our problem. Then we think this is Dharma, this is the Buddha Way—and we cling to it. Even if the teaching is not mistaken, our clinging is mistaken. We are tied to this pole and walk around it the rest of our life. Even if the pole is a true teaching, a post is just a post. This is the idea of the "golden chain."

Before we practice we are bound with an iron chain, but when we start to practice we find the truth in Buddha's teaching and somehow this teaching becomes a golden chain. It's gold, but it's still a chain. We are chained by Dharma—but that's still a limitation. We are circling around our understanding like a donkey tied to a pole. That is the point of this story.

> Then Decheng said, "You've let down a thousand-foot line. You're fishing very deep, but your hook is still shy by three inches. Why don't you say something?"

You've reached a thousand feet but you need three more inches. How can we go three more inches? The final three inches are the most difficult to reach. Thinking and understanding can't help us there.

> As Jiashan was about to speak, Decheng knocked him into the water with the oar. When Jiashan clambered back into the boat Decheng yelled at him, "Speak! Speak!"
> Jiashan tried to speak, but before he could do so, Decheng struck him again. Then suddenly Jiashan attained great enlightenment. He then nodded his head three times.

He stopped speaking. He was free from thinking about the water because he was completely in the water. He found he didn't need to say anything. Now he's got it.

> Then Chuanzi [Decheng] said, "Now you are the one with the pole and line. Just act by your own nature and don't defile the clear waves."
> Jiashan asked, "What do you mean by 'throw off the line and cast down the pole'?"

This means that Decheng is giving his pole and line to Jiashan and Jiashan asks why he does such a thing.

Chuanzi said, "The fishing line hangs in the green water, drifting without intention."

This is what Decheng had been doing by the river: just drifting without intention because he was an "undisciplined" person who did not want to leave the mountains and waters and go out to the world. Once he gave the pole and line away, he did not fish anything anymore.

Jiashan said, "There is no path whereby words may gain entry to the essence. The tongue speaks, but cannot speak it."

Using words we cannot get into the mountains and waters. To say that we cannot say anything is the right way to express the Dharma.

Chuanzi said, "When the hook disappears into the river waves, then the golden fish is encountered."

When we stop fishing, the golden fish comes up. What is this golden fish? The Dharma body of Buddha. In order to fish the Dharma body we should stop fishing, stop hooking; then the golden fish appears. Not "I get" or "I catch" or "I own" the dharmakāya, but the dharmakāya manifests itself when we stop fishing. This is the way we fish the dharmakāya.

Jiashan then covered his ears.

He didn't need to hear any more.

Chuanzi said, "That's it! That's it!"

The transmission of Dharma is completed. And Decheng gives some admonitions to Jiashan:

He then enjoined Jiashan, saying, "Hereafter, conceal yourself in a place without any trace."

This is an expression Dōgen used before in "Sansuikyō." We should
hide ourselves in a place without any trace. That means our practice
should be traceless—no attachment, no clinging.

"If the place has any sign don't stay there. I stayed with
Yaoshan for thirty years and what I learned there I have passed
to you today. Now that you have it stay away from crowded
cities. Instead, plant your hoe deep in the mountains."

"Any sign" means a sign of germination. Earlier Daowu said that
Decheng didn't have a place to plant his hoe. Now Decheng asks his
disciple to plant his hoe in the deep mountains—to establish a monastery to fish bodhisattvas.

"Find one person or one-half a person who won't let it die."

Transmit this Dharma to one person or even half a person; the number of people is not important. You don't have to establish a huge monastery, but you should transmit this Dharma to one true practitioner
of the way. Decheng urged Jiashan to follow his style of life, hiding
himself in the mountains or by the river, and yet transmit the Dharma
to even one-half person. Within Zen Buddhism, this style has been
transmitted until today. When monasteries became too institutional
and lose the genuine spirit of practice, people from this mountains and
waters way of life criticize them and help restore the original spirit.

This is the same admonition Dōgen's teacher, Tiantong Rujing,
gave him before Dōgen returned to Japan. According to the *Kenzeiki*,
Dōgen's biography, Rujing said,

When you return to your country, do not associate closely
with the emperor and ministers. Do not live in a city, a

town, or a village. Live in a deep mountain or a quiet valley. You don't have to collect many people like clouds. Having many fake practitioners is inferior to having a few genuine practitioners. Choose a small number of true persons of the way and become friends of them. Teach one person or even half a person and continue the wisdom life of buddhas and ancestors.

This must have been a significant teaching for Dōgen. Later people thought that this advice was one of the reasons Dōgen moved from near the capital, Kyōto, to Echizen and established Eiheiji in the remote mountains.

> Is this not hooking a fish? Is it not hooking a person? Is it not hooking water?

Decheng hooked a true disciple. Actually, Decheng hooked the water, the true reality of all beings.

> Is it not hooking himself?

This reality of all beings is none other than himself. He hooked himself.

> That the person got to see Decheng is [because he was] Decheng;

"The person" means Jiashan. Jiashan went to see Decheng, the boatman, because Decheng was actually Jiashan himself. When Jiashan first heard of Decheng from Daowu, he might not have felt that way, but from Dōgen's point of view Jiashan's true self is Decheng. This is a genuine relationship between a teacher and student. Dharma transmission is possible between such a teacher and student.

Sometimes Dōgen used the expression *tanden*. *Tan* means single or singular, and *den* means transmission. I discussed this in the introduction of *The Wholehearted Way*.[114] It can be interpreted in a few ways. One way is that only one thing, one Dharma is transmitted from teacher to student. Another is that teacher and student are one and there's nothing to transmit. We can see both sides. Jiashan was Decheng.

> Decheng's acceptance of Jiashan is his meeting the person.

This meeting is essential. How can we really meet a person? Meeting is an action of "contact"; it could be the cause of problems. But when we meet and have real, intimate contact, also called no-contact, then this meeting does not create poison. Decheng meets Decheng and Jiashan meets Jiashan. There is no separation between subject and object. This kind of meeting is possible when both have no fixed views and no attachments.

A meeting or contact without poison is a real meeting. How is this possible? How can we meet people without producing poisons? This is an important point, not only in our practice of Zen but also in our daily life outside the zendō.

In the ideal meetings between teachers and students, there's no separation. Teachers are ordinary human beings, so between teachers and students we could have a conflict; sometimes we create poisons. But the idea is that Dharma transmission from teacher to student, or the relationship between teacher and student, should be without separation. It's like water: we are all in the water. So water hooks the water or the wave hooks the wave; there's no separation.

How can we meet not only with teachers but with others without separation? When we meet this way, "contact" is the cause not of problems but of nirvāṇa. Depending upon our way of meeting it, our life and this world become saṃsāra or nirvāṇa.

The meaning of Decheng's name is important. In Japanese, Decheng is Tokujō: *toku* (徳) or "virtue" and *jō* (誠) or "sincerity." So we can also read "That the person got to see Decheng is [because he was] Decheng" as "That the person (Jiashan) got to see Decheng is because Jiashan was virtuous and sincere." Or we could say that both Decheng and Jiashan were virtuous and sincere.

The point is that to meet with others without poisoned minds, we must meet them with virtue and sincerity. This is the same as meeting without separation. Specifically we are meeting them with the virtues of the way: abiding peacefully and always walking. When we maintain our awareness of these two virtues and we are sincere, then we can meet others without poison. In the English translation Decheng is simply the boatman's name. This is a difficulty in understanding Dōgen only through translation.

## A WORLD IN WATER

> (44) It is not the case simply that there is water in the world; within the world of water there is a world.

Here "water" means the reality of all beings. The true reality of beings is not a part of the world, but the world is a part of the reality of all beings.

> And this is true not only within water: within clouds as well there is world of sentient beings; within wind there is world of sentient beings; within fire there is world of sentient beings; within earth there is world of sentient beings. Within the Dharma realm there is a world of sentient beings; within a single blade of grass there is world of sentient beings; within a single staff there is a world of sentient beings.

The world of sentient beings is everywhere, and the reality of all beings pervades every part of the universe. Each element of the universe and the universe as a whole permeate each other. This is the world of sentient beings for us sentient beings.

"A single blade of grass" refers to work in our daily lives. "A single staff" refers to the Zen masters' teaching; the abbot usually holds a whisk or a staff when ascending the platform in the Dharma hall to

give a formal discourse. "A single staff" can also refer to monks' practice, since they used their staffs to travel to visit teachers.

> And wherever there is a world of sentient beings, there, inevitably,
> is the world of buddhas and ancestors. The reason this is so, we
> should study very carefully.

We usually think the world of sentient beings is saṃsāra, but wherever
saṃsāra is, there is also nirvāṇa, because saṃsāra and nirvāṇa are not
two separate places. Depending upon whether or not we encounter
other people and situations with virtue and sincerity, we create nirvāṇa
or saṃsāra. Wherever we are can be a world of sentient beings and also
a world of buddhas and ancestors. Wherever we are, even in a Buddhist
community, we may create saṃsāra. It really depends on what attitude
we maintain or what kind of spirit we have. Any community can be
saṃsāra or nirvāṇa or both or neither. We must study carefully how
our lives become the burning house of saṃsāra, and how can we extin-
guish this fire with the fire of wisdom.

## TRUE DRAGON, TRUE PERSON

> (45) In this way, water is the palace of the "true dragon"; it is not
> flowing away.

Dōgen's *Fukanzazengi* tells us what the true dragon means.[115] In
ancient China, there was a person who loved dragons. He collected
all kinds of carved dragons and put them in his room. One day a true
dragon thought that because this person loved dragons—even imita-
tion ones—he would be very happy to receive a visit from a real dragon.
But when the dragon visited his house, the person was frightened and
ran away.

In *Fukanzazengi* Dōgen used this metaphor for zazen. We like the
idea of it, but we don't like actually sitting zazen.

The water Dōgen is discussing here is the palace of the true dragon, or in this case the true person of the way who lives in the water style. The person who really lives within the water, who is awakened to the reality of all beings, is a true dragon. This person and this water are not flowing away; they manifest eternity in each moment. Until this point Dōgen has been discussing the flowing of water, the way water moves; he hasn't said anything about the way water doesn't move, or about no flowing. But here he says that as a palace of the true dragon the water doesn't flow. The fish or dragon sees the water as their home. Impermanence is the stable dwelling, the home of a bodhisattva.

> If we regard it only as flowing, the word "flowing" is an insult to water; it is like imposing "not flowing."

We should remember the "not flowing" aspect of water. Water has the virtues of flowing and not flowing, of constantly moving and peacefully abiding in each Dharma position.

> Water is nothing but water's "real form just as it is."

This "real form just as it is" is a translation of *nyoze-jissō,* the true reality of thusness. *Nyoze,* which we discussed in detail in chapter 2, appears in the very beginning of Dongshan's "Hōkyōzanmai": *nyo-ze no hō,* "the Dharma of thusness."[116] *Jissō* is a part of the long name of *Shōbōgenzō: Shōbōgenzō nehanmyōshin jissōmusō mimyō no hōmon.* The subtle (*mimyo*) Dharma-gate (*hōmon*) of true form (*jissō*) and no form (*musō*) is what has been transmitted through teachers and students. This is what the *Lotus Sūtra* is saying: to show this true form, and allow all beings to see, it is the only reason buddhas appear in this world. This is an essential point of Mahāyāna Buddhism and the Zen tradition. Dōgen says that water is nothing other than this thusness (nyo-ze no hō) and true form (jissō) that have been transmitted.

> Water is the virtue of water; it is not flowing.

Just being water *as it is* is the virtue of water. Maybe we should say "it is not simply flowing," because it also has a virtue of not flowing.

> In the thorough study of the flowing or the not-flowing of a single [drop of] water, the entirety of the ten thousand things is instantly realized.

Here a "single drop of water" means each and every thing including ourselves. Each one of us is a single drop of water. We appear, stay for a while, and go away. When we see the "true virtue of flowing and not-flowing," we see the true reality of our lives. That means change, improvement, progress, and also the side of not-flowing that is peacefully resting. We find peacefulness with this not-flowing side of water. This is what Dōgen meant when he says in "Genjōkōan,"

> When a person attains realization, it is like the moon's reflection in water. The moon never becomes wet; the water is never disturbed. Although the moon is a vast and great light, it is reflected in a drop of water. The whole moon and even the whole sky are reflected in a drop of dew on a blade of grass.[117]

In each tiny drop of water, eternal and boundless moonlight is reflected. This is the image of eternity manifesting itself within impermanence.

These two virtues are not only present in the truth transmitted from teacher to student in the Zen tradition; within our personal life there are also the two virtues of flowing and not-flowing. We need peace in each moment, and we need progress. We need to walk in a certain direction. This reality of beings is not an abstract truth outside of ourselves; it is very real in this daily life. Dōgen is discussing this person's life, body, and mind. How can we live this person's impermanent life expressing eternity?

"Instantly realized" here is also *genjō*. When we really, deeply, thoroughly investigate the reality of this being we can study the entirety of the ten thousand things, and the reality of the ten thousand things is immediately realized within our own lives.

> Among mountains as well, there are mountains hidden in jewels; there are mountains hidden in marshes; mountains hidden in the sky; there are mountains hidden in mountains. There is a study of mountains hidden in hiddenness.

"Hidden" is a translation of *zō* (蔵) in *Shōbōgenzō*. In the case of *Shōbōgenzō*, *zō* means "storehouse" or "treasury." "Hidden" could mean something is stored. A mountain is hidden within the mountain; we are hidden in ourselves; trees are hidden in the trees. When we are really one with the mountain, we are hidden within the mountain, the mountain is hidden within the mountain, and the mountain is hidden within ourselves. It's not an idea; it is our practice. Within our practice—for example, chopping vegetables or cleaning rooms—Buddha is hidden, or treasured; within Buddha, we are hidden.

# Conclusion:
## Mountains Are Mountains, Waters Are Waters

(46) An old buddha has said, "Mountains are mountains and waters
are waters."

I HAVE HAD MANY difficulties trying to understand what Dōgen
writes, and then explain it in English. I have been trying to report
on seeing the thousand peaks from inside the mountains. This is
the same thing I have been doing since I became Uchiyama Rōshi's
disciple. This is just a report. Please don't think that what I am saying
is exactly what Dōgen is writing. This is just my tunnel-visioned view.
Some places are very difficult and some places are beautiful. I feel as
if I have been looking, paragraph by paragraph, at Sesshū's long-scroll
painting of mountains and waters.

This scroll is sixteen meters (about fifty-three feet) long, so it is not
possible to see the entire painting at once. We need to see it part by part.
Each part looks like a complete independent painting, yet all these
parts are connected. We see the changes of scenery of mountains and
waters in space, and also the changes of seasons in time from spring to
winter. In the continuous mountains and waters, some people appear,
but they are tiny beings: this helps us understand how ancient Chinese
and Japanese people saw boundless nature—and tiny human beings in
it. Human beings cannot be the owners of the mountains and waters;
they are only a tiny part of the network of interdependent origination.

After all these discussions of the virtues of mountains and waters, now Dōgen says that a mountain is just a mountain and water is just water. He is an outrageous Zen master.

When he speaks about mountains just being mountains, Dōgen is quoting Chinese Zen masters. For example:

> Having entered the Dharma Hall for a formal instruction Master Yunmen said, "You monks must not think falsely; heaven is heaven, earth is earth, mountain is mountain, river is river, monk is monk, and layperson is layperson."[118]

In his discourse Yunmen exclaimed, "*Sho oshō! Maku mōzō!* (諸和尚、莫妄想)" or "All monks! Don't be lost in wild fantasy!"

*Mōzō* (妄想) is "a fantasy" or "a wild fantasy." *Mō* (妄) is "unreal" or "illusory," and *zō* or *sō* (想) is used as a translation of "perception," the third of the five aggregates. In a short sutta in the *Suttanipāta*, this word is used with "nāmarūpa."

*Maku* (莫) is "not" or "never," so *maku mōzō* is "don't be given to delusional thinking," or "don't indulge in wool gathering."

I think *maku mōzō* is what Śākyamuni Buddha meant when he said in the *Suttanipāta*, "Without ordinary perception, without disordered perception, without no perception, without any annihilation of perception." This mōzō is wild fantasy, disordered perception. But ordinary perception is also mōzō; as Nāgārjuna said, all discriminating thoughts are productions of our mind. So mōzō is both ordinary and disordered perception.

Then Yunmen said, "Heaven is heaven. Earth is earth. Mountain is mountain. Water is water. A monk is a monk and a lay person is a lay person." He is pointing out the true reality of heaven, earth, mountain, and water before these are processed within our mind to become perceptions and concepts.

Another person who stated this, probably the source of Dōgen's reference here, is Qingyuan Weixin (in Japanese, Seigen Ishin, 1044–1115), a

Dharma successor of Chinese Linji Zen master Huitang Zuxin (Kaidō Soshin, 1025–1100). He says:

> Thirty years ago when I had not studied Zen, I saw that mountains are mountains and waters are waters. Later I intimately met my teacher and entered this place. I saw mountains are not mountains and waters are not waters. Now I have attained the place of resting. As before I simply see that mountains are mountains and waters are waters.[119]

After a long discussion about what mountains and waters are and how we should enter them, finally Dōgen says that water is just water and mountains are just mountains.

## SHIKAN: JUST DOING

> (47) These words do not say that mountains are mountains; they say that mountains are mountains.

Dōgen has given us another kōan. What does this mean? One possible interpretation is that the first "mountains are mountains" is how Qingyuan Weixin saw the mountains as nāmarūpa before he practiced Zen. The second "mountains are mountains" is how he saw them after he became liberated from so-called Zen or enlightenment, when mountains were just mountains again. Maybe these two "mountains are mountains" are before and after—before this Zen master studied Zen and after he was liberated from Zen. This is the same as the word *shusshin* in the question to Yunmen regarding the place from whence all the buddhas come.

    Why does Dōgen quote this sentence as the conclusion of this sūtra on mountains and waters? I think he wants to express the spirit of *shikan* in *shikantaza*, just sitting. This word "just" or "simply" is the cornerstone of Dōgen's teaching. Mountains are just mountains and waters are just waters. In the case of zazen, we just sit; we do nothing else, really nothing else.

Shikantaza is often used as an approach to meditation practice, meaning sitting without using kōans or other techniques. I don't think that is what Dōgen meant when he used the expression. I think this word *shikantaza* is the final answer to his question: why do we have to practice if we are already in Dharma nature, if we are enlightened from the beginning? Why do we have to go through the long and hard study and practice?

Originally this expression *shikantaza* was used not by Dōgen himself but by his teacher Rujing. We not only just sit—when we eat, we just eat; when we work in the kitchen, we just cook; when we clean, we just clean; when we chant, we just chant.

This attitude of "just" is the answer Dōgen discovered through seeing the two virtues of mountains and waters. It means the reality of all beings: abiding peacefully in their Dharma positions and also constantly walking. These are the contradictory aspects of one reality. When we see both sides of our life, what can we do? What kind of attitude should we maintain toward our lives? The answer is to just be attentive and put our whole energy into whatever we are doing right now. When we are sitting in the zendō we just sit, one hundred percent there, nothing else. This is one aspect of "just sitting."

Yet we cannot cling to this Dharma position; we also have to go to other places. That is the meaning of "constantly walking": we cannot cling to who I am or what I do. We often say, "I want to be a teacher" or "I'd like to be a tenzo" or "I'd like to become abbot." We try to find a role we want, and once we attain it, we want to stay there; but we cannot, we have to flow. "Just" or *shikan* means we just do what we are supposed to do at this moment, completely, without attachment, without clinging to what we are doing. This is the meaning of *shikan* in *shikantaza* or "just sitting."

Shikantaza is not a method of sitting; shikantaza is the only thing we can do when we face the dual reality of peacefully abiding and constantly walking. Be here, but within being here, somehow we are moving. We cannot cling to this Dharma position; we have to go to the next Dharma position. This shikan, this just doing something, is very important, not only in zazen but in our entire life.

Finally what Dōgen wants to say is, "Just be as it is": "Just do it." We want to do many things at the same time. Just be in one place at one time. Just do one thing at one time. This "just doing" naturally brings us to the next stage. Our practice is not a preparation for the next stage, but by doing what I am doing now this practice brings us to the next moment.

We might wonder why Dōgen has to discuss such a simple thing. Why did he have to say "just sit," just do things? Of all Dōgen's writings, I think this fascicle is where he devoted his energy to explaining why we have to just do things one at a time.

## A CAUTION

> Therefore we should thoroughly study these mountains.

If we take this teaching of "just doing" carelessly, it becomes another poison. When Dōgen teaches "just doing," we have to understand what he means. As an explanation of the profound meaning of "just be as-it-is," he has to write these strange, difficult, almost nonsensical words to enable us to be free from our fixed, karmic, tunnel views.

We need to understand this practice of "just doing" in the context of all Dōgen's teachings and practice. This attitude becomes a poison when we can say that wherever we are, Buddha is hidden: in war, in vermin, in selling drugs, or whatever. If "just doing" lacks the context of Dōgen's teaching, it can be used to justify killing in war, or in many other harmful contexts. That is not what Dōgen is saying. He's teaching this attitude in the context of mountains and waters as the true reality of all beings. In the context of the Buddha's teaching this is how we can avoid harm, in which contact with others causes argument and fighting, tears and anguish.

To be a Buddhist student we have to receive precepts. Precepts are the guidelines for our way of life. We should understand this "just doing" teaching within the context of receiving precepts and studying Buddha's teachings of how to live peacefully, in harmony with all beings.

Robert Aitkin discusses the importance of the precepts in *The Mind of Clover: Essays in Zen Buddhist Ethics*. He quotes Japanese Rinzai Zen master Takuan Sōhō:

> The uplifted sword has no will of its own, it is all of emptiness. It is like a flash of lightning. The man who is about to be struck down is also of emptiness, as is the one who wields the sword. . . .
>
> Do not get your mind stopped with the sword you raise; forget about what you are doing, and strike the enemy. Do not keep your mind on the person before you. They are all of emptiness, but beware of your mind being caught in emptiness.[120]

Aitken comments about Takuan's teaching to the samurai:

> The Devil quotes scripture, and *Māra*, the incarnation of ignorance, can quote the *Abhidharma*. The fallacy of the Way of the Samurai is similar to the fallacy of the Code of the Crusader. Both distort what should be a universal view into an argument for partisan warfare. The catholic charity of the Holy See did not include people it called pagans. The vow of Takuan Zenji to save all beings did not encompass the one he called the enemy.[121]

And:

> The first point is that in the world of nirvāṇa, the real world of empty infinity, there is nothing to be called death. From this point of view, Takuan Zenji is right: there is no one

killing, no killing, and no one to be killed. The peace of infinite emptiness pervades the universe.

I discussed the risk of this absolute position, when taken exclusively, in "The Nature of the Precepts." If there is no sword, no swing of the sword, no decapitation, then what about all the blood? What about the wails of the widow and children? The absolute position, when isolated, omits human details completely.[122]

Japanese Zen deeply influenced the samurai. In the Tokugawa period this influence, so-called *bushidō* or "the way of warriors," was just an idea. For almost three hundred years in Japan we had no wars. The way of samurai was an idea of how samurai should train themselves and what kind of attitude the warriors should maintain. They did not actually use this idea "a sword and Zen are one" in the battlefield. But after the Meiji period (1868–1912 CE), Japan experienced many wars. The idea that "the sword and Zen are one" was finally put into practice. This was a poison, a misuse of Zen. If we miss the context of this practice and apply this attitude of "just doing" to any situation, it becomes a terrible weapon that has nothing to do with the Buddha's teaching. The Japanese people used this attitude in war without the vow of not killing.[123] I think Zen and Buddhism were twisted because of national egoism.

When we thoroughly study the mountains, this is the mountain training.

Dōgen asks us to thoroughly study mountains. Without studying mountains, this idea of "just doing" may become a poison. We need to thoroughly study what this mountain is: our living together with all beings. Then this practice or study is the mountain training. I think this means the mountains are training the mountains.

Such mountains and waters become wise men and sages.

The true reality of all beings becomes wise men and sages, people of the way.

## FINAL NOTE

What I've written here is my current report of studying Dharma through Dōgen's writings. Please don't take this as my final understanding. I will continue to study more deeply. Next year I may write in a completely different way. What you have read from me is one point of view; please don't just trust it. Please read Dōgen's writings or any Buddhist writings through your own understanding and experience.

I FIRST ENTERED into the Mountains and Waters at Tassajara
thirty years ago, when I was young and foolish. After that, I wandered off, into the halls of academe, getting gradually old and foolish. And now it seems I've circled back, to start all over again. Odd how my life somehow got bound up with this old book by Dōgen.

I set out to translate the book in 1971, when I was a student at Berkeley and studying Zen with Shunryū Suzuki in San Francisco. At the time, I was looking to try out my new knowledge of Japanese on Dōgen, and Suzuki suggested that I take a look at the "Mountains and Waters Sūtra." A look convinced me it was much too hard for me, but Suzuki said I should do it anyway and offered to help. I had one short, sweet summer at Tassajara, sitting in the sycamore shade with my books and meeting with the man to go over the text. Then, the man was gone, and I was off to classrooms in Tōkyō. I figured that was more or less the end of it.

However, a few years ago, one of my students at Stanford, Mark Gonnerman, got an idea for a seminar on Gary Snyder's long poem *Mountains and Rivers Without End*. When Gary came down from the Sierras to read for us, he talked about how that old Tassajara translation had worked its way into his work on the book. Sure enough, if you follow Gary's trail through the book, you can see Dōgen's mountains walking across the landscape of the poems. So Mark asked me to rework my translation and give a talk on the sūtra for his seminar. And there I was, a lifetime later, back where I started—but with many more books and no man to help.

Meanwhile, around the same time, the Sōtōshū Shūmuchō had the idea of starting up the Sōtō Zen Text Project to translate the entire *Shōbōgenzō*, and somehow I got involved, even though I still couldn't understand what Dōgen was talking about. I used to think that I shouldn't try to translate the *Shōbōgenzō* till I understood Dōgen, but recently I've come to realize that I can't wait for that anymore and should just do it anyway, as Suzuki said. I figure that he must have understood what Dōgen was getting at and, if he had just lived a little longer, could have used even a poor translation of the "Mountains and Waters Sūtra" to explain it to people. I figure others probably understand and may be able to use whatever I can do now to explain it to people. Anyway, with a book like the *Shōbōgenzō*, you can't have too many translations.

There are already several translations of the *Shōbōgenzō*, and more are coming out now all the time. Some of them seem pretty poor, but some are really good. I don't think my own translations will be better than the good ones, but I want to try something a little different from most of what I've seen so far. Of course, there are lots of ways to translate, each with its own virtues and vices. When the translator doesn't understand what the author is talking about, probably the safest approach is to keep as close as possible to the author's language. Every translator has to cook her text, but the trick in this approach is to try for no more than medium rare, so the reader can still taste some of the raw juices of the original words.

The chief virtue here, at least when all goes well, is that the translation will have less of the translator's own ideas. The chief vice is that the translation will be hard to read, with a foreign feel, full of odd diction and unusual syntax. Sometimes, this minimalist approach may catch more of the author's style; other times it can distort the style, making what may originally have been smooth and flowing for the native reader into something twisted and clunky. Sometimes, it can make a passage seem more difficult or more exotic than it really is, turning what was fairly easy and idiomatic into something strange and fraught with unintended mystery; but it can also preserve some of the original strangeness and keep open mysteries that are inherent in the text.

Every translation is a bunch of trade-offs, every translator is a negotiator between author and audience. But when the negotiations get tough, as they often do with Dōgen, I guess I'd rather let the reader wrestle with the difficulties of his medieval Japanese diction and syntax than make her read my own ideas in easy English paraphrase. Dōgen loved his language, and he was a master of it. He had his own ways of saying things, strange, powerful ways, notoriously demanding of the reader. The language of his *Shōbōgenzō* has been boggling minds in Japan for almost eight hundred years now, and it seems only fair to let it boggle us for a while. Anyway, in another hundred years or so, today's elegant English translations will probably look just as cramped and quaint as the clunky ones that stick closer to the text.

The point of avoiding easy paraphrase and sticking close to the language of the text is not just to keep the translation as difficult for the reader as the original but to make it easier for the reader to get behind the translation to the original difficulties. And for this, I want to have as many notes as possible. Not just the usual notes on Buddhist technical terms and Zen masters' names but all sorts of notes on interesting words and ambiguous phrases, on ordinary idioms and obscure allusions, on puns and word plays. Notes that warn when the translation doesn't really get it or is just a guess; notes that give other options than the one I end up choosing. I want notes that say things like "The antecedent of the pronoun here isn't clear, but Menzan's commentary says it's X."

One of the things I like best about the Shūmuchō translation project is that it allows me to indulge this footnote fetish. Publishers, even academic presses, don't like a lot of notes; they make a book too bulky and expensive. But right from the start of the Sōtō Zen Text Project, we decided that, in addition to publishing our work as a book, we'd have an electronic version of our translations that includes all our notes on the texts. Most people probably won't care about them, but at least they'll be there for anyone who really wants to get into the *Shōbōgenzō*. Maybe teachers can use them sometimes to prepare lectures; maybe people can use them to make better translations.

It's one of the great luxuries of academic life that one can while away half a day tracking down a single strange word in old books. Of course, this way of doing things means you go pretty slowly. At this point, I guess our project has about one-fourth of the *Shōbōgenzō* in draft form, but it will still be several years before we can go to press. Meanwhile, we wanted to start making some of our work available, in order to see how people like it and get suggestions on what we might do better. We're happy that the Education Center have offered us space in *Dharma Eye* to run a series of our translations. As you might guess, I'm especially happy that we're starting off the series with my old friend, the "Mountains and Waters Sūtra."

The translations we put in *Dharma Eye* can't include all our notes. But as we publish our work in *Dharma Eye*, we'll be putting it on the internet, together with our annotation. The Stanford Center for Buddhist Studies has kindly let us use a corner of their server to put up a Sōtō Zen Text Project website, where you can find the translations, as well as news of the project and a handy email form for sending us messages. Please come and visit us.

Prof. Carl Bielefeldt
Stanford University

Carl Bielefeldt is an American scholar specializing in East Asian studies, editor of the Sōtō Zen Text Project, and in 1971 was the first translator of *Sansuikyō* into English. This essay first appeared in *Dharma Eye*, no. 9, October 2001.

# Appendix 2. Mountains Hidden in Mountains:
## Dōgen Zenji and the Mind of Ecology

## Prologue: Serving Sentient Beings

*In what manner should one accommodate and serve sentient beings? To do so, one should think: "Throughout the realm-of-dharmas and the realm-of-space, in the ocean-like cosmos in the ten directions, there are infinite kinds of sentient beings; some are born of eggs, some are born of the womb, of wetness, or of metamorphosis; . . . some live by earth, some by water, fire, wind, space, trees, or flowers. . . . O countless are their kinds and infinite are their forms, shapes, bodies, faces, life-spans, races, names, dispositions, views, knowledge, desires, inclinations, manners, costumes, and diets. They abide in numerous kinds of dwellings: in towns, villages, cities, and palaces. They comprise the devas, the nagas, the heavenly musicians, the tree nymphs . . . humans, nonhumans, beings without feet, beings with two, four, or many feet; some are with form, some are without form, some with or without thoughts, or neither with nor without thoughts. To all these infinite kinds of beings, I will render my service and accommodate them in whatever way is beneficial to them."*

*Why should we cherish all sentient beings?*
*Because sentient beings are the roots of the tree-of-awakening.*

*The Bodhisattvas and the buddhas are the flowers and fruits.*
*Compassion is the water for the roots.*
                                                    —Hua-yen Sūtra

## I. OPENING THE MOUNTAIN

I grew up on a farm in the eastern Pacific, western North America, in the Puget Sound area of Washington State. I worked as a kid caring for the family milk cows and entering the forest, and as I grew older I explored the vast Cascade range. I become an avid backpacker, mountain climber, and amateur naturalist. I also witnessed excessive exploitation of the forests and began to do environmental politics while still in high school.

Puget Sound in the 1930s was about like Yayoi, Japan: some parts developed but much wild land left. Today it is 90 percent logged. As I studied history and literature, both occidental and oriental, I learned that Hinduism and Buddhism shared the ethical precept of *ahimsā*, nonharming, and that this was meant to embrace not just human beings but all living beings. This definitely tilted me toward Asia. This proclivity was reinforced by seeing East Asian landscape paintings, by reading Chinese and Japanese poetry in translation, and by the Daoist writings of Lao-tzu and Chuang-tzu. I discovered Indian mythology and cosmology and yoga practice. I went on to read up on early Indian Buddhism, Mahayana sūtras, and Zen. When I arrived at Zen I finally saw the connections between the insights of Mahāyāna sūtras, Daoist thought, *sumi* painting, poetry, Indian yoga, and zazen practice.

It was a few more years before I discovered Dōgen. By that time I was living in Kyōto studying at Daitoku-ji with the *sōdō-rōshi*,[124] Oda Sessō. I was introduced to Dōgen by the elderly Morimoto-Rōshi of Nagaoka Zenjuku, with whom I occasionally visited, and who once admiringly said: "Dōgen! You should look at Dōgen. He gives Zen away, he tells everything! Dōgen is like a clam. He opens his mouth and you can see down to the bottom of his stomach. Read the *Shōbōgenzō*." There was not much Dōgen in translation then. I found an early translation of the *Zuimonki* in Kyōto. Back in the States I ran into Dr. Carl Bielefeldt's translation of "Sansuikyō" when it was still part of his M.A. draft. (Someone at Page Street, I think, smuggled it to me.)

Once I had read the "Sansuikyō" and gotten a little sense of Dōgen's approach to both practice and the phenomenal world of nature, I knew I was dealing with something far richer than just an East-Asian nature sensibility, far more than "love of nature" with its limited and chosen range of subjects, but with a great mind that played across all the realms. As a person who had worked outdoors for the Forest Service and logging companies, and as one who had lived for months in remote mountaintop fire-lookout cabins, I also took mountains and rivers pretty literally. They were the wildest and most exciting features of the landscape, waiting to be traveled on foot or by canoe.

You cannot see the landscape with accuracy and clarity if you just drive across it in a train or car. The only way a landscape can be known is by walking across it, day after day. I realized that Dōgen knew his mountains and rivers not only from zazen but from his own walking—starting with his hike up Mount Hiei when he was nine or ten. Like everyone in those days, he was doubtless walking hundreds of miles, up hill and down, in both Japan and China, for most of his life.

## II. Billions of Beings See the Morning Star, and They All Become Buddhas

There have been many Dōgens brought forward in this century: the strict monk, the big-spirited teacher, the philosopher, the aristocrat, and the poet. And maybe I should suggest the peripatetic, the walker, the hiker. These facets of the great teacher are called forth of course by different constituencies, groups with different views, who "construct" Dōgen to fit their needs. No blame for this; it happens constantly everywhere.

Now it becomes possible for contemporary environmentalists, of wide and compassionate view, also to think of Dōgen as a kind of ecologist. An *ecologist*, not just a Buddhist priest who had a deep sensibility for nature, but a proto-ecologist, a thinker who had remarkable insight deep into the way that wild nature works. At the risk of saying what's already known, I'll say a few words about ecology as a scientific discipline.

Ecology is originally based on biology. It now incorporates methods and information from physics, mathematics, and even engineering. The English word was created in the nineteenth century from the Greek root *oikos*, which means "household," plus the Greek *logos*. In this case "ecology" simply implies "thinking about the household." It's close to the word "economics," which means "the rules of the household"— from *nomos*, laws or rules. The formal Japanese word for ecology is *seitaigaku*, which has the sense of "life situation study" or "living conditions." *Ekorojii* might have more public currency these days.

Scientific ecology is a very sophisticated field. It is based on the accumulation and analysis of real-world data, involving living organisms on every scale, plus tracking the inorganic materials such as carbon and oxygen that cycle in and out of living systems. Over that, it analyzes the flow of energy through living systems, energy that takes its start from a variety of chemical and solar sources. Evolutionary ecologists look at the interconnectedness of plants, creatures, clouds, sunshine, and so forth as it works through time, and how the whole planetary web of life-and-death is manifesting constant change, constant adaptation, and in some organisms at least an apparent self-organizing dynamic. No one would try to say, though, where it's all going. The contemporary ecological scientists are in the forefront of high-level computer use, by which they model the various possibilities of major switches and changes in processes both great and small, and they try to predict various outcomes in the real world. The degree of complexity witnessed in the workings of living systems has contributed to the emergence of chaos and complexity theorizing. All these organic and inorganic realms interacting is what we call the biosphere and would be referred to in Buddhism as "all sentient beings." It can be called a community of practice. It is a huge lineage, of which we are all members. Dōgen Zenji is one of its fruits.

This demanding science of the planetary household has precursors throughout the world in the hands-on practical proto-scientific knowledges of pastoralists, horticulturalists, agriculturalists, wild-plant gatherers, fisher-people, and hunters, for all of hominid history. Our ancient ancestors had a deep understanding of the cycles of the seasons, animal behavior, plant and animal properties, and of course they realized that human beings are also creatures and are inevitably members of the communities of nature. Today we call them ecosystems. They could see that life and death flowed on like a river, and that suffering and impermanence were sooner or later everyone's lot—the fate of cranes and foxes, of whales and mice, as well as humans.

The study of ecology is truly the study of *shōji*, of *saṃsāra*, "the wheel of life and death" in the *kāmadhātu*, the realm of desire, or of metabolic beings. But ecologists do not lament it or seek to flee it but to investigate and analyze it, to hope to know what goes on inside. Need I say, this does no harm to nature? If the analytic mode is spiritually problematic, it is only so for the analyst. And some scientists will marvel at it. The ecological view, like the Dharma view, can appreciate the flowers and the moon, but it also sees parasites, bacteria, cancers, and baby birds eaten by snakes with a nondiscriminating eye that grasps the many roles in the community of life-and-death.

For some time now ecological scientists have been telling us all that the way humans and their economies are treating the planet is destructive and dangerous in the extreme. This is known. But scientific information in itself does not move governments, world leaders, or masses of people. To transform public policy in regard to the oceans and air, forests, and population questions, and to move toward saving endangered species, both require reaching the very hearts of whole societies.

This is not a work for the scientists. Their research is essential to us, but to change the way contemporary human beings live on earth is a kind of Dharma work, a work for dedicated followers of the Way who because of their practice and insight can hope to balance wisdom and compassion and help open the eyes of others. I think that Buddhism, and especially old Shamon Dōgen, has something to show us in the matter of how to go about this.

In "Mountains and Waters Sūtra," Dōgen says, "although mountains belong to the nation, they really belong to the people who love them." This is weirdly cogent for us as we debate about land-use policies with the governments and corporations of the world. In a sense it can be read as a permission to engage with, intervene in, the behavior of governments and corporations alike when they abuse the resources entrusted to them.

But that's not what I really want to say right now. I want to get back to Dōgen as a proto-ecologist whose words speak to both spiritual and secular affairs. In "Sansuikyō" he says:

> Now when dragons and fish see water as a palace, it is just like human beings seeing a palace. They do not think it flows . . .

And,

> You who study with buddhas should not be limited to human views when you are studying water.

And,

> There is also a world of sentient beings in clouds. There is a world of sentient beings in the air. There is a world of sentient beings in fire. . . . There is a world of sentient beings in a blade of grass.

Here Dōgen causes us to look at the world in many layers, from many sides, on all scales, with both the spiritual eye and the eye of the nonhuman all-species ecological imagination—calling for a mind that can know that a rocky island in the offshore Pacific covered with breeding sea lions, full of racket and an incredibly foul odor, is for sea lions a jeweled palace, redolent with the sweetest of perfumes.

In Buddhist psychology we speak of the "six roads," *rokudō*, which constitute the spiritual and biological inventory of possible states of being. Not only the familiar human and nonhuman sentient beings (animals) are on the "roads"—but *devas* (gods and spirits), *asuras* (angry intelligent demons), hungry ghosts (greed-obsessed spirits), and hell-dwellers as well. Each of these zones is a mythological habitat, a part of the ecology of the mind.

We of the cusp of the third millennium, puppets of Late Capitalism, might also identify with the best-known facet of Dōgen, that is, Dōgen as a teacher who helps us skillfully grasp the truth that all realms are authentic and then teaches how to overcome human-species ego, as well as personal ego.

To recapitulate, I would suggest that Dōgen's nature sensibility can be seen in his poetry, the richness of his many levels and realms of mind can be seen in texts like the "Sansuikyō," but his *Instructional Text for Forest Management, Ocean and Wetland Restoration, and Third World Crisis Intervention* would be that guide for Dharma activists and administrators, the *Tenzo Kyōkun, Instructions for the Cook.*

But then I am speaking as a person from a backward society that is equally far from the land of the Buddha and the Land of Plato—inhabited by self-righteously ignorant people, some of whom don't even want to hear about Darwinian evolution, let alone the Dharma.

### III. Decomposed

*Hungry ghosts see water as raging fire*
*or pus and blood....*

Life in the wild is not just eating berries in the sunlight. I like to imagine a "depth ecology" that would go to the dark side of nature—the ball of crunched bones in a scat, the feathers in the snow, the tales of insatiable appetite. Wild systems are in one elevated sense above criticism, but they can also be seen as irrational, moldy, cruel, parasitic. Jim Dodge told me how he had watched—with fascinated horror—orcas methodically batter a gray whale to death in the Chukchi Sea. Life is not just diurnal and a property of large interesting vertebrates; it is also nocturnal, anaerobic, cannibalistic, microscopic, digestive, fermentative: cooking away in the warm dark. Life is well maintained at a four-mile ocean depth, is waiting and sustained on a frozen rock wall, and is clinging and nourished in hundred-degree desert temperatures. And there is a world of nature on the decay side, a world of beings who do rot and decay in the shade. Human beings have made much of purity and are repelled by blood, pollution, putrefaction. The other side of the "sacred" is the sight of your beloved in the underworld, dripping with maggots. Coyote, Orpheus, and Izanagi cannot help but look, and they lose her. Shame, grief, embarrassment, and fear are the anaerobic fuels of the dark imagination. The less familiar energies of the wild world, and their analogs in the imagination, have given us ecologies of the imagination.

Here we encounter the peculiar habitat needs of the gods. They settle in on the summits of mountains (as on Mount Olympus), have chambers deep below the earth, or are invisibly all around us. (One major deity is rumored to be domiciled entirely off this earth.) The Yana said that Mount Lassen of northern California, "Waganupa" in Ishi's tongue—a ten-thousand-foot volcano—is a home to countless *kukini* who keep a fire going inside. (The smoke passes out through the smoke hole.) They will enjoy their magical stick-game gambling until the time that human beings reform themselves and become "real people" whom spirits might want to associate with once again.

The spirit world goes across and between species. It does not need to concern itself with reproduction, it is not afraid of death, it is not practical. But the spirits do seem to have an ambivalent, selective interest in cross-world communication. Young women in scarlet and white robes dance to call down the gods, to be possessed by them, to speak in their voices. The priests who employ them can only wait for the message. (I think it was D. H. Lawrence who said, "Eat and carouse with Bacchus, or munch dry bread with Jesus, but don't sit down without one of the gods.")

Where Dōgen and the Zen tradition would walk, chant a sūtra, or do sitting meditation, the elder vernacular artisans of soul and spirit would also play a flute, drum, dance, dream, listen for a song, go without food, and be available to communicate with birds, animals, or rocks. There is a story of Coyote watching the yellow autumn cotton-wood leaves float and eddy lightly down to the ground. He said it was so lovely to watch, and he asked the cottonwood leaves if he might do it too. They warned him, "Coyote, you are too heavy and you have a body of bones and guts and muscle. We are light, we drift with the wind, but you would fall and be hurt." Coyote would hear none of it, and insisted on climbing a cottonwood, edging far out onto a branch, and launching himself off. He fell and was killed. There's a caution here: Do not be too hasty in setting out to "become one with." But, as we have heard, Coyote will roll over, reassemble his ribs, locate his paws, make do with a pebble with a dot of pitch on it for an eye, and trot off again.

Narratives are one sort of trace that we leave in the world. All our literatures are leaving, of the same order as the myths of wilderness peoples who leave behind only stories and a few stone tools. Other orders of being have their own literatures. Narrative in the deer world is a track of scents that is passed on from deer to deer, with an art of interpretation, which is instinctive. A literature of blood stains, a bit of piss, a whiff of estrus, a hit of rut, a scrape on a sapling, and long gone. And there might be a "narrative theory" among these other beings—they might ruminate on "intersexuality" or "decomposition criticism."

I suspect that primary peoples all know that their myths are some-how "made up." They do not take them literally and at the same time they hold the stories very dear. Only upon being invaded by history and whipsawed by other and unfamiliar values do a people begin to declare that their myths are "literally true." This literalness in turn provokes skeptical questioning and the whole critical exercise. What a final refinement of confusion about the role of myth it is to declare that they are not to be believed but are nonetheless aesthetic and psycho-logical constructs that bring order to an otherwise chaotic world, and to which we should willfully commit ourselves! Dōgen's "You should know that even though all things are liberated and not tied to any-thing, they abide in their own phenomenal expression" is medicine for that. The "Mountains and Waters Sūtra" is called a "sūtra" not to assert that the "mountains and rivers of this moment" are a text, a system of symbols, a referential world of mirrors but that this world in its actual existence is a complete presentation, an enactment—and that it stands for nothing.

## IV. Walking on Water

There's all sorts of walking—from heading out across the desert in a straight line to a sinuous weaving through undergrowth. Descending rocky ridges and talus slopes is a specialty in itself. It is an irregular dancing—always shifting—step of walking on slabs and scree. The breath and eye are always following this uneven rhythm. It is never paced or clocklike but flexing—little jumps, sidesteps—going for the well-seen place to put a foot on a rock, hit flat, move on, zigzagging along and all deliberate. The alert eye looking ahead, picking the footholds to come, while never missing the step of the moment. The body-mind is so at one with this rough world that it makes these moves effortlessly once it has had a bit of practice. The mountain keeps up with the mountain.

In 1225 Dōgen was in his second year in South China. That year he walked out of the mountains and passed through the capital of the Southern Sung Dynasty, Hang-chou, on his way north to the Wan-shou monastery at Mount Jing. The only account of China left by Dōgen are notes on talks by the master Ju-ching.[125] I wonder what Dōgen would have said of city walking. Hang-chou had level, broad, straight streets paralleling canals. He must have seen the many-storied houses, clean, cobbled lanes, theaters, markets, and innumerable restaurants. It had three thousand public baths. Marco Polo (who called it Quinsai) visited it twenty-five years later and estimated that it was the largest (at least a million people) and most affluent city in the world at that time.[126] Even today the people of Hang-chou remember the lofty eleventh-century poet Su Shi, who built the causeway across West Lake when he was governor. At the time of Dōgen's walk North China was under the control of the Mongols, and Hang-chou would fall to the Mongols in fifty-five more years.

The South China of that era sent landscape painting, calligraphy, teachings from both the Sōtō and Rinzai schools of Zen, and the idea of that great southern capital Hang-chou, to Japan. The ideal of Hang-chou shaped both Osaka and Tōkyō in their Tokugawa-era evolution. These two positions—one the austere Zen practice with its spare, clean halls, and the other the possibility of a convivial urban life rich in festivals and theaters and restaurants—are two potent legacies of East Asia to the world. Zen stands in a way for the Far Eastern love of nature, and Hang-chou stands for a world-scale vision of the city. Both are brimming with energy and life. Because most of the cities of the world are now mired in poverty, overpopulation, gridlock, and pollution, there is all the more reason to recover the dream. To neglect the city (in our hearts and minds for starters) is deadly, as James Hillman has said.[127]

"Mountains and Waters Sūtra" goes on to say:

> All waters appear at the foot of the eastern mountains. Above all waters are all mountains. Walking beyond and walking within are both done on water. All mountains walk with their toes on all waters and splash there.

Dōgen finishes his meditation on mountains and waters with this: "When you investigate mountains thoroughly, this is the work of the mountains. Such mountains and waters of themselves become wise persons and sages"—become sidewalk vendors and noodle-cooks, become brokers and street-people, become marmots, ravens, graylings, rattlesnakes—*all* beings are "said" by the mountains and waters—even to the clanking tread of a Caterpillar tractor, to the gleam of the keys of a clarinet.

## V. WE WASH OUR BOWLS IN THIS WATER

*"The 1.5 billion cubic kilometers of water on the earth are split by photosynthesis and reconstituted by respiration once every two million years or so."*

A day on the ragged North Pacific coast get soaked by whipping mist, rainsqualls tumbling, mountain mirror ponds, snowfield slush, rock-wash creeks, earfuls of falls, sworls of ridge-edge snowflakes, swift gravelly rivers, tidewater crumbly glaciers, high hanging glaciers, shore-side mud pools, icebergs, streams looping through the tideflats, spume of brine, distant soft rain drooping from a cloud,

sea lion lazing under the surface of the sea—

> *ga shi sempassui*
> *nyo ten kanro mi*
> *We wash our bowls in this water*
> *It has the flavor of ambrosial dew—*
> .

Beaching the raft, stagger out and shake off wetness like a bear, stand on the sandbar, rest from the river    being

upwellings, sideswirls, backswirls
curl-overs, outripples, eddies, chops and swells
wash-overs, shallows        confluence turbulence        wash-seam
wavelets, riffles, saying

"A hydraulic's a cross between a wave and a hole,
        —you get a weir effect.
Pillow-rock's a total fold-back over a hole,
        it shows spit on the top of the wave
a haystack's a series of waves at the bottom of a tight channel
        there's a tongue of the rapids—the slick tongue—the 'v'—
some holes are 'keepers,' they won't let you through;
eddies, backflows, we say 'eddies are your friends.'
Current differential, it can suck you down
vertical boils are straight-up eddies spinning,
herringbone waves curl under and come back.
Well, let's get going, get back to the rafts."

Swing the big oars,
   head into a storm.


*Seyo kijin shu*
*Shitsuryo toku ho man*
*Om makura sai sowaka*
*We offer it to all demons and spirits*
*May all be filled and satisfied.*


*Om makula sai svaha!*
 •

Su Tung-po sat out one whole night by a creek  on the slopes of
Mount Lu.
Next morning he showed this poem to his teacher:

 The stream with its sounds  is a long broad tongue
 The looming mountain is a wide-awake body
 Throughout the night song after song
 How can I speak at dawn.

Old Master Chang-tsung approved him. Two centuries later Dōgen
said,
 "Sounds of stream and shapes of mountains.
 The sounds never stop and the shapes never cease.
 Was it Su who woke
 Or was it the mountains and streams?
 Billions of beings see the morning star
 and all become Buddhas!
 If *you*, who are valley streams and looming
 mountains, can't throw some light on the nature of ridges and rivers,

 *who the hell can?"*

              Gary Snyder

Gary Snyder is best known as a poet, essayist, lecturer, and environmental activist, and he spent years in Japan studying Zen. His writings influenced the Deep Ecology movement. He served as a faculty member at the University of California, Davis, for many years.

Sections III and IV of this paper are from Gary Snyder's book of essays *The Practice of the Wild* (New York: North Point Press, 1990). Section V is from Gary Snyder's book-length poem *Mountains and Rivers without End* (Washington, D.C.: Counterpoint, 1996). This paper was presented to the symposium "Dogen Zen and Its Relevance for Our Time," Stanford University, October 23–24, 1999. The full proceedings of the symposium have been published as *Dōgen Zen and Its Relevance for Our Time*, ed. Shōhaku Okumura (San Franciscio: Soto Zen Buddhism International Center, 2003).

# APPENDIX 3. THE MEANING OF THE TITLE *SHŌBŌGENZŌ*

THE TERM *Shōbōgenzō* first appeared in 801 in the *Baolin Zhuan* (in Japanese, *Horin Den*), a Chan record that established a genealogy of Dharma transmission from Śākyamuni Buddha to Huineng, the Sixth Ancestor of Chinese Zen.[128] Some Zen scholars consider this writing to be the beginning of the formation of Zen as a school. The next collection of transmission stories was in 952, the *Zutang ji*, followed in 1004 by the *Jingde Chuandeng Lu*. The genealogy mentioned in *Jingde Chuandeng Lu* has been the authoritative history of Zen since the Song Dynasty.

In the *Zutang ji* and *Jingde Chuandeng Lu*, the Dharma that has been transmitted through thirty-three ancestors from Mahākāśyapa to Huineng is called by various names in the sections of the various ancestors. For example, we have *Shōbōgen* (正法眼, true Dharma eye), *hōgen* (法眼, Dharma eye), *hō* (法, Dharma), *Daihōgen* (大法眼, great Dharma eye), *Shōbōgenzō* (正法眼蔵, true Dharma eye treasury), *Jōhōgen* (淨法眼, pure Dharma eye), *Shōbō* (正法, true Dharma), *hōgenzō* (法眼蔵, Dharma eye treasury), *Daihōgenzō* (大法眼蔵, great Dharma eye treasury), and *shōgen* (正眼, true eye). Since *Shōbōgenzō* was one of these names, we can be certain that this expression existed from the beginning of the ninth century and remained in use through the eleventh as a synonym of "Dharma eye" and other similar expressions.

The story of Dharma transmission from Śākyamuni Buddha to

Mahākāśyapa is always introduced as the origin of the word *Shōbō-genzō*. The most popular version is in the thirteenth-century *Wumen-guan* (*The Gateless Barrier*, or in Japanese *Mumonkan*), case 6:

> One day at Vulture Peak, in front of many people in his assembly, the World-Honored One picked up one stalk of a flower, without saying anything. Everyone in the assembly was silent. But Venerable Mahākāśyapa broke into a smile. The World-Honored One said, "I have the true Dharma eye treasury, the marvelous mind of nirvāṇa, the subtle Dharma-gate that shows the true form of the formless, independent of words and letters and transmitted outside the verbal teachings.[129] I entrust it to Mahākāśyapa."

However, this story, called *nenge-mishō*, or "holding flower and smiling," was written long after the expression *Shōbōgenzō* appeared in the genealogies. It is said that the story appeared in the sūtra titled *Daibonten-ō-monbutsuketsugi-kyō*, which means "The Great Brahma Gave a Question to Buddha and Resolved His Doubt," but that sūtra was written in China, not India. We can be sure that this story did not exist when *Jingde Chuandeng Lu* was compiled in the beginning of the eleventh century, so this story is not the origin of the term *Shōbōgenzō*.

The earlier story of the Buddha's transmission to Mahākāśyapa, in the *Zutang ji*, is as follows:

> Śākyamuni Buddha was about to pass away in Kuśinagara, but Mahākāśyapa was not there. So he said to the monks in the assembly there, asking them to tell Mahākāśyapa, "I have the pure Dharma eye, the marvelous mind of nirvāṇa, and the subtle true Dharma, which in its authentic form is formless. You must cherish it and maintain it."

And then the transmission verse is introduced.

In the later *Jingde Chuandeng Lu*, the text quotes the Buddha as saying exactly the same words as in the *Zutang ji* version, but the location and situation are simply omitted, and it does not mention whether Mahākāśyapa was present or absent. Probably the author thought that the Dharma should be transmitted face to face and made a story to match this.

In both texts, the Dharma transmitted from the Buddha to Mahākāśyapa is called "*Shōjō-hōgen, nehan-myōshin, jissō-musō, mimyōno shōbo* (清浄法眼、涅槃妙心、実相無相、微妙正法)." The parts with bold font are different from the *Wumenguan* version. And the final two phrases, *mimyōno shōbo*, were added.

*Shōjō-hōgen*, "clear and pure Dharma eye," is an expression used since early Buddhism. There is a story in the *Dhammacakkappavattana Sutta* (*The First Discourse of the Buddha: Turning the Wheel of Dhamma*) that I think is its origin. After Śākyamuni Buddha's first teaching of the Four Noble Truths, he said about himself:

> "Indeed a vision of true knowledge arose in me thus: My mind's deliverance is unassailable. This is the last birth. Now there is no more becoming."
>
> Thus the Buddha spoke. The group of five bhikkus was glad and acclaimed his words. While this doctrine was being expounded, there arose in the Venerable Kondañña the pure, immaculate vision of the truth and he realized, "Whatsoever is subject to causation is also subject to cessation."[130]

The original meaning of this expression is that Venerable Kondañña's eye was open and he could see the reality (Dharma) of dependent origination that is the basis of the Four Noble Truths. It refers to the wisdom eye, undefiled by the three poisons, that can see objects as they truly are.

In Mahāyāna sūtras the expression *hōgen* (Dharma eye) is used quite often. For example, in the *Diamond Sūtra*, section 18, this word is used as one of the five eyes: the physical eye, divine eye, prajñā eye, Dharma eye, and buddha eye.[131] The first two are discriminating eyes. Nāgārjuna explains the prajñā eye as follows:

> The prajñā eye does not see beings, for all common and differentiating characteristics are extinguished. It is free of all attachments and immune to all Dharmas, including prajñā itself. But because it does not distinguish anything, the prajñā eye cannot liberate other beings. Hence, a bodhisattva gives rise to the Dharma eye.

And he said of the Dharma eye, "The Dharma eye enables a bodhisattva to cultivate a Dharma and to realize a path as well as to know the expedient means by which other beings can do so."[132]

In the later version of the story of the transmission to Mahākāśyapa, *shōjō-hōgen* (clear and pure Dharma eye) was replaced with *Shōbōgenzō* (true Dharma eye treasury). Why? Here is my guess. If the Dharma transmitted from Śākyamuni to Mahākāśyapa is shōjō-hōgen, it was identical to what Koṇḍañña attained at the first discourse, which would mean that all the Buddha's disciples who attained arhathood got the same hōgen (Dharma eye). When the Buddha passed away, there were five hundred arhats; if Mahākāśyapa had been only one of five hundred monks with the same status, there would be no reason to call him the First Ancestor. Probably the person or people who made this change wanted to make a clear distinction between the attainment of those five hundred monks and the Dharma transmission to Mahākāśyapa. Although Mahākāśyapa was not considered to be the second Buddha, Zen people wanted to make him the First Ancestor, and therefore he must have received something different from the Buddha's other disciples.

*Nehan-myōshin*, the next part of the name of this Dharma, is "marvelous or wondrous mind of nirvāṇa." Nirvāṇa is the opposite of saṃsāra. "Mind" is Buddha mind. Uchiyama Rōshi often said, "This is not psychological mind; this is life." Life includes both body and mind. *Nehan-myōshin* actually means "the wondrous life in nirvāṇa."

The next part, *jissō musō*, is "true form of the formless." *Jissō* is "true form" and *musō* is "no form." *Jissō musō* means that the true reality of all beings is no form. This is an expression of emptiness, from before the term *emptiness* was used.

Dōgen often discusses the "true form of all beings" or *shohōjissō*. *Jissō* includes both *sō*, "form," and *mu-sō*, no form. Thus, *shohōjissō* has both form and no form; no form *is* true form. Dōgen often said that we should see both sides; they are two sides of one reality. This is the way all things are according to Mahāyāna Buddhism. This teaching was transmitted from Buddha to Mahākāśyapa and later generations.

*Shōbōgen* is clear: "true Dharma eye" is Buddha's wisdom, which sees all things as they are, without distortion. But what does *zō*, "treasury," mean? I have been asking this question for a long time.

The Chinese word *zō* (蔵) is used as a translation of at least four Indian words: *piṭaka, kośa, ālaya,* and *garbha. Piṭaka* is often translated into English as "basket" and refers to any of three categories of Buddhist scriptures. *Kośa* literally means "barrel," "box," "container," "storage," or "treasury," and is used in the title of texts, for example, *Abhidharma-kośa. Ālaya* is used in *ālayavijñana* or "storehouse consciousness," the eighth consciousness in Yogācāra teachings, in which all our experiences are stored as seeds. *Garbha* means womb or embryo and is used in the term *tathāgata-garba* (in Japanese, *nyrai-zō*), womb or embryo of Tathāgata, another name for buddha nature. All of these words mean some kind of container, and any of them could be the original meaning of the *zō* in *Shōbōgenzō*: basket, container, treasury, storehouse, or womb.

*Hō-zō* (法蔵, *dharma-kośa*) is also an expression from India, and means "treasury of Dharma." It has three possible meanings: the Dharma teaching itself, the sūtras that contain the Dharma teaching, or an actual building for storage of sūtras.

But what is a treasury of the "true Dharma eye"? Tanahashi and Bielefeldt interpreted this as "treasury of true Dharma eye," and Nishiyama thought this is "the treasury" and "the eye" of true Dharma.

"Treasury of Eyes of True Dharma" or "treasury of true Dharma eye" suggests that this treasury holds the eye that sees the true Dharma. If scriptures are stored, it is very clear. But in what "treasury" could the "true Dharma eye" be stored?

If, however, this refers to two separate things, "true Dharma eye" and "true Dharma treasury," to me it is not the right name of the Dharma transmitted from a teacher to a disciple through generations, outside of teaching.

Another thing about this expression is that *Shōbōgenzō* was used by a Chinese Rinzai Zen master named Dahui Zonggao (in Japanese, Daie Soko, 1089–1163), who lived about a hundred years before Dōgen, for his collection of six hundred kōan stories. Dahui was a close friend of Sōtō Zen master Hongzhi Zhengjue, but they had a famous argument: Dahui called Hongzhi's way of practice *mokushō ja zen*, which means "evil silent illumination Zen." Hongzhi ignored Dahui's criticism and took this word *mokushō* as a positive expression of his style of practice. He even wrote a long poem entitled "Mokushō Mei."

Dōgen's lineage came from Changlu Qingliao (Chōro Seiryō, 1089–1151), Hongzhi's Dharma brother, who may have been Dahui's actual target. Dōgen criticized Dahui very strongly, but still he borrowed Dahui's title *Shōbōgenzō* for the collection of three hundred kōan stories he made during his thirties. Much later he also used the title for the collection of his Japanese essays.

So there are actually three *Shōbōgenzō*s: one is by Dahui, the first one by Dōgen is simply the collection of three hundred stories, and the most famous one is the text we are reading now.

Here is one last possibility. "*Shōbōgenzō*" could mean the treasury of what Dōgen is seeing by the true Dharma eye, that these words he has written contain the truth that he has seen. This seems contradictory with the Zen idea of "independent of words and letters and transmitted outside the verbal teachings." This contradiction might be acceptable because Dōgen criticizes this idea as a mistaken view.[133] But in the rest of Zen this expression is used to show the superiority of Zen to the teaching schools that transmitted Buddha's words. I think it is not correct to understand this as "the eye" and "the treasury" of "true Dharma."

Honestly speaking, I still don't understand exactly what *Shōbōgenzō* means. It is certain, however, that this word is used as the name of the Dharma that has been transmitted from Śākyamuni to Mahākāśyapa, then through each generation to Bodhidharma, finally reaching Dōgen himself.

*Shōbōgenzō* was written in Japanese. I think this is a very important point. Even up to the seventeenth or eighteenth century many Japanese Buddhist scholars wrote in Chinese. For Japanese of that time, not only Buddhists but Confucianists as well, Chinese was the formal language, like Latin in medieval European countries. So Dōgen did something very unusual by writing in Japanese. Some parts of the original text remain in Dōgen's own handwriting.

The Japanese language has changed a lot, and these days there are more than ten published translations of *Shōbōgenzō* into modern Japanese. Except for scholars who have thoroughly studied Buddhism and Chinese and Zen literature, Japanese people need both commentaries and modern translations to read *Shōbōgenzō*.

There are four basic collections of *Shōbōgenzō*. One collection is called the seventy-five-volume version; another is called the twelve-volume version. Traditionally it is said that the seventy-five-volume version was compiled by Dōgen, and the twelve-volume version was written after he finished the seventy-five volumes. Dōgen wanted to make a hundred-volume version but couldn't complete it because he died so young. So only eighty-seven were written. These two collections are considered original, collected by Dōgen himself.

There is heated controversy over which version is Dōgen's final teaching. Some scholars say the last-written twelve volumes supersede the earlier seventy-five. Others say that even though sometimes they seem opposite, all the volumes should be regarded as Dōgen's true teaching and should be used to illuminate each other.

There is also a sixty-volume version, thought to have been compiled by Giun (1253–1333), the fifth abbot of Eiheiji. It is said that Giun tried to remove all the fascicles in which Dōgen criticized Linji and Rinzai Zen masters. There is also a twenty-eight-volume version, possibly left over when Giun made the sixty-volume version.

Until recently *Shōbōgenzō* was essentially hidden in various Sōtō Zen temples. It was studied by a small circle of Zen masters, who almost worshiped Dōgen as a great Zen master and the founder of Sōtō Zen. Now many people read and interpret *Shōbōgenzō*, and the discussions of scholars are very interesting. But from my point of view, we can't really understand Dōgen's writings without zazen practice—meaning without shōbōgen, without the "true Dharma eye." We cannot acquire that eye by intellectual study; seeing things with the true Dharma eye is the process of our practice.

# APPENDIX 4. FURONG DAOKAI

FURONG DAOKAI is an important master in our Sōtō Zen lineage. He lived in the eleventh and twelfth centuries: 1043–1119. In "Sansuikyō" Dōgen calls him Dayang Daokai, but we commonly call him Furong. Both names are from places he lived: the Dayang and Furong mountains. Furong Daokai's teacher was Touzi Yiqing (Tōsu Gisei, 1032–1183). Furong is the seventh generation from Dongshan Liangjie (Tōzan Ryōkai, 807–69), the founder of the Sōtō lineage.

There is a curious story about Furong's teacher Touzi Yiqing. Touzi's teacher Dayang died five years before Touzi was born, so Touzi never studied with him. All Dayang's heirs had died before him, but he had a student in a Rinzai lineage, so he asked that student to pass on his Sōtō lineage so he could have an heir. Touzi became that person. This interruption was controversial later; in the seventeenth century many scholar-monks wanted to change the story to include face-to-face transmission. But actually the whole lineage is a fiction; they invented a good lineage for Zen because in Chinese culture the lineage of a family is very important.

In the Song Dynasty Zen was part of the Buddhist establishment, both supported and controlled by the government. Most prestigious monasteries were headed by Zen masters. The abbots of the major monasteries, called the Five Mountains, were appointed by the emperor. Anyone who wanted to be a Buddhist monk or priest in Chinese society needed permission from the government.

Because Furong Daokai was a virtuous and well-known teacher, the emperor asked him to be the abbot of a certain monastery, with the honorific title of Great Teacher. But Furong rejected the emperor's offer because he had vowed to be free of fame and profit. In ancient China, such a refusal would end in punishment. The emperor's messenger tried to save him by asking if he was sick. Furong refused the help, saying, "I was sick, but now I am fine." Since the messenger couldn't elicit any excuse, Furong was exiled to his hometown. There he established another monastery, on Mount Furong, when he was about sixty-six or sixty-seven years old. His popularity grew as a result of this incident, and many students came to practice with him. According to the record he had ninety-three disciples, of whom twenty-nine received Dharma transmission and became abbots of temples or monasteries. In this way, because of Furong Daokai the Sōtō lineage revived and restored its popularity.

# NOTES

1. Beata Grant, *Mount Lu Revisited: Buddhism in the Life and Writings of Su Shih* (Honolulu: University of Hawaii Press, 1994), 125.
2. *Dharma Eye* (October 2001), 5.
3. Francis Dojun Cook, *How to Raise an Ox: Zen Practice as Taught in Zen Master Dōgen's Shōbōgenzō* (Los Angeles: Center Publications, 1978), 102.
4. Kazuaki Tanahashi, trans., *Enlightenment Unfolds: The Essential Teachings of Zen Master Dōgen* (Boston: Shambhala, 1999), 60.
5. Gudo Nishijima and Chodo Cross, trans., *Master Dōgen's Shōbōgenzō* (Woking, Surrey: Windbell Publications, 1994), book 1, 86.
6. My translation, unpublished. Unless otherwise noted, all translations are my own.
7. Described in John Stevens, *The Marathon Monks of Mount Hiei* (Boston: Shambhala, 1988), 58.
8. This is a part of Shenxiu's (in Japanse, Jinshu) verse in the *Platform Sūtra*. This translation is by John McRae in *Seeing through Zen: Encounter, Transformation, and Genealogy in Chinese Chan Buddhism* (Berkeley and Los Angeles: University of California Press, 2003), 61.
9. "Preceptor Kai of Mount Dayang" is better known as Furong Daokai (or in Japanese Fuyō Dōkai) (1043–1118), the seventh ancestor after the founder Dongshan of Dōgen's Caodong House of Chan.
10. "Swift as the wind" alludes to a line in the *Lotus Sūtra* describing the speed of the supreme buddha vehicle. "A flower opening within the world" probably alludes to the line "A flower opens and the world arises," in the transmission verse attributed to Bodhidharma's master, Prajñātārā.
11. Dōgen is playing here with the term "stepping back," often used in Chan texts in the sense of "returning the mind to its enlightened source."
12. The four views of mountains here are probably drawn from a similar list in Buddhist scripture.
13. Dōgen is here playing with the term "stone woman," a standard idiom for a barren woman. The references to male and female, heavenly and earthly stones invoke passages in Chinese literature.

14. "The Great Master Yunmen Kuangzhen" is better known as Yunmen Wenyan (in Japanese, Ummon Bunen) (864–949), founder of the Yunmen House of Chan.

15. "Nanquan's 'sickle'" refers to a well-known conversation attributed to the early ninth-century master Nanquan Puyuan; "Huangbo's 'stick' and Linji's 'roar'" refer to the famous Chan teaching techniques of beating and shouting attributed to these two ninth-century masters.

16. "Son of Māra" ("The Evil One") is a standard Buddhist term of condemnation; "gang of six" refers to a notorious group of lawless monks among the followers of the Buddha.

17. Or "children of a non-Buddhist naturalism." "Naturalism" here may well refer to what Buddhists consider the false view that things arise, not from cause and conditions but spontaneously.

18. "Seven high and eight across" indicates a state of total spiritual freedom; "practice and verification are not nonexistent" is an expression from a dialogue between the Sixth Patriarch, Huineng, and his disciple Nanyue Huairang, often used by Dōgen to indicate the mystery of enlightened spiritual practice.

19. These various ways of seeing are based on the Vijñānavāda teaching known as "the four views of water": gods see water as jewels; humans see it as water; hungry ghosts, as blood; and fish, as a dwelling.

20. Buddhist cosmology posits a set of disks, or "wheels," beneath the earth, composed of, in descending order, the "elements" water, wind, and space.

21. The exact source of this saying is unidentified.

22. After a line in book one of this Daoist classic (also spelled *Wenzi*).

23. Avīci hell is the worst of the eight traditional hells of Buddhism.

24. From the *Zheng dao ge* (*Song of Verification of the Way*) attributed to the early eighth-century Chan figure Yongjia Xuanjue.

25. Dōgen seems to be running together two stories from the ancient Daoist classic the *Zhuangzi*, one dealing with the Yellow Emperor's interview with Guangchengzi of Mount Kongtong, the other with Emperor Yao's instruction by the Hua Guard.

26. At the time of the Tang government persecution of Buddhism (845) Chuanzi Decheng left his teacher Yaoshan Weiyan and became a boatman on the Huating River. There he met Jiashan Shanhui. After transmitting the Dharma to Shanhui by throwing him in the river, Decheng himself leaped into the water and disappeared.

27. There are several possible sources for this saying, such as the early tenth-century figure Yunmen Wenyan: "Monks, do not have deluded notions. Heaven is heaven, earth is earth; mountains are mountains, waters are waters; monks are monks, laymen are laymen."

28. In *Shōbōgenzō* "Kenbutsu" ("Seeing Buddha"), Dōgen wrote, "In seeing Buddha there are many forms that are seen and no-form that is seen; that is 'I do not understand the Buddhadharma.' In not seeing Buddha there are the many forms that are not seen and no-form that is not seen; that is, 'People who understand the Buddhadharma have attained it.'"

    Dōgen's usage of "understand" and "not-understand" came from the conversation between the Sixth Ancestor, Huineng, and a monk that appears in *Shinji Shōbōgenzō*, case 59:

    > A monk asked, "Who attained the meaning of Huangmei [the Fifth Ancestor]?"
    > Huineng said, "Those who understood the Buddhadharma attained it."
    > The monk asked, "Did you attain it, master?"
    > Huineng said, "No, I did not attain it."

The monk asked, "Why didn't you attain it?"
Huineng said, "I don't understand the Buddhadharma."

29. Shohaku Okumura, *Realizing Genjōkōan: The Key to Dōgen's Shōbōgenzō* (Boston: Wisdom Publications, 2010), 1.

30. Kazuaki Tanahashi, *Enlightenment Unfolds: The Essential Teachings of Zen Master Dōgen* (Boston: Shambhala, 1999), 10.

31. Beata Grant, *Mount Lu Revisited: Buddhism in the Life and Writings of Su Shih* (Honolulu: University of Hawaii Press, 1994), 125.

32. Taigen Leighton and Shohaku Okumura, trans., *Dōgen's Extensive Record: A Translation of the Eihei Kōroku* (Boston: Wisdom Publications, 2004), vol. 9, 552.

33. Ibid.

34. "Uji," in Norman Waddell and Masao Abe, trans., *The Heart of Dōgen's Shōbōgenzō* (Albany: State University of New York, 2002), 47.

35. "Uji," in Waddell and Abe, *The Heart of Dōgen's Shōbōgenzō*, 50.

36. Ibid.

37. Ibid.

38. Ibid.

39. Ibid.

40. Ibid.

41. Ibid.

42. Ibid., 51.

43. Menzan's eighteenth-century commentaries on *Shōbōgenzō*. No English translation exists.

44. Carl Bielefeldt, "Kobutsu shin" ("Old Buddha Mind"), *Dharma Eye* 13 (autumn 2003):16.

45. Ibid., 17.

46. Okumura, *Realizing Genjōkōan*, 2.

47. Ibid., 3.

48. My translation. Shohaku Okumura, "Gakudō-yōjin-shū" in *Heart of Zen: Practice without Gaining-mind* (Tōkyō: Sōtōshū Shūmuchō, 1988), 6.

49. Daitsu Tom Wright and Shohaku Okumura, trans., *Life-and-Death: Selected Dharma Poems by Kōshō Uchiyama Rōshi*. This collection of Uchiyama Rōshi's poems was printed as a commemoration of the tenth anniversary of Sanshinji in Bloomington in 2013.

50. Translated from Chinese by the Buddhist Text Translation Society, Dharma Realm Buddhist University (Talmage, CA: City of Ten Thousand Buddhas, 1999). http://cttbusa.org/bequeathed_teaching/sutra.htm.

51. Gene Reeves, trans., *The Lotus Sūtra: A Contemporary Translation of a Buddhist Classic* (Boston: Wisdom Publications, 2008), 114.

52. My translation, unpublished, from the section of Prajñātārā, in the third chapter of *Jingde Chuandeng Lu* (*Keitoku Dentoroku*, Taisho 2076:216b.15).

53. Taigen Leighton and Shohaku Okumura, trans., *Dōgen's Extensive Record: A Translation of the Eihei Kōroku* (Boston: Wisdom Publications, 2010), 164, 223, 279, 318, 361, 451. Dharma discourses 136, 213, 297, 360, 406, 506.

54. "Jijuyū Zanmai" is a part of *Bendōwa*. Shohaku Okumura and Taigen Leighton, trans., *The Wholehearted Way* (Boston: Tuttle, 1997), 21–24.

55. The ten names of Buddha are part of the meal chant in the Sōtō Zen tradition. See *Sōtō School Scriptures for Daily Services and Practice* (Tōkyō: Sōtōshū Shūmuchō, 2001), 75.

56. Gene Reeves, trans., *The Lotus Sūtra,* 83.

57. Ibid.

58. Ibid., 75.

59. Ibid., 76.

60. Ibid.

61. Ibid.

62. Shohaku Okumura, *Realizing Genjōkōan,* 215–16.

63. Kenneth K. Inada, trans., *Nāgārjuna: A Translation of His Mūlamadhyamakakārikā with an Introductory Essay* (Tōkyō: The Hokuseido Press, 1970), 74–75.

64. Taigen Leighton and Shohaku Okumura, *Dōgen's Pure Standards for the Zen Community: A Translation of Eihei Shingi* (Albany: State University of New York Press, 1996), 38.

65. This is a paraphrase of Robert Thurman, trans., *The Holy Teaching of Vimalakīrti: A Mahāyāna Scripture* (University Park, PA: Pennsylvania State University Press, 1976), 52–53.

66. *The Śūraṅgama Sūtra: With Excerpts from the Commentary by the Venerable Master Hsuan Hua* (Ukiah: The Buddhist Text Translation Society, 2009), 65.

67. Kazuaki Tanahashi, trans., *Enlightenment Unfolds: The Essential Teachings of Zen Master Dōgen,* 6–7. In this translation, the translator mistakes the *Śūraṅgama Sūtra* for the *Laṅkāvatāra Sūtra.* In this quote, I corrected the name of the sūtra.

68. The seven buddhas before Śākyamuni Buddha.

69. Leighton and Okumura, trans., *Dōgen's Extensive Record,* 341–42.

70. Dōgen also uses these terms in question 10 of the eighteen questions in the second half of *Bendōwa.* Okumura and Leighton, trans., *The Wholehearted Way,* 32.

71. Dōgen Zenji discusses satori in *Shōbōgenzō* "Daigo," "Great Realization."

72. *Sōtō School Scriptures for Daily Services and Practice* (Tōkyō: Sōtōshū Shūmuchō, 2001), 36.

73. My translation, unpublished. Another translation is in Nishijima and Cross, trans., *Master Dōgen's Shōbōgenzō,* book 2, 214.

74. Shohaku Okumura, *Living by Vow: A Practical Introduction to Eight Essential Zen Chants and Texts* (Boston: Wisdom Publications, 2012), 208.

75. Leighton and Okumura, trans., *Dōgen's Extensive Record,* 76.

76. Ibid.

77. Kōshō Uchiyama, *How to Cook Your Life* (Boston: Shambhala, 2005), 39.

78. Urs App, trans., *Master Yunmen: From the Record of the Chan Master "Gate of the Clouds"* (New York: Kodansha America, 1994), 94.

79. Leighton and Okumura, trans., *Dōgen's Extensive Record,* vol. 8, 532.

80. See Thomas Cleary, trans., *The Blue Cliff Record* (Boston: Shambhala, 1992), case 67, 376.

81. App, *Master Yunmen,* 94 (footnote).

82. In *Shōbōgenzō* "Kōmyō" ("Radiant Light"), Dōgen discusses the same point regarding the expression from the *Lotus Sūtra*: "This light illuminates the eighteen thousand Buddha lands in the East." See Nishijima and Cross, trans., *Master Dōgen's Shōbōgenzō,* book 2, 239.

83. See Akira Sadakata, *Buddhist Cosmology: Philosophy and Origins* (Tōkyō: Kosei Publishing, 1997), 25–30.

84. See Nishijima and Cross, trans., *Master Dōgen's Shōbōgenzō,* book 3, 37.

85. Shohaku Okumura, trans., *Shōbōgenzō-zuimonki: Sayings of Eihei Dōgen Zenji Recorded by Koun Ejō* (Tōkyō: Sōtōshū Shūmuchō, 1988), 171.

86. Ibid., 172–73.

87. Francis Dojun Cook, trans., *The Record of Transmitting the Light: Zen Master Keizan's Denkoroku* (Boston: Wisdom Publications, 2003), 258.

88. In the *Wumenguan* (*The Gateless Barrier*, or in Japanese *Mumonkan*), the kōan text of the Rinzai tradition, the *mu* kōan is "Does a dog have Buddha-nature?" to which Jōshū answered, "Mu"—which means "no." In *Congronglu* (*Book of Serenity*, or in Japanese *Shōyōroku*), the conversation is longer, and when another monk asked the same question to Jōshū, he answered, "Yes." Another famous kōan is Hakuin's "What is the sound of one hand clapping?"

89. Kōshō Uchiyama, *The Zen Teaching of "Homeless" Kodo* (Tōkyō: Sōtōshū Shūmuchō, 1990), 87.

90. The excerpts from the *Suttanipāta* over the next few pages are all from H. Saddhatissa, trans., *The Sutta-Nipāta* (Surrey: Curzon Press 1994), 101–2.

91. Inada, trans., *Nāgārjuna*, 39.

92. Burton Watson, trans., *The Zen Teaching of Master Lin-chi* (Boston: Shambhala, 1993), 21.

93. Ibid., 23.

94. H. Saddhatissa, trans., *The Sutta-Nipāta*, 102–3.

95. Cleary, *Book of Serenity*, case 98, 423.

96. John Keenan, trans., *The Summary of the Great Vehicle by Bodhisattva Asaṅga, Translated from the Chinese of Paramartha (Taisho, Volume 31, Number 1593)* (Berkeley: Numata Center for Buddhist Translation and Research, 1992), 98.

97. This is how he read the sentence from the *Diamond Sūtra* that is commonly read, "To see all forms as no-form is seeing Tathāgata."

98. Akira Sadakata, *Buddhist Cosmology: Philosophy and Origins* (Tōkyō: Kosei Publishing, 1997), 27.

99. Loori, *The True Dharma Eye: Zen Master Dōgen's Three Hundred Koans*, case 19, 26.

100. Okumura, *Realizing Genjōkōan*, 2.

101. Okumura, *Realizing Genjōkōan*, 3.

102. Okumura, *Realizing Genjōkōan*, 13–19.

103. The *Suvarṇaprabhāsottama Sūtra* (金光明最勝王経, *The Sūtra of Most Superior King of Golden Radiant Light*), Taisho, 665, vol. 16:424b. To my knowledge, it has not been translated into English.

104. Okumura, *Realizing Genjōkōan*, 3.

105. Leighton and Okumura, trans., *Dōgen's Pure Standards for the Zen Community*, 156–57.

106. Nishijima and Cross, trans., *Master Dōgen's Shōbōgenzō*, book 1, 111.

107. Okumura, *Realizing Genjōkōan*, 4.

108. Okumura and Leighton, trans., *The Wholehearted Way*, 36.

109. Cook, *The Record of Transmitting the Light*, 29.

110. According to *Zengakudaijiten* (*Large Dictionary of Zen Study*), the name of the mountain came from a sūtra on the Buddha's practice in previous lifetimes, the *Rokudoshūkyō* (*The Sūtra of the Collection of the Practices of the Six Pāramitās*). In this sūtra, there is a story of a bodhisattva, Prince Sudana, which was Śākyamuni's name in one of his previous lifetimes, who practiced in Mount Dantaloka. It seems this story got mixed up with Buddha's practice before his awakening. Neither of these texts have been translated into English.

111. Shohaku Okumura, *Realizing Genjōkōan*, 1.

112. The following story, over the next few pages, of Daowu, Jiashan, and Decheng are from Andy Ferguson, *Zen's Chinese Heritage* (Boston: Wisdom Publications, 2011), 163–66.

113. Shohaku Okumura, *Realizing Genjōkōan*, 3.

114. Okumura and Leighton, trans., *The Wholehearted Way*, 14–15.

115. Leighton and Okumura, *Dōgen's Extensive Record*, vol. 8, 535.

116. *Sōtō School Scriptures for Daily Services and Practice*, 33.

117. Okumura, *Realizing Genjōkōan*, 3.

118. App, *Master Yunmen*, 111.

119. Xu-Chuandeng-lu, *Zoku Dentoroku,* vol. 22, Taisho #2077, vol. 52, 0614 b29. English translation in App, *Master Yunmen*, 111–12, footnote.

120. Robert Aitken, *The Mind of Clover: Essays in Zen Buddhist Ethics* (San Francisco: North Point Press, 1984), 5. This is a quotation from D. T. Suzuki's *Zen and Japanese Culture* (New York, Pantheon, 1959), 114–15.

121. Ibid., 5–6.

122. Ibid., 17.

123. Brian Victoria wrote about this in *Zen at War* (New York: Weatherhill, 1997).

124. Master of a Rinzai monastery.

125. Takashi James Kodera, *Dōgen's Formative Years in China* (Boulder, CO: Prajna Press, 1980).

126. Jacques Gernet, *Daily Life in China: On the Eve of the Mongol Invasion* (Stanford, CA: Stanford University Press, 1962).

127. James Hillman, *Blue Fire* (New York: Harper & Row, 1989), 169.

128. I cannot take a look at this text but I was taught this by Yukako Matsuoka, an eminent Dōgen scholar.

129. *Shōbōgenzō, nehan myōshin, jissō musō, mimyō hōmon, furyū monji kyōge betsuden* (正法眼蔵、涅槃妙心、実相無相、微妙法門、不立文字、教外別伝).

130. Rewata Dhamma, *The First Discourse of the Buddha* (Boston: Wisdom Publications, 1997), 20.

131. Red Pine, *The Diamond Sūtra*, 19.

132. Ibid., 312.

133. "Bukkyo" in Gudo Nishijima and Chodo Cross, trans., *Master Dōgen's Shōbōgenzō* (Woking, Surrey: Windbell Publications, 1994), book 2, 55–57.

**Avalokiteśvara** (Skt.): One of the most important bodhisattvas of the Mahāyāna Buddhism, considered to be the symbol of Buddha's compassion.

**Chuanzi Decheng** (Sensu Tokujō, 780–850): The "boat monk" of Huating River. Heir of Shitou Xiqian and teacher of Jiashan.

**Daowu Yuanzhi** (Jap. Dōgo Enchi, 769–835): A Dharma heir of Yaoshan Weiyan, Dharma brother of Yunyan Tansheng, and teacher of Dongshan, a founder of the Sōtō school.

**Decheng**: See *Chuanzi Decheng.*

**Dōgen**: See *Eihei Dōgen.*

**Dongshan Liangjie** (Jap. Tōzan Ryōkai, 802–69): The founder of the Chinese Caodong School. Dongshan was a Dharma heir of Yunyan Tansheng.

**Eihei Dōgen** (1200–1253): The founder of Japanese Sōtō Zen Buddhism, Dōgen became a Tendai monk at age twelve, then changed to Rinzai Zen as a student of Myōzen. Together with Myōzen he traveled to China. He was seeking a true teacher and became Dharma heir of Tiantong Rujing. On his return he promoted zazen practice, was critical of the establishment, and eventually founded Eiheiji deep in the mountains. He was highly literate and wrote extensively, yet insisted that "between the dull and the sharp-witted there is no distinction."

**Emperor Wu** (464–549): The first emperor of the Rian Dynasty. He supported Buddhism and he himself lectured on Buddhist sūtras such as *Mahāparinirvāṇa Sūtra*. In Zen tradition, it is said that he met Bodhidharma.

**Guangchengzi** (Jap. Koseishi 広成子): The mountain hermit who taught the Yellow Emperor. He lived in the Kongtong Mountains.

**Guishan Lingyou** (Jap. Isan Reiyu, 771–853): A Dharma heir of Baizhang Huihai. Together with his disicple, Yangshan Huiji, Guishan is considered the founder of one of the five schools of Chinese Zen, Guiyang School.

**Hongzhi Zhengjue** (Jap. Wanshi Shōgaku, 1091–1157): A famous Chinese Caodong (Sōtō) Zen master who served as abbot of Tiantong monastery. Hongzhi was well known for the excellence of his poetry, and he composed verses to supplement a hundred kōans. Wansong Xingxie later wrote commentaries on these verses and created the *Congronglu* (*Book of Serenity*, or in Japanese *Shōyōroku*).

**Huike** (Dazu Huike, Jap. Taiso Eka, 487–593): The Second Ancestor of Chinese Zen, successor of Bodhidharma, and teacher of Sengcan, he is known for standing in the snow waiting for Bodhidharma to accept him as a student, and finally being accepted after cutting off his own arm.

**Huineng** (Jap. Enō, 638–713): The Sixth Ancestor of Chinese Zen, considered to be the founder of the Southern School of Chinese Zen. He was the Dharma heir of the Fifth Ancestor, Daman Hongren.

**Jiashan Shanhui** (Jap. Kassan Zenne, 805–81): Heir of Decheng.

**Jōshin Kasai.** Jōshin-san was Kōdō Sawaki Rōshi's disciple, Uchiyama Rōshi's Dharma sister, a nun, and also Rev. Zenkei Blanche Hartman's sewing teacher. Jōshin-san was ordained first by Ekō Hashimoto Rōshi.

**Katagiri, Dainin** (1928–90): The founder of Minnesota Zen Meditation Center. He came to San Francisco Zen Center in 1963, staying until Suzuki Rōshi's death in 1971. He moved to Minneapolis to establish MZMC in 1972 and traveled widely in North America to teach.

**Mahākāśyapa:** One of the ten major disciples of Śākyamuni Buddha, famous for his strict discipline. After the Buddha's death, he became the leader of the saṅgha and took the leadership for the first council of five hundred arahats. In Zen tradition, he is considered as the First Ancestor who received Dharma transmission from the Buddha.

**Menzan Zuihō** (1683–1769): One of the important Sōtō Zen monk scholars in the Tokugawa period (1603–1868). Dharma heir of Sonnō Shūeki. He studied Dōgen extensively and wrote many commentaries on *Shōbōgenzō* and other writings of Dōgen.

**Myōzen** (1184–1225): A disciple of Myōan Eisai who transmitted Rinzai Zen tradition to Japan and was Dōgen's first Zen teacher in Japan. Myōzen and Dōgen went to China together, but Myōzen died while practicing at Tiantong monastery.

**Nāgārjuna:** One of the most important philosophers of Buddhism and the founder of the Madhyamaka school of Mahāyāna Buddhism. His most important work is the *Mūlamadhyamakakārikā*. In Zen tradition, he is considered the Fourteenth Ancestor.

**Nanyue Huairang** (Jap. Nangaku Ejo, 677–744): A Tang Dynasty Zen master. He was Dharma heir of the Sixth Ancestor Huineng and the master of Mazu Daoyi.

**Never-Despise Bodhisattva:** A character in the twentieth chapter of the *Lotus Sūtra*, he continually praises people and predicts their future buddhahood, even though he is ridiculed and reviled for doing so.

**Prajñātārā** (Jap. Hannyatara): Twenty-seventh Ancestor in India, teacher of Bodhidharma. May have been a woman, according to traditions from India. According to the story of Prajñātārā from Kerala, originally she was a homeless waif who wandered western India and called herself Keyura, which means "necklace" or "bracelet." One day she met Master Punyamitra and became his student and successor.

**Śākyamuni Buddha:** The founder of Buddhism. *Śākyamuni* means "the sage from the Sakya clan."

**Sawaki, Kōdō** (1880–1965): A modern Sōtō Zen master and Kōshō Uchiyama's teacher. He was a professor at Komazawa University but never had his own temple or monastery. He was called "Homeless Kōdō" because he traveled throughout Japan to teach.

**Shitou Xiqian** (Jap. Sekitō Kisen, 700–790): A Tang Dynasty Zen master. The Dharma heir of Quingyuan Xingsi and the master of Yaoshan Weiyan, he is famous for his poems "Merging of Difference and Unity" ("Sandōkai") and "Song of the Grass Hut."

**Suzuki Rōshi, Shunryū** (1905–71): A Japanese Sōtō Zen master who traveled to the United States. He founded San Francisco Zen Center and Zenshinji, the first Sōtō Zen monastery in the West, usually known by its place name of Tassajara.

**Tiantong Rujing** (Jap. Tendo Nyojo, 1163–1227): A Song Dynasty Zen master who was the abbot of Tiantong monastery when Dōgen practiced in China. Dōgen received Dharma transmission from Rujing.

**Uchiyama, Kōshō** (1912–98): Kōdō Sawaki's Dharma heir who succeeded Sawaki at Antaiji. He wrote many books, and several of them were translated into English and other languages. He was the teacher of Shohaku Okumura.

**Yaoshan Weiyan** (Jap. Yakusan Igen, 745–828 or 750–834): Chinese Zen master, Dharma heir of Shitou Xiqian, also studied with Mazu. Teacher of Decheng and other notable masters.

**Yellow Emperor:** The legendary emperor of China who invented Chinese characters, the calendar, music, and medicine.

**Yunmen Wenyan** (Jap. Unmon Bunen, 864–949): Important Chinese Zen master, founder of the Yunmen House of Chan (one of the five houses of Chan in China, later absorbed into Rinzai Zen). He was a Dharma heir of Xuefeng Yicun, the originator of the teaching method using sayings from old masters, which evolved into kōan study, and known for forceful, direct, and subtle teaching.

**Yunyan Tansheng** (Jap. Ungan Donjō, 780–841): A Tang Dynasty Zen master. A Dharma heir of Yaoshan Weiyan, Dharma brother of Daowu Yuanzhi, and the teacher of Dongshan Liangjie, the founder of Chinese Caodong (Sōtō) School of Zen.

**(A)**

**an** (案): Paper or desk. This is the *an* usually used in *kōan*, giving the usual meaning "public case."

**an** (按): The left side of the character (手) means "hand" and the right (安) "to place hand on something." This *an* has the connotation of doing something to solve a problem, such as healing in *anma*, massage. This is the *an* in Dōgen's *kōan*.

**ancient buddha** (Jap. *kobutsu*古仏): Dōgen used this expression as a title of the Zen masters who truly attained the Dharma.

**Antaiji**: A Sōtō Zen temple located in Kyōto, Japan, where Kōdō Sawaki Rōshi and Kōshō Uchiyama Rōshi taught. It moved to Hyōgo Prefecture in 1976.

**(B)**

**bodhisattva**: In Early Buddhism, *Bodhisattva* refers to Śākyamuni Buddha when he practiced before he attained buddhahood. In Mahāyāna Buddhism, a bodhisattva is a person who has aroused bodhicitta (aspiration to seek the Way), taken the bodhisattva vows, and is walking the bodhisattva path.

**bodhisattva vows**: Vows taken by Mahāyāna Buddhists as the bases for life and practice:

> Beings are numberless; I vow to free them
> Delusions are inexhaustible; I vow to end them
> Dharma gates are boundless; I vow to enter them
> The Buddha's way is unsurpassable; I vow to realize it.

**buddha land**: The realm influenced by one Buddha's teaching. In the *Lotus Sūtra*, the various buddhas are said to each have a buddha land.

**buddha mudra**: *Mudra* means hand shape, and there are various mudras associated with Buddhist practice. "Buddha mudra" refers to the life that expresses Buddha's Way, using the hand shape as analogy for the shape of a life.

**buddha nature**: In Mahāyāna teaching, the true nature of all beings that enables them to become buddhas. In Dōgen's teaching, buddha nature is manifested in practice and is none other than reality itself.

**Buddha Way**: The concrete life experience of practice. In "Genjōkōan" Dōgen Zenji says, "to study the Buddha Way is to study the self," and this self is the self that includes the entire network of interdependent origination as *jijuyū zanmai* (see below).

**buddhahood** (Jap. *Bukka* 佛果): The realization of perfect enlightenment. In Zen, every sentient being is already Buddha; thus, buddhahood cannot be attained but only realized.

**buddhas and ancestors**: The masters who passed down the teaching from Buddha's time to this day. They are called buddhas because they express their buddha nature visibly. They are called ancestors because the process of passing down knowledge from one generation to the next, through face-to-face transmission, is like the generations of a family.

**Buddhist psychology**: Over the course of several centuries up to about 450 CE, Buddhist psychology and philosophy were compiled, systemetized, and codified in Abhidharma. There are two different versions, Theravādan and Sarvāstivādan, each of which includes discussion of the elements of the teaching, aggregates, meditations, and other points for study.

## (C)

**consciousness** (Skt. *vijñāna*): The fifth of the five aggregates (*skandhas*). When the six sense organs encounter their objects, six consciousnesses arise: eye consciousness, ear consciousness, nose consciousness, tongue consciousness, body consciousness, and mind consciousness. In Yogācāra teaching, two deeper consciousnesses are added: *manas* (ego consciousness) and *ālayavijñāna* (storehouse consciousness).

## (D)

**Daruma-shū**: The school of Zen founded by Dainichi Nōnin, who emphasized *kenshō jōbutsu* (becoming Buddha by seeing nature), transmitted from Chinese Rinzai Zen.

**desire** (Jap. *shu*, Pa. *upādāna*, Ch. *qu* 取): The ninth of the twelve links of causation. English translations include craving, attachment, or clinging.

**Dharma**: The Buddha's teaching; truth or law; the way all things are. The term "dharmas" not capitalized means all things or objects of thought.

**Dharma body** (Skt. *dharmakāya*): In the beginning, the Buddha's Dharma body referred to the Dharma (teachings) of the Buddha. However, later in Mahāyāna Buddhism the Dharma body is considered to be the reality of all things as they are. The other two bodies are saṃbhogakāya (reward body) and nirmāṇakāya (transformation body).

**Dharma eye** (Skt. *prajñā*): Buddha's wisdom, what is seen when letting go of thoughts.

**Dharma gate** (Skt. *Dharma mukha*): The teachings of the truth. The gate to the truth.

**dharmakāya** (Skt.): See *Dharma body*.

**Dharma King**: Śākyamuni Buddha.

**Dharma nature** (Skt. *dharmatā*, Jap. *hosshō* 法性): The true nature of all beings; thusness or emptiness.

**Dharma position, Dharma state**: A translation of *hō-i* (法位) from the *Lotus Sūtra*—each and every being dwells within its own *hō-i*.

*Diamond Sūtra* (Skt. *Vajracchedikā Prajñāpāramitā Sūtra*): *Sūtra of the Diamond-Cutter of Supreme Wisdom.* One of the sūtras in the group of prajñāpāramitā sūtras. It shows that all the forms of phenomenal beings are not ultimate reality but rather illusions, projections of one's own mind.

**dō** (道): Way, enlightenment, or speech.

## (E)

**Echizen**: The western province in Japan where Dōgen built his monastery Eiheiji, in modern Fukui Prefecture.

**ehō** (依報): Circumstances. Dōgen uses it here to indicate objective versus the subjective shōhō.

**Eiheiji**: Temple of Eternal Peace, formerly called Daibutsuji, founded by Dōgen in 1244 at Fukui Prefecture. One of two principal monasteries of the Japanese Sōtō School of Zen.

**emptiness** (Skt. *śūnyatā*): Emptiness is an expression used in Mahāyāna Buddhist texts such as the prajñāpāramitā sūtras for the nonexistence of the permanent self (*anātman*) and interdependent origination.

**explaining the mind and explaining the nature** (Jap. *sesshin sesshō* 説心説性): Daruma-shū teaching, seeing buddha nature by stopping thoughts and seeing deeply. Mind is *shin* and nature is *shō*. Dōgen had many students who came from Daruma-shū, and he vigorously corrected their misunderstandings.

**(F)**

**form** (Skt. *rūpa*): The first of the five aggregates. Material element, in the case of human beings; body is rūpa and the other four aggregates are functions of the mind.

**(G)**

**gang of six**: A group of the Buddha's disciples who did outrageous things such as manipulating people to give them money and persuading other monks to commit suicide. Their actions were the occasion for many of the specific precepts in early Buddhism and today's Vinaya.

**gen** (現): To appear; present or actual.

**gen** (験): Supernatural powers attained by various practices in the mountains (in *Shugendō*, 修験道).

**Genzō-e** (Jap. 眼蔵会): A gathering for studying Shōbōgenzō.

**go** (吾): Self; see also *go-uji*.

**go** (語): Word, as in *ikku gattō no go*.

**gō** (劫): Kalpa.

**go-uji** (Jap. 吾有時): This reality-self and all other beings and all time. *Uji* means "being-time" and *go* means "self."

**golden chain**: Becoming attached to the truth in Buddha's teaching, so the teaching does not make us free.

**gu** or **kyu** (求): To seek.

**gū** or **kyū** (窮): To penetrate.

**Gyōbutsu** (Jap. 行佛): Practice Buddha, a buddha name invented by Dōgen from the words *gyō*, practice, and *butsu*, buddha.

## (H)

*Heart Sūtra*: The shortest of the prajñāpāramitā sūtras, the important Mahāyāna sūtras expounding the teachings of emptiness. The *Heart Sūtra* contains the "heart" of the teaching of ultimate wisdom. See also *prajñāpāramitā*.

**heavenly beings:** In the six realms (human, animal, hungry ghost, hell-dweller, jealous gods, and heavenly beings), the heavenly beings are those whose good karma has resulted in a very pleasant place called heaven. However, as their karma is used up, eventually they fall from heaven and must take a new rebirth. It is considered more fortunate to be born as a human, with the possibility of awakening.

**hīnayāna** (Skt.): Literally meaning "narrow vehicle," *hīnayāna* is a pejorative term used by Mahāyānists for practitioners who are considered to be on the narrow path of individual liberation. Occasionally erroneously and insultingly equated with Theravāda.

**Huating River:** A river in China where Decheng was a boat man. See also *Chuanzi Decheng*.

**hungry ghosts** (Skt. *preta*): In the six realms (human, animal, hungry ghost, hell-dweller, jealous gods, and heavenly beings), hungry ghosts are those who are always hungry and thirsty but never able to be satisfied. They are pictured as beings with big bellies and skinny necks. The only nutrition they can receive are the water offerings from Buddhist meals.

## (I)

**impermanence** (Skt. *anitya*): One of the three marks of all beings; the other two are suffering (*dukkha*) and no-substance (*anātman*).

**Indra's net:** A metaphor used to illustrate the concepts of emptiness, interdependent origination, and interpenetration that first appeared in *Avataṃsaka Sūtra*. The metaphor shows that all phenomenal beings are intimately connected. Indra's net has a multifaceted jewel at each vertex, and each jewel is reflected in all of the other jewels.

**interdependent origination** (Skt. *pratītyasamutpāda*, Jap. *engi*): The teaching that all things and phenomena are the product of an infinite number of causes and conditions. All these causes and conditions are also infinitely interconnected and constantly changing, hence all things are impermanent and lack independent existence; they are empty. Not the same as the teaching of "dependent origination" in early Buddhism, even though the Sanskrit word is the same.

**iron chain:** Before we practice we are said to be bound with an iron chain. After we have had some insight and become attached to it, we are said to be bound with a golden chain. See also *golden chain*.

# (J)

**Jambudvīpa:** See *Mount Sumeru*.

**jō** (成): To become, accomplish, achieve, complete.

**jō** (情): Sentiment.

**jō** (常): Constantly.

**jō** (上): To go high up.

**jō** (生): To live, living; living beings (in *shu jō*).

**jō** (誠): Sincerity.

**joyful mind:** One of the three minds discussed in Dōgen's *Tenzo Kyōkun*. The other two are magnanimous mind and nurturing mind.

**just sitting** (Jap. *shikantaza* 只管打坐): Wholeheartedly sitting in the middle of everything, in the middle of our life.

## (K)

**kalpa** (Skt.): An endlessly long period of time, used in Buddhism to measure time. To express the length of a kalpa two similes are used: (1) One kalpa is the length of time to empty a ten-cubic-mile container of poppy seeds by taking one seed every one hundred years. (2) Every hundred years, a heavenly woman comes to rub a solid one-cubic-mile rock with her silk sleeve; one kalpa is the length of time the rock is worn away by this.

**ke** (繫): To tie.

**ke** (化): To teach.

**Kenninji:** The monastery in Kyōto, Japan, where Dōgen studied with his Rinzai master Myōzen, and to which he returned temporarily after his travels in China.

**kōan** (Jap. 公案): The same expression as in kōan stories. This word is used in China to mean a public document in a government office. In ancient China all government documents were issued in the name of the emperor and had absolute power and authority. No one could question them or complain. From this meaning the word evolved to mean the absolute truth expressed by Chinese Zen masters. That is one of the meanings of kōan in Zen literature—the expression of absolute reality with absolute authority. We have to study and master this teaching, and try to live based on it. (See *an* for a discussion of Dogen's use of *kōan*.)

**kobutsu** (Jap. 古仏): Ancient buddhas or old buddhas.

**Kongtong and the Hua Guard:** An old story explaining that earthly rulers should pay respect to spiritual teachers. Involves the Yellow Emperor and the hermit Guangchengzi.

**Kōshōji:** Dōgen's first monastery, founded in Kyōto in 1233.

**ku** (功): Function or ability.

**kyu:** See *gu*.

**(L)**

**land of Song:** Refers to China under the Song Dynasty, meaning the China of Dōgen's time. See also *Song Dynasty*.

**links of causation:** See *twelve links of dependent origination*.

***Lotus Sūtra*** (Skt. *Saddharmapuṇḍarīka Sūtra*, Jap. *Myō hō renge kyō*): One of the most important sūtras in Mahāyāna Buddhism, especially popular in China and Japan. The Tiantai (Tendai) and Nichiren School are based on its teachings. Since Dōgen was originally ordained and trained in the Tendai tradition before starting to practice Zen, he valued *Lotus Sūtra* as the king of all sūtras.

**(M)**

**magnanimous mind:** One of the three mental attitudes all Zen practitioners need to maintain mentioned in Dōgen's *Instructions for the Cook* (*Tenzo Kyōkun*). The other two are nurturing mind and joyful mind. Magnanimous mind is the mind like a mountain or ocean, immovable and without discrimination.

**mahāsattva** (Skt): Great being; another word referring to bodhisattva. Implies fearlessness, being like a lion.

**Mahāyāna** (Skt.): Literally "Great Vehicle." It is a branch of Buddhism that arose during the first century CE and developed, first in India and later in China, as the foundation of many schools of Buddhism including Tendai, Pure Land, and Zen. Mahāyāna Buddhism, which stresses the possibility of buddhahood for all beings, likely developed in reaction to the highly insular and monastic practices of early Buddhism. Ideal Mahāyāna practice is embodied in the bodhisattva, a being who practices for the awakening of both self and others.

**mani gem:** Wish-fulfilling jewel. A metaphor for the teachings and virtues of Buddha.

**Meiji period** (1868–1912 CE): A period in Japan during which Japan moved from being an isolated and feudal society to roughly its modern form. The term *meiji* means "enlightened rule." The role of the emperor was strengthened, and the era of the samurai ended. Limited representation was instituted, a modern currency was established, the Industrial Revolution occurred, and attention turned toward Europe. Buddhism, always associated with the aristocracy (shogunate), was separated from Shintōism and suffered some violence.

**merit:** "To gain merit" is a common expression in Buddhism. It means that our practice or offering brings about some virtue or merit, which we accumulate to become a buddha. Sometimes we offer this merit to all beings.

**Mount Dantaloka** (Jap. *Dantokusan* 檀特山): A mountain in Gandhara, northern India, where Buddha was said to have cut off his hair.

**Mount Dayang:** The site of an important Chan Buddhist monastery and thus the setting for many classical kōans.

**Mount Hiei:** The mountain located northeast of Kyōto, Japan, where the main monastery of Japanese Tendai School, Enryakuji, is located. Eihei Dōgen originally became a monk at the monastery.

**Mount Lu:** A sacred mountain in China, famous for its beauty.

**Mount Sumeru:** The center of this entire universe, according to the Buddhist cosmology described in *Abhidharmakośa*. Around Mount Sumeru there are nine mountains, like a square of mountains, and the other mountain ranges are beyond that. Our continent, Jambudvīpa, is south of Mount Sumeru.

**mountains:** In this text, "mountains" refers to this entire world, the network of interdependent origination in which we take part. This entire network becomes buddhas and ancestors.

**mountain training**: Life as practice.

**mountain way of life**: The way of life that is completely present with ordinary life; life as practice.

**mujō** (無常): Impermanent.

**mujō** (無情): Insentient.

**myriad dharmas**: All phenomenal beings.

## (N)

**name and form** (Skt. and Pāli *nāmarūpa*, Ch. *mingse* 名色): The fourth link in the twelve links of causation.

**nikon** (而時): This present moment, the intersection of impermanence and eternity, discontinuation and continuation, phenomenal beings and ultimate truth.

**nirvāṇa** (Skt.; Jap. *nehan*): Literally "extinction" or "blowing out" of the fires of greed, anger/hatred, and ignorance; the state of perfect peace of mind. In Early Buddhism, it meant departure from the cycle of rebirth in saṃsāra and entry into an entirely different mode of existence. Nirvāṇa is unconditioned, beyond arising, abiding, changing, and perishing. In Mahāyāna, nirvāṇa is not different from saṃsāra or from the ultimate nature of the dharmakāya.

**not understanding** (Jap. *fue suru* 不会する): In common usage this means "I don't understand," and is negative. Dōgen used it to mean "do not-understanding" or "go beyond understanding," a positive thing.

**nurturing mind** (Jap. *rōshin* 老心): One of the three minds mentioned in Dōgen's *Tenzo Kyōkun*. Other possible translations are parental mind or grandmotherly mind; the mind that takes care of others for others' sake as parents nurture their children. The characters literally mean "old mind."

## (O)

**one bright jewel**: An expression affirming the nature of saṃsāra as nirvāṇa. "The entire ten-direction world is one bright jewel." The word can be translated as either "pearl" or "jewel."

**ōryōki** (応量器, Skt. *patra*): A set of eating bowls, which Zen monks receive at their ordination. In India, Buddhist monks were allowed to have only one very large bowl called *patra* used for begging and eating foods.

**oshō** (和尚, Skt. *upādhyāya*): A common word for Buddhist priests and monks. It is sometimes translated as "preceptor" but is not limited to a person who can give precepts (ordain someone).

## (P)

**pāramitā** (Skt.): Perfection (literally, "that which has gone beyond") of certain virtues. In Mahāyāna Buddhism, the six pāramitās—giving, morality, patience, diligence, concentration, and wisdom—are considered to be the bodhisattva practice.

**perception** (Skt. *samjna*, Jap. *zō* or *sō* 想): The third of the five aggregates. Perception is not only the capture of mental images and the action of forming concepts but also the concepts themselves.

**person in the mountains**: This expression appears in the verses on Mount Lu by Su Shi, Hongzhi, and Dōgen. Su Shi said that he could not see the mountains' true face because he was in the midst of them.

**phenomenal beings** (Skt. *samskṛta*, Jap. *ui-hō*): Conditioned beings. All interdependent and conditioned phenomenal beings, which arise, abide, change, and perish. Everything conditioned is empty, impermanent, without substance.

**phenomenal thought construction**: See *thought construction*.

**practice and verification** (Jap. *shu shō* 修証): Dōgen's fundamental teaching is that practice and verification, *shu* and *shō*, are one, though in ordinary understanding *shu* is a cause and *shō* is the result.

**practice-enlightenment**: See *practice and verification*.

**prajñā** (Jap. *hannya*): A central concept of Mahāyāna Buddhism. One of the six pāramitās of bodhisattva practice. The wisdom that sees emptiness, the true reality of all things.

**prajñāpāramitā** (Skt.; Jap. *hannya haramita*): Wisdom beyond wisdom or perfection of wisdom. Mahāyāna Buddhism has a body of prajñāpāramitā literature, and Prajñāpāramitā is also personified as a female bodhisattva, the mother of wisdom.

**pratyekabuddha**: See *three vehicles*.

**precept** (Skt. *śīla*): One of the six pāramitās of bodhisattva practice; the perfection of morality, ethics, virtue, proper conduct.

**prior to the kalpa of emptiness**: Before anything happened. Also "before the germination of any subtle sign."

## (R)

**realization**: Actualization or practice-enlightenment.

**repentance** (Skt. *ksana*, Jap. *Sange* 懺悔): The practice of repentance has been an important part of Buddhism from its earliest beginnings. Twice a month each sangha gathered for *uposatha*. During the gathering, the leader of the sangha recited the Vinaya precepts and monks who violated the precepts made repentance. See also *vow*.

## (S)

**samādhi**: Concentration of the mind, one of the three foundations of the study of Buddhism: precepts (*śīla*), samādhi, and wisdom (*prajñā*). Dōgen called his practice of zazen *jijuyū zanmai* (samādhi).

**saṃsāra:** Literally "continuous flow"; that is, the cycle of birth, life, death, and rebirth within the six realms. This cycle ends in the attainment of liberation and entrance into nirvāṇa. However, Zen considered that saṃsāra and nirvāṇa are interpenetrating.

**saṅgha:** The Buddhist community. In a narrower sense, the saṅgha consists of monks, nuns, and novices. In a wider sense the saṅgha also includes lay followers or even all sentient beings.

**sanshin** (three minds): The three mental attitudes for the practitioners in a Zen monastery mentioned in Dōgen's *Tenzo Kyōkun*: joyful mind, nurturing mind, and magnanimous mind.

**sense organ:** The five sense organs are eyes (sight), ears (hearing), nose (smell), tongue (taste), and body (touch). In addition, the thinking mind is sometimes treated as a sense organ, with thoughts as its object.

**sentient beings** (Jap. *ujō* 有情): *Jō* (情) means "sentiment," "feeling," "emotion." A being with emotions is a sentient being, while a being without emotions is insentient (Jap. *mujō* 無情). *Sentient beings* refers to the mass of living beings subject to illusion, suffering, and transmigration within saṃsāra.

**sesshin:** Literally "touching or embracing the mind/heart." This refers to intensive practice period in Zen monastery during which monks focus on sitting meditation practice.

**seven treasures:** Precious gems and substances; one list includes gold, silver, lazuli, moonstone, agate, coral, amber.

**seventh consciousness** (Skt. *manas*): Ego consciousness.

**shavepates** (or shavelings): People who become monks but have no idea of the Dharma.

**shin** (心): Heart/mind or mind/heart.

**shin** (身): Body.

**Shintō:** The original religion of Japan, a nature religion with components added from Confucianism and later Buddhism. Literally "Shintō" means "Way of the gods."

**sho** (処): Place.

**sho** (諸): All, various (in *shohō* 諸法).

**shō** (性): Nature.

**shō** (正): Interior.

**shohō** (諸法): All dharmas.

**shōhō** (正報): Conditioned body and mind; Dogen uses it here to indicate the subjective, opposed to the objective *ehō*.

**shu** (主): Owner, lord, or host.

**shu** (修): Practice.

**shusshin** (Jap., 出身): Emancipation. Literally *shutsu* means "to exit" or "get out," and *shin* is "body."

**single staff:** The staff or whisk is used by an abbot when giving a formal discourse; thus, the master's teaching. Can also refer to monks' practice.

**sixth consciousness** (Skt. *manovijñāna*): The discriminating mind, our usual psychology.

**skin, flesh, bones, and marrow:** Expression referring to each and every aspect of practice and movement within the network of interdependent origination; based on Bodhidharma's discussion with his four disciples. The first attained his skin, the second his flesh, the third his bones, and finally Huike attained his marrow.

**Song Dynasty:** The Song Dynasty ruled China 960–1279, including the time of Dōgen's life.

**śrāvaka** (Skt.): See *three vehicles*.

**stepping forward and stepping backward** (Jap. *shinpo taiho* 進歩 退歩): Stepping forward is to study myriad external things and to work together with other people in society; stepping backward is to inwardly illuminate and study the self.

*Suttanipāta*: A collection of short suttas. One of the oldest scriptures of Buddhism included in Khuddaka Nikāya.

**swift as the wind**: From the *Lotus Sūtra*; refers to a wind that carries all living beings to buddhahood.

## (T)

**Tathāgata** (Skt.): One of the ten epithets for the Buddha, literally the "thus-come one" or "thus-gone one."

**ten-direction world**: The whole world, east, west, south, north, between each of them, and up and down.

**Tendai school**: The school of Buddhism into which Dōgen was first ordained. Japanese counterpart to Tiantai school in China, emphasizing the *Lotus Sūtra*. Brought to Japan by Saichō in the ninth century.

*Tenzo Kyōkun* (*Instructions for the Cook*): The first section of *Eiheishingi*. Eihei Dōgen wrote about cooking in the kitchen to teach the importance of communal work as a practice.

**thought construction** (Skt. *vikalpa,* Jap. *keron*): One of the important expressions in Nāgārjuna's teachings on emptiness. It refers to the deluded conceptualization of the world through the use of ever-expanding language and concepts, all rooted in the delusion of self. Other translations are conceptual proliferation and self-reflexive thinking.

**three poisons**: Greed/attraction, hate/anger/aversion, delusion.

**three times**: Past, present, and future.

**three treasures:** Same as Three Jewels, Triple Gem. The three things in which a Buddhist takes refuge and looks to for guidance. Buddha, Dharma, and Saṅgha.

**three vehicles:** *Śrāvaka* or word-hearers, *pratyekabuddha* or self-enlightened ones, and *bodhisattva* or a being who delays nirvāṇa until all can enter together.

**to** (斗): Dipper.

**to** (途): Path.

**tō** (頭): Head.

**tō** (透): To permeate.

**tō** (等): Equal.

**tōdatsu** (透脱): Liberated. As a Zen expression this compound means freely penetrating, going through any barriers, and totally liberated. *Tō* is "to penetrate" and *datsu* is "to drop off" or "take off."

**toku** (徳): Virtue.

**toku** (得): Get or attain.

**transmigration:** Transmigration or reincarnation is believed to occur when the soul or spirit, after the death of the body, comes back to life in a newborn body. This doctrine is a central tenet within the majority of Indian religious traditions, such as Hinduism, Jainism, and Sikhism, and early Buddhism was similar.

**true Dharma wheel:** The teaching of Buddha.

**true self:** See *buddha nature*.

**turning the object and turning the mind:** A practice of the Daruma school, founded by Dainichi Nōnin, to stop the cognitive mind and attain enlightenment.

**twelve links of dependent origination:** The final version of the teaching of dependent origination. It shows the cause of old age and death, accompanied in its full recital by sorrow, lamentation, pain, grief, and despair. It says the first cause of suffering is ignorance.

# (V)

**Vajrayāna:** A school of Buddhism that emerged around the sixth or seventh century in India. This school is also called esoteric Buddhism or Tantric Buddhism. It developed out of the teaching of Mahāyāna Buddhism influenced strongly by Hinduism. It reached into China, Japan, and Tibet. The Shingon School founded by Kūkai is a Japanese form of Vajrayāna Buddhism.

**Vinaya:** One of the three *piṭaka* (baskets) of Buddhist scriptures. Vinaya is a collection of the rules and regulations for the communal life of monks and nuns.

**vital path of emancipation** (Jap. *shusshin no katsuro* 出身の活路): *Katsuro* is "vital path," *shusshin* is "emancipation." This means going beyond awakening, going beyond Buddha.

**vow** (Skt. *pranidhana*): In Mahāyāna Buddhism, bodhisattvas take a vow stating that they will strive for as long as saṃsāra endures to liberate all sentient beings from saṃsāra and lead them to enlightenment. A Bodhisattva does not seek to awaken solely for himself or herself but rather to free all beings and help them into nirvāṇa.

**Vulture Peak** (Skt. *Gṛdhrakuṭa*, Pa. *Gijjhakūṭa*): A mountain near from the city of Rajagriha. Śākyamuni Buddha often gave discourses on this mountain. It is said that the *Lotus Sūtra* was expounded on this mountain. In Zen tradition, the transmission from the Buddha to Mahākāśyapa took place there when Buddha held up a flower and smiled.

# (Y)

**Yogācāra**: Literally "application of yoga," Yogācāra is one of the two Mahāyāna schools in India founded by Maitreynātha, Asaṅga, and Vasubandu. Characterized by "mind-only" teachings.

# (Z)

**zendō** (Jap. 禅堂): Meditation hall in Zen tradition; a hall for zazen practice.

Aitken, Robert. *The Mind of Clover: Essays in Zen Buddhist Ethics*. San Francisco: North Point Press, 1984.

App, Urs, trans. *Master Yunmen: From the Record of the Chan Master "Gate of the Clouds."* New York: Kodansha America, 1994.

Cleary, Thomas, trans. *The Blue Cliff Record*. Boston: Shambhala, 1992.

Cleary, Thomas, trans. *Book of Serenity: One Hundred Zen Dialogues*. Hudson, NY: Lindisfarne Press, 1990.

Cook, Francis Dojun. *How to Raise an Ox: Zen Practice as Taught in Zen Master Dogen's Shobogenzo*. Los Angeles: Center Publications, 1978.

Cook, Francis Dojun, trans. *The Record of Transmitting the Light: Zen Master Keizan's Denkoroku*. Boston: Wisdom Publications, 2003.

Ferguson, Andy. *Zen's Chinese Heritage: The Masters and Their Teachings*. Boston: Wisdom Publications, 2011.

Grant, Beata. *Mount Lu Revisited: Buddhism in the Life and Writings of Su Shih*. Honolulu: University of Hawaii Press, 1994.

Inada, Kenneth K., trans. *Nāgārjuna: A Translation of His Mūlamadhyamakakārikā with an Introductory Essay*. Tōkyō: The Hokuseido Press, 1970.

Kodera, Takashi James. *Dogen's Formative Years in China*. Boulder, CO: Prajna Press, 1980.

Leighton, Taigen, and Shohaku Okumura, trans. *Dōgen's Extensive*

*Record: A Translation of the Eihei Kōroku.* Boston: Wisdom Publications, 2004.

Leighton, Taigen, and Shohaku Okumura, trans. *Dogen's Pure Standards for the Zen Community: A Translation of Eihei Shingi.* Albany: State University of New York Press, 1996.

Leighton, Taigen, and Shohaku Okumura, trans. *The Wholehearted Way.* Boston: Tuttle, 1997.

McRae, John. *Seeing Through Zen: Encounter, Transformation, and Genealogy in Chinese Chan Buddhism.* Berkeley and Los Angeles: University of California Press, 2003.

Nishijima, Gudo, and Chodo Cross, trans. *Master Dogen's Shobogenzo.* Windbell Publications 1994.

Okumura, Shohaku. *Living by Vow: A Practical Introduction to Eight Essential Zen Chants and Texts.* Boston: Wisdom Publications, 2012.

Okumura, Shohaku. *Realizing Genjōkōan: The Key to Dogen's Shobogenzo.* Boston, Wisdom Publications, 2010.

Okumura, Shohaku, trans. *Shōbōgenzō-zuimonki: Sayings of Eihei Dōgen Zenji Recorded by Koun Ejō.* Tōkyō: Sōtōshū Shūmuchō, 1988.

Red Pine (Bill Porter). *The Diamond Sutra: The Perfection of Wisdom: Text and Commentaries Translated from Sanskrit and Chinese.* New York: Counterpoint 2001.

Reeves, Gene, trans. *The Lotus Sutra: A Contemporary Translation of a Buddhist Classic.* Boston: Wisdom Publications, 2008.

Saddhatissa, H., trans. *The Sutta-Nipāta.* Surrey: Curzon Press, 1994.

Stevens, John. *The Marathon Monks of Mount Hiei.* Boston: Shambhala, 1988.

Tanahashi, Kazuaki, trans. *Enlightenment Unfolds: The Essential Teachings of Zen Master Dōgen.* Boston, Shambhala, 1999.

# ABOUT THE AUTHOR

 SHOHAKU OKUMURA was born in Osaka, Japan, in 1948. He received his education at Komazawa University in Tōkyō, Japan, where he studied Zen Buddhism. On December 8, 1970, Okumura was ordained at Antaiji by his teacher Kōshō Uchiyama, and he practiced there until Uchiyama retired in 1975. He then traveled to the United States, where he cofounded Valley Zendō in Massachusetts and continued Uchiyama's style of zazen practice. In 1981 he returned to Japan and began translating the writings of Uchiyama and Eihei Dōgen from Japanese into English. He taught at the Kyōto Sōtō Zen Center in Japan and the Minnesota Zen Meditation Center in Minneapolis, and was the director of the Sōtō Zen Buddhism International Center (previously called Sōtō Zen Education Center) in San Francisco from 1997 to 2010.

He is the founding teacher of Sanshin Zen Community, based in Bloomington, Indiana, where he lives with his family.

Okumura is the author of *Realizing Genjōkōan: The Key to Dōgen's Shōbōgenzō* and *Living by Vow: A Practical Introduction to Eight Essential Zen Chants and Texts*. His books of translation include *Dōgen's Extensive Record: A Translation of the Eihei Kōroku*; *Shikantaza: An*

*Introduction to Zazen*; *Shōbōgenzō Zuimonki: Sayings of Eihei Dōgen Zenji*; *Heart of Zen: Practice without Gaining-mind* (previously titled *Dōgen Zen*); *The Zen Teaching of Homeless Kodo*; *Opening the Hand of Thought: Foundations of Zen Buddhist Practice*; *The Wholehearted Way: A Translation of Eihei Dōgen's Bendōwa with Commentary by Kōshō Uchiyama Rōshi*; and *Dōgen's Pure Standards for the Zen Community: A Translation of Eihei Shingi*. He is also an editor of *Dōgen Zen and Its Relevance for Our Time*; *Sōtō Zen: An Introduction to Zazen*; *Nothing Is Hidden: Essays on Zen Master Dōgen's Instructions for the Cook*; and *Dōgen's Genjōkōan: Three Commentaries*.

## EDITOR

SHODO SPRING is a Sōtō Zen priest and Dharma heir of Shohaku Okumura. Before encountering Zen in 1983 she had studied physics and social work, and she practiced as a psychotherapist before beginning Zen training. She met the Dharma through Dainin Katagiri in Minnesota, studied at San Francisco Zen Center, and finally trained with Okumura Rōshi. She has been interim priest at Anchorage Zen Community, and she volunteered with Brahmavihara Cambodia in 2014. In 2013 she organized and led the Compassionate Earth Walk, a three-month spiritual walk along the proposed Keystone XL pipeline route.

She is the author of *Take Up Your Life: Making Spirituality Work in the Real World* and blogs at https://vairochanafarm.wordpress.com.

Currently Spring hosts a small sitting group (Sansuiji), sits monthly Antaiji-style sesshins in the tradition of her lineage, and has founded the Mountains and Waters Alliance to work together with all beings for the welfare of the whole earth. She spends time with her children and grandchildren.

WHAT TO READ NEXT
FROM WISDOM PUBLICATIONS

**Realizing Genjōkōan**
*The Key to Dōgen's Shōbōgenzō*
Shohaku Okumura
Foreword by Taigen Dan Leighton

"A stunning commentary. Like all masterful commentaries, this one finds in the few short lines of the text the entire span of the Buddhist teachings."—*Buddhadharma: The Practitioner's Quarterly*

**Dōgen's Extensive Record**
*A Translation of the Eihei Kōroku*
Translated by Taigen Dan Leighton and Shohaku Okumura
Foreword by Tenshin Reb Anderson

"Taigen and Shohaku are national treasures."—Norman Fischer, author of *Training in Compassion*

**Deepest Practice, Deepest Wisdom**
*Three Fascicles from Shōbōgenzō with Commentary*
Kōshō Uchiyama
Translated by Tom Wright and Shohaku Okumura

"Real Dharma. The mingled voices of these teachers—inspiring, challenging, sage, and earthy—shake dust from the mind so we may see more clearly what's right here."—Ben Connelly, author of *Inside Vasubandhu's Yogacara: A Practitioner's Guide*


**Living by Vow**
*A Practical Introduction to Eight Essential Zen Chants and Texts*
Shohaku Okumura

"An essential resource for students and teachers alike."—Dosho Port, author of *Keep Me in Your Heart a While*


**The Zen Teaching of Homeless Kodo**
Shohaku Okumura and Kosho Uchiyama

"Kodo Sawaki was straight-to-the-point, irreverent, and deeply insightful—and one of the most influential Zen teachers for us in the West. I'm very happy to see this book."—Brad Warner, author of *Hardcore Zen*


**Being-Time**
*A Practitioner's Guide to Dogen's Shobogenzo Uji*
Translated by Shinshu Roberts
Foreword by Norman Fischer

"This book is a great achievement. Articulate, nuanced, and wonderful."
—Jan Chozen Bays, author of *Mindfulness on the Go*

**Dōgen's Shōbōgenzō Zuimonki**
*The New Annotated Edition—Also Including Dōgen's Waka Poetry with Commentary*
Translated by Shohaku Okumura

"This translation is not only Dōgen's instructions, handwritten by his successor Ejo and transmitted to us. It's as if the reader were there over and over again with the myriad examples and instructions straight from Dōgen. With the combination of Dōgen's poetry, this gives a light and creative quality. I was struck by the simplicity of Okumura-roshi's presentation, which is the profundity of Zen. This book will stand and speak as a classic—openly shared and digested for the true Zen student."—Jakusho Kwong-roshi, author of *No Beginning, No End*; *Breath Sweeps Mind*; and *Mind Sky*

## About Wisdom Publications

Wisdom Publications is the leading publisher of classic and contemporary Buddhist books and practical works on mindfulness. To learn more about us or to explore our other books, please visit our website at wisdomexperience.org or contact us at the address below.

Wisdom Publications
199 Elm Street
Somerville, MA 02144 USA

We are a 501(c)(3) organization, and donations in support of our mission are tax deductible.

Wisdom Publications is affiliated with the Foundation for the Preservation of the Mahayana Tradition (FPMT).